Healing the Hurt
RESTORING THE HOPE

'This book deals with grief and loss in children and adolescents and offers the reader sound, practical advice. Suzy Marta is an authority on this subject and the book stems from some 25 years experience of working with bereavement. It represents a significant resource for both parents and professionals and is written with clarity, sensitivity and insight into this most important of subjects.'

Professor John A. Collings, *Consulting Psychologist.*

'This inspirational, sensitive and highly practical book has been written with such great skill and empathy by Suzy Yehl Marta. It is essential reading for all who accompany children and young people as they weather the storm of loss. It is an invaluable aid which deepens our understanding of the trauma of grief and is packed with practical strategies that help create a brighter future. It deserves a place in every school in the country.'

Frank J. McDermott, *Director of Schools in the diocese of Hallam, Sheffield.*

Healing the Hurt
RESTORING THE HOPE

How to guide children and young people
through times of divorce, death and crisis
with the RAINBOWS approach

SUZY YEHL MARTA

Founder of RAINBOWS, the world's largest grief support organization
for children and young people

RODALE

This edition first published in the UK in 2004 by
Rodale Ltd
7–10 Chandos Street
London WIG 9AD
www.rodale.co.uk

Printed and bound in the UK by CPI Bath using acid-free paper
from sustainable sources.

1 3 5 7 9 8 6 4 2
A CIP record for this book is available from the British Library

ISBN 1–4050–4191–9

This paperback edition distributed to the book trade by Pan Macmillan Ltd

Book design by Leanne Coppola and Tara Long

Notice
The medical information in this book is for reference only. It is designed to help you make
informed decisions about your child's behaviour and emotional health. It is not intended as a
substitute for any treatment that may have been prescribed by your child's doctor or
psychologist. If you suspect that your child has a medical or psychological problem, we urge you
to seek competent medical help.

Internet addresses and telephone numbers given in this book were accurate
at the time it went to press.

RODALE
WE INSPIRE AND ENABLE PEOPLE TO IMPROVE
THEIR LIVES AND THE WORLD AROUND THEM

To Michael, Tom, Tim, Peter, David and Katie,
my beloved children, who have been vulnerable with their pain
and unbelievably candid with their needs, and who have taught me
how to love unconditionally.

To Marty,
my husband, whose boundless love fills my soul with strength.
From the beginning, you have been unfailingly supportive
of me both personally and professionally.

To Tommy, Samantha and Emma,
my grandchildren, whose hugs dissolve my stress
and fill my heart with love.

To my friends,
who patiently cheered me on during times of exhaustion
and celebrated with each accomplishment.

A waterfall begins with a single drop.
In writing this book, my hope is to unlock a cascade
of compassion that will flow into all of our communities
through our homes, schools and communities.

Contents

Foreword

Every year thousands of children face bereavement through the death of a parent, grandparent, sibling or friend. Young people will also encounter many life events that have no connection with the death of a person. The effects of family breakdown extend far beyond the social wellbeing of children. Verbal and physical conflict between two people a child loves is emotionally painful and upsetting. Other children are the victims of war and political strife. Their homes have been destroyed and their parents may have been abducted, tortured, imprisoned or killed. Some will have witnessed emotional or physical abuse, rape, famine and material deprivation. They may have no language with which to talk about what has happened and harbour horrendous memories.

Bereavement rocks the foundations of children's lives; their confidence in the world they know is destroyed and they experience confusion and anguish. It can be an acutely sad and difficult time, to the point of being overwhelming. Emotional responses can be particularly confusing when young people are also experiencing rapid physical growth and bodily change. Grief interferes with the normal process of growing up.

Everyone has different needs when faced with loss. When someone dies, adults are understandably so engrossed in their own grief that children's emotional pain may not be noticed. No amount of silence or secrecy can hide the fact that something is wrong. Overheard conversations, glimpses of adults in tears and changed routines can make children fearful.

Much has changed in recent years in our understanding of childhood and in children's experiences of death, dying and bereavement. We no longer treat children as miniature adults. We know that children's concepts of death are more complex than is sometimes acknowledged and that it is dangerous to oversimplify emotional responses in two or three watertight stages. Finally, much has been learned about interventions that are appropriate to the specific needs of children and young people.

The belief that given time children are able to reach a healthy resolution to their grief, is often understood to mean that they have a capacity to 'get over' the event without being helped to do so. RAINBOWS does not subscribe to this view.

Rather the organization believes that, like adults, children and young people are deeply affected by loss and they need to be given opportunities to resolve their lives so that they are able to develop coping strategies.

> 'Children are not rubber bands that can be stretched out of shape and then be expected to snap back into position. They are living beings with their own feelings.'

The way in which children are helped when sad things happen may have a profound effect on how they are able to adapt to loss and change throughout their lives. The relationship that exists between compassionate carers and children is often an unbalanced one, where carers do most of the giving and the child and their family do a large proportion of the receiving. Many professionals suffer from personal stress as a result of a commitment to caring for somebody else. Suzy Yehl Marta reminds readers that looking after other people is emotionally demanding and that carers owe it to children to recognise their own emotional depletion. A person's willingness to support others should not cause them to neglect their own needs.

Many books have been published about loss and change. This book will be of interest to all professional adults who come into contact with bereaved children. Parents and other adults who are faced with children suffering loss will also find that the suggested games and activities will support them in helping to provide children with effective and age-appropriate activities.

Written with tremendous insight into children's experience of loss and change, the text brings together Suzy Yehl Marta's unique experience of working with bereaved children and their families. Compassionate carers will find they are able to develop their own practice within the RAINBOWS framework, building on individual strengths and skills.

The text does not purport to make every reader an expert in dealing with children's grief, but to increase their awareness of the impact of bereavement on children's holistic development. Suzy has done children and professionals a great service in writing this readable, accessible and helpful book.

Erica Brown, Head of Research and Development in Care, Acorns Children's Hospice Trust, Birmingham, UK; former Head of Special Education at Oxford University; and author of *Loss, Change and Grief* and *Supporting Children with Post-Traumatic Stress Disorder.*

Acknowledgements

During my 25 years of working with bereaved children and young people, I never aspired to write a book. The work of RAINBOWS challenged my limits, stretched my boundaries and humbled me. Yet through the years, many people suggested that I should put my experiences and knowledge into a format that could be shared with others.

Finally, after significant prodding from people I trust, I gathered 20-plus years of notes from workshops, seminars and training sessions I had given and took them home to begin this venture. In all, the material weighed 52 pounds (nearly 25 kg)! My plan was to synthesize these notes into a single book. During the years of work with RAINBOWS, my routine response to every challenge was to pose the question: 'How difficult can this be?' All too soon, I realized how extraordinarily challenging this project was going to be! Writing a book is an altogether different process than giving a presentation to 15 or 3,000 people or even creating a curriculum for a generation of youth.

In the ensuing months, I quickly realized that all I know, all that I have written or spoken about, is the compilation of the real-life experiences of thousands of children and teenagers who trusted me with their pain and the heart-rending stories of parents who shared their losses with me in the hope of getting some insight on how to strengthen their bereaved families. They have deepened my capacity for compassion and empowered me not to rest until society has tended to its bereaved youth!

In addition, I must acknowledge the support of the RAINBOWS Board of Directors, the National and State Chapter Directors, and the hundreds of thousands of RAINBOWS volunteers — Registered Directors, Coordinators and Facilitators — who have brought the message of this book to life through their involvement in RAINBOWS and their steadfast commitment. They have been soldiers on the front lines of grief, restoring hope into the hearts of the bereaved.

Once this daunting task began to take shape, Patricia Skalka offered her guidance and book-development expertise. She has been a colleague and friend during the past 10 years, constantly helping spread the word about RAINBOWS. Through this entire project, she was instrumental in weaving my thoughts and feelings into a 'seamless garment'. We did it!

Also key to making the dream a reality were my agent, Stephanie von Hirschberg, and editor, Lou Cinquino, both of whom recognized the value of and need for this book.

Finally, without the competence of the RAINBOWS executive staff — Laurie Olbrisch, who carried the additional burdens and responsibilities during my absence, and the unflagging support of Eleanor Langton, Chris Ardornetto, Evelyn Maier, Stacey Daccardo, Jennifer Sweborg, Susan Ruddy, Lesley Roberts and Charlie Procter — I could have never stayed away from the office all of these months to stay focused on this project. Thank you all!

Introduction

My Personal Journey

D ON'T WORRY ABOUT THE CHILDREN. They're resilient. They'll bounce back.'

These reassuring words were salve to my wounds. My husband Jim and I had recently divorced. At the time, my children were young — 5, 6 and 7 — too young, I hoped, to comprehend and be seriously affected by the enormous changes that had taken over our lives. Despite my own deep emotional pain, I clung to the belief that my sons would move through the upheaval in their lives relatively unscathed. 'They'll be fine,' I told myself.

After the divorce, everything in our household changed. For a while, I held down three jobs just to make ends meet. My time for parenting was drastically reduced. The little touches of family were no longer there — time to cuddle, watch television together or play in the park. Most days, I felt like a machine that was running on drained batteries. Every task was a struggle.

I just didn't seem to have enough time or strength to organize the house, feed the children and get them to and from school on time. But the kids? They seemed to be just fine. Doing better than I was, actually.

As it turns out, I was naïve and I was dead wrong. My sons were not just fine. They were grieving terribly, but I was in such pain that I wasn't even aware of their distress. In addition, everyone — my friends, family doctor, counsellor and even parish priest — assured me that my boys would handle the situation and move on. 'Kids bounce back,' they said. In the midst of my own agony, I took comfort in their words. In retrospect, I find the very notion absurd. Children are not rubber bands that can be stretched out of shape and then expected to snap back into position. They are living beings with their own feelings. Like adults, they are deeply affected by loss.

I remained in an emotional daze for nearly a year after my husband moved out, numbed by my own pain and oblivious to my sons' grief. Then, one day, for the first time in many months, I sat down and took a long, hard look at my children. They're just fine, right? The unmistakable pain in their eyes shocked me. I felt a searing ache in my heart. How could I have missed this?

In the past, the boys had been active in their school functions, participated in local sports, and had lots of friends. This last year had been different. They'd become withdrawn, sullen and angry. They fought constantly among themselves. They were cruel to each other — punching and shoving one another so much that I lost track of the number of trips we'd made to the local hospital for stitches. Occasionally they were verbally nasty to me as well.

Even worse, Michael had started to shoplift sweets from the local corner shop. Tom was getting into scrapes at school with his closest friends. And Tim had started spending all his free time watching television or curled up in bed, asleep.

Academically they were struggling, too. Their grades were spiralling downwards. In class, the boys daydreamed; they weren't 'applying' themselves to their work, their teachers said.

My children — the most precious beings on earth to me — had been hurting all this time and no one, not one single adult, had made the connection between the divorce, their behaviour and their emotional pain. Even today, I cannot imagine how they must have felt, torn by unfamiliar emotions and yet completely ignored. Divorce was the most significant event that had occurred in their lives, and no one — not me, their dad, their grandparents, their teachers or their doctor — had asked them how they felt about it.

That night, I vowed that I would *talk to them* about the divorce.

Knowing that children chatter best around food, I made a big bowl of popcorn and sat us all down around it on the rug in the living room. As the boys munched their snack, I fired questions at them.

'How do you feel now that your father isn't living with us?'

Michael shrugged his shoulders.

'Do you mind going to your dad's at the weekend?'

Tom stared at the floor.

'Does it bother you that I'm working so much?'

Tim avoided my gaze and snatched a handful of popcorn.

I didn't know what to do. I'd been advised to put on a strong appearance in front of my children. I was counselled to be brave, allow no tears, voice no fears and never complain. My strength would inspire the children to be strong as well. Sitting with the boys that evening, I realized that I had been living a lie.

So I decided (or was inspired) to *share with them* what was going on inside me. I started with what was most important: I told them how much I loved them. I apologized for not talking to them openly and honestly about what had happened to our family. I admitted that this new status of divorced single parent was embarrassing and awkward for me. I went on to say that I often wasn't sure how my friends would treat me or how the neighbours would act around me. I even told them that I was still concerned about my family's reaction. Finally, I told them that I was scared because I didn't know how to be a single parent.

I cried as I talked. Yet my vulnerability and openness was the catalyst for them to open up. One by one, the boys shared their confusion, pain and embarrassment — in school, in the playground, where we lived. Mike pleaded with me not to tell his teachers about the divorce. He was convinced that they would give him extra homework as a 'punishment' — and then mark him down anyway. Tom thought that the divorce meant that something was wrong with our family. He begged me not to say anything to the neighbours for fear that they wouldn't let him play with their children any more. Tim listened, absorbing all that was being relayed, but didn't say a word.

It quickly became evident how much anguish my beloved children were in. I began to wonder how resilient these youngsters were and if they would ever bounce back.

That night, we sat together for hours. We wept; we yelled at each other; we laughed together; and we hugged. By the end of the evening, we had taken our first steps to healing the wounds left by the divorce. We were still unclear about the direction we were taking, and we weren't sure of all the steps needed, but we were determined to triumph, both as individuals and as a new family, and to do it together.

As the days moved into weeks and then months, we grew stronger. Along the way, we made many mistakes, but we learned from them. We had no role models. We were self-taught, and eventually we began to teach others.

There Were So Many ...

In 1978, I tried to find a support programme for my children so that they could talk about their feelings concerning the divorce. No matter where I called — my doctor's office, church, school, community mental health organization, every source I could conjure up — the answer was invariably the same: no, we have nothing for children. Not knowing what else to do, I turned to my local church and a group of concerned parents and, with their backing, offered to help organize weekend retreat support groups for children.

The response was incredible. Some children came to the weekend retreats because of divorce; others had been abandoned or had lost a parent to death. All of these children were from our local suburban communities, and there were so many! We offered six to eight weekends a year for three years — helping more than 800 children during that time.

Though each child was unique, they all echoed the same sense of loss that my sons had experienced; they endured the same pain and had similar needs. I remember two young sisters, Anna Marie, 6, and Sydney, 8 — beautiful, shy children with big innocent brown eyes whose parents had divorced. They came to several retreats and cried the whole time they were there.

Another child, Taylor, was an infant when his father walked out on the family. Growing up, he had seemed unaffected by the situation. Then he reached adolescence and became obsessed with uncovering his personal history. He peppered his mother with questions about his dad, but she refused to tell him anything. By the time Taylor came to us at 14, he had already attempted suicide twice.

Then there was Bryan, a quiet, earnest 17-year-old. Two years earlier, Bryan's brother had been killed in a car crash. Since then, his father had been drinking heavily, and his heartbroken mother rarely got out of bed, leaving Bryan to care for his three younger siblings. 'I can't go anywhere with my friends or do anything I want,' he told me bitterly. 'My brother died, but I lost my childhood.' His parents, he said, didn't care about anyone but their dead son.

It was evident that all of these children were in great crisis — and that no one was paying attention. Many of these youngsters were dressed in black, depressed and angry. Too many had already flirted with drugs, alcohol and even suicide. And these were kids from 'good' suburban families.

At the end of each weekend, I was overwhelmed with sadness and frustration. I knew that we had helped many of the participants, both young children and teenagers. But I knew also that there were many more children out there suffering in silence — or acting out their pain in very serious and destructive ways. 'What will happen to these children?' I wondered. I knew that they were not as strong as society assumed. In their own way, each of them was floundering emotionally, looking for someone to acknowledge their feelings, and desperately trying to understand what their loss meant to them. At the end of the retreats, the children left us realizing that they could move beyond their pain. They discovered new possibilities within themselves and in their lives. They felt empowered! Yet it was clear that they, and countless other grieving children, needed more.

The hours spent with these children changed who I was as a person and what I was going to do with my life.

If our weekend retreats could do this much, I thought, surely an ongoing programme could accomplish so much more. Again, I searched both locally and nationally for community support groups for young people who had experienced a loss in the family. Still, nothing was available. Although some school social workers ran their own grief-support programmes, they had never been formalized and produced in a format that could be used by others.

Finally, I began to wonder if I could devise such a programme — using what the children had shared at the retreats and knowing what they needed to learn from the caring adults in their lives.

This was the beginning of RAINBOWS, an international, non-profit organization that fosters emotional healing among children and adults grieving the loss created by a life-altering crisis. RAINBOWS believes that *the pain of loss does not need to hurt forever.* To carry out its mission, we have developed five age-directed, community-based grief support programmes. Three of these serve children and teenagers, from pre-school age to adolescence, and two serve young adults and single parents and step-parents. Since 1983, the RAINBOWS network of trained volunteers has helped more than one million young people around the world.

The Four Central Principles of the RAINBOWS Programme

Grieving children have taught me four valuable lessons that now form the guiding principles of RAINBOWS.

Adults often don't recognize when children are grieving. At a local nursery, a young mother had just finished telling her daughter's teacher how well the child was adjusting to her divorce when the curly-haired, blonde, blue-eyed 4-year-old began pummelling a child-size punchbag that hung in the corner of the classroom. 'I'm angry because my daddy didn't come to see me when he was supposed to,' the little girl said with the first jab. 'I hate having two houses,' she announced with the second. Despite the mother's protests, the child kept hitting the bag and reciting her litany of despair. Finally, the parent stepped away, head down, embarrassed and subdued.

Grief is often misunderstood. It is a powerful and *natural* emotion. Yet, in the midst of loss, each child's experience is unique. How a child grieves depends on the loss, the amount of love invested in what has been taken away, the relationship that was shared, and how the loss occurred. Life teaches its own valuable lessons about recognizing and coping with this powerful emotion. Children and teenagers, however, haven't lived long enough to gain this perspective.

When loss occurs, children are hit by a myriad of emotions. Their minds and hearts are battered by an onslaught of strange, scary, unpredictable feelings. They are frightened by the intensity of their anguish and confusion.

Children don't know how to grieve, and the consequences of this can be devastating. Children and teenagers often are left with no one guiding them through the turbulent seas of grief. After a life-altering crisis, natural caregivers — mums, dads and extended family — are immersed in their own pain and usually cannot help their children. Alone, many of

19

our young people turn to destructive behaviour as a means of 'coping' with overwhelming emotional pain. The results can be tragic.

• In many incidences of school violence, the attackers had experienced a major loss or change in a significant relationship prior to the school attack.

• Children of separated families have a higher probability of learning, emotional or behavioural problems due to the family system changing.

• The majority of of teenage pregnancies are among adolescents from single-parent homes.

• Many children in drug-dependence clinics are from single-parent families.

• A large proportion of suicides tend to be from single-parent families.

These unfortunate statistics speak for themselves. They are the sad harvest of society's neglect.

Children don't distinguish between the pain of loss that results from death and the pain of loss that results from divorce, separation, or abandonment. Adults do, but kids don't. Children of divorced parents grieve just as deeply as children who have had a loved one die. Further, children and teenagers don't see the differences among each other — they are able to respond compassionately to the loss events of their peers as being similar to their own. No matter what event precipitates loss, children's needs are the same.

Children are not conceptual thinkers. They cannot differentiate between the loss of divorce or death and any other major loss. Children only know that something is missing.

In RAINBOWS, we see this time and again. The calls we received for help after the shooting rampage at Columbine High School in Colorado were essentially the same as the requests that came in after the Gulf War pulled thousands of soldiers — both men and women — away from their children.

Children can be healed from loss. While the pain of loss cannot be avoided — and children go through life experiencing many losses — it doesn't need to hurt for ever.

Some experts suggest that children can never escape the long-term negative effects of divorce. While I respect their work, I disagree with their conclusions. I *know* that children can recover from the painful effects of divorce and other family loss, because I have seen it happen countless times. Grieving children and teenagers need adult guidance and help — they can't negotiate grief's emotional abyss alone — but they can survive and thrive if they are supported and given the tools to grieve.

These final two lessons — that grief springs not only from death but also from all other life-altering loss events, and that children can be healed — are the most important things to remember about the way children deal with loss. Over the past 20 years, these have become the primary themes of RAINBOWS' grief support efforts. Helping adults understand these realities and showing them our proven path to healing are the underlying reasons for this book.

Healing the Hurt, Restoring the Hope

The book you are reading is a direct result of RAINBOWS. It's based on the experiences shared by participants, parents and RAINBOWS volunteers and on material used successfully year after year at RAINBOWS sites.

Grieving youngsters often feel that adults don't care that their hearts are broken, won't talk with them about their feelings and fears, and avoid listening to their concerns. In fact, parents and other concerned adults may simply be overwhelmed, or they may not know what to do. Parents and caring adults struggle with what to say and how to say it; they may even wonder if they should say anything at all. This book helps to bridge the gap between children and adults.

Whether you are a parent, teacher or other caring adult, this book is written as a guide for you. All of you — grandparents, extended family members, neighbours, teachers, social workers, doctors, nurses and even law enforcement personnel — witness the pain of grieving children, but you may not have been given the permission or direction to help in a meaningful way. This book recognizes the important influence you have in children's lives and welcomes you into the role of a compassionate guide who can provide needed support and encouragement.

The book is divided into three parts to cover three distinct elements: The Hurt, The Healing and The Hope.

• Part One, The Hurt, helps adults to recognize grief in kids. It looks at loss from a child's perspective, details the tragic toll that unresolved grief extracts from young people, and explores the fears and problems that they encounter when the family structure is radically changed. It also debunks the myth that children and teenagers are resilient and naturally able to bounce back from significant loss on their own.

• Part Two, The Healing, provides effective, age-appropriate grief-recovery strategies, including activities and games from RAINBOWS. Each chapter in this section includes practical checklists or guidelines to help you implement its suggestions.

• Part Three, The Hope, helps grieving children understand, appreciate, and accept their altered family units. Here, they learn how to let go of the family structure that they had before the loss, adapt to their new lives, and move forward.

Curing the Epidemic of Grief

Today, we walk amidst a burgeoning population of grieving children and teenagers. We are in a grief epidemic.

The types of losses young people may suffer include the loss of a parent due to death, divorce, separation or abandonment, Increasingly, young people are living in non-traditional families. According to the latest Census data, almost one in four children now lives in a one-parent family.

Young people endure other losses as well. These may include a parent who has lost a job, or the sadness of saying goodbye to friends, teachers and schools as they move to new areas with their families. Whether it is the death of a grandparent or family pet, or the more traumatic loss of a sibling, friend or parent, most children will at some time experience the pain and loss of death. Thousands of children may be affected by injury or illness that debilitates a loved one, or may be themselves incapacitated. They may suffer emotional distress as a result of damage to homes and communities due to natural disasters such as flooding. Or children may experience other types of community crisis, such as the death of a beloved teacher.

Indeed, virtually all children will encounter some significant loss or family transition while growing up. I believe that no child should have to face these events alone.

Throughout my years of work with bereaved youngsters, I've seen at first hand the critical difference that caring adults can have on a child's grieving process. As president and founder of RAINBOWS, I talk about children and loss every day with parents, teachers, and

> A child's life is like a piece of paper … where each person met leaves a mark.

other caregivers. Every year, I conduct seminars on grief issues for families, teachers and counsellors across the country. The overwhelming, positive response I receive has compelled me to write this book to empower parents and other caregivers of children to be a source of strength and support for our emotionally overburdened young people.

Our children need us now more than ever. We are essential to their healing and resolution of loss. *We* are the cure for the global grief epidemic.

Part One
The Hurt

Companions on a Journey

All of you reading this book
Really are compassionate companions.

To children,
To teenagers,
Who are on a pilgrimage to a land called loss.

A pilgrimage is a journey
To a holy place of historic value …
And this place of loss
Is the holiest of all …
Deep in the soul where the beloved lived.

For most people, this journey is perilously frightening
Because they are not prepared to navigate
The turbulent waters
Of grief …

They don't know how
To manoeuvre through these emotions
That seem to shadow the bereaved every day
For years to come.

The signs of healing are initially
Small and undetectable.
Nevertheless,
If you look diligently,
The signs are unmistakably present.

Remember, grief is a process,
Recovery is a choice,
But it takes hard work.

All of the bereaved need and
Deserve a support team to cheer them on!

Chapter 1

Inside the Hearts of Grieving Children

ON A CRISP AUTUMN DAY IN THE MID-1980S, I drove to an old, red brick school for my first meeting with a group of five grieving children. The students were 13-year-olds who had enrolled in one of RAINBOWS' pilot programmes for children struggling with family loss and change. I didn't know the youngsters who had signed up, but as the group's facilitator, my job was to guide them through the grief process.

Anxious to have everything in place and ready to go, I arrived early. After checking in at the main office, I walked to the library, where the group was scheduled to meet, and looked for a comfortable spot. Bookshelves lined the walls and filled a third of the room. Two tidy rows of sturdy wooden tables occupied the rest of the space. I chose a table at the far end of the room, away from the door. Four chairs were in place already. I pulled two more up to it, set out the papers and materials I'd brought, then sat down and waited. The muted voices of children echoed up and down the hall, but the room itself was quiet, save for the steady, quiet ticking of a clock on the wall.

As I glanced nervously at the door, I wondered about the children with whom I was going to be working. Why had they enrolled in RAINBOWS? What type of loss was each one contending with? Were they at different levels of dealing with their grief? Had parents pressured the children to participate, or did they really want to be here? Would they like each other? Would the personalities mesh well or clash?

Finally, the participants arrived. Mark sauntered through the door first. He was a tall, blonde, smart-looking boy, a football player, with a strong profile, a reserved manner and a hint of peach fuzz on his cheeks. Mark said that he had joined RAINBOWS because his father had died recently. John, the second to show up for the session, had long, stringy hair and was dressed

WHAT IS RAINBOWS?

RAINBOWS is an international grief-support charity for children, adolescents and adults who are confronting a death, divorce, or some other painful family transition. RAINBOWS offers support and direction as the bereaved journey towards acceptance of their loss. Tragically, most of our children are left to mourn alone in silence. For those who have suffered a significant loss, RAINBOWS provides a bridge to emotional healing.

To carry out its mission, RAINBOWS has developed five age-directed programmes: SunBeams for very young children; Rainbows for children of primary school age; Spectrum for adolescents; Kaleidoscope for college students and adults; and Prism for single parents and step-parents. These peer-support programmes provide the participants with the opportunity to share and resolve their feelings in an accepting, non-judgemental environment.

RAINBOWS began by serving young people, and today the majority of our efforts remain focused on children and teenagers. All youth sessions are offered at no charge to participants and completely in black. His attitude was sullen, with an obvious chip on his shoulder. 'My old man divorced my mother. I live with her and my annoying little sister,' John muttered as he plopped down as far away from me as possible. Josh was the third to arrive. He waltzed in full of confidence and good cheer and pushed his thick wire-rimmed glasses up the bridge of his nose as he slipped into the centre seat. Nonchalantly, Josh announced that his parents had divorced two years earlier and that since then his father had disappeared and his mother remarried.

The last two participants walked in together. Red-haired, freckle-faced Brian trained his bright blue eyes on me and in a voice full of false bravado announced that his mother was serving a three-year prison sentence for fraud. In the meantime, he said, he and his dad were having a great time together. Jeff, the last to introduce himself, spoke with a hint of defiance in

---

most are located in schools, churches, synagogues and other convenient community sites, making it easy for children to attend.

RAINBOWS trains the sites' volunteer coordinators and the facilitators that guide each group. They help the participants to grapple with their immediate acute grief and deal with hidden and often simmering emotions, as well as teaching positive coping strategies that will support them throughout life. Each cycle is completed in 12 weeks, but the youngsters can return as often as they wish year after year. It's not unusual for children and teenagers to attend RAINBOWS for two or more cycles – or to return years later and rejoin a group after another family change, such as a remarriage.

Founded in 1983, we began with three sites in the Chicago area. Today, RAINBOWS has more than 8,500 sites in seventeen countries and has served more than one million children and teenagers. For more information, have a look at our website, *www.rainbows.org*, or *www.rainbowsgb.org* in the UK.

his voice. A slender child with an olive complexion, the shadow of a moustache over his upper lip and a head of thick, curly brown hair, Jeff said he'd never had a dad and had always lived with his mother.

There they were. Five adolescents. All boys! Each one 13 years old, gangly, awkward in a different way, voice cracking. Each one affected by loss, mired in grief and not even aware of it. That first day, the young teenagers made it clear that, despite the losses they'd endured, they were 'cool' and everything was 'OK'. As if to underline the point, the boys acted bored and distracted. Throughout the session, they fidgeted in their seats and often stared past each other. But behind the youthful panache, I knew other feelings were simmering. It was my responsibility to encourage these young men to acknowledge and talk about them.

Not an easy task. Working as the facilitator with such a diverse group was difficult. I wanted the meetings to matter for each boy. Given their varied situations, I knew that we needed to spend time on death, divorce, abandonment and even stepfamilies. I worried that, because their losses were so different, the members in the group would not understand or relate to each other.

I was wrong.

Many Losses, One Grief

Over the course of the many hours they spent together, these five boys — Mark, John, Josh, Brian and Jeff — forged a remarkable bond with each other. And, yes, sometimes they teased one another. At first, the boys denied or downplayed their personal upheavals. They either would not or could not acknowledge their emotional distress or hurt feelings. But as they grew to trust each other — and me — they dropped the pretence that all was well.

It became obvious that each boy wanted — desperately needed — to tell his individual story and was grateful that the others were there to listen.

Week after week, these youngsters shared their deepest fears and most personal experiences with each other. As they did so, the 'natural' divisions that I had anticipated never materialized. In revealing the intimate details of their lives, the boys did not distinguish between the source or degree of pain they felt. Not one of them saw his personal loss as harder or easier to bear than anyone else's loss. Each young man hurt deeply and needed to share his private pain. Each one needed the others to acknowledge his situation and feelings. It was as simple and as complicated as that.

The boys in that early group didn't compare scars; they helped each other heal. They also taught me more about loss and grief than any psychology class I've ever taken or any research study I've ever read. As I listened to their stories and heartaches, I came to understand the simple, underlying reality of children's grief: any life-altering loss can generate grief in a child or adolescent. It doesn't matter who or what is missing from their lives. Why someone is gone is irrelevant. What took them away doesn't matter in the innermost, deepest recesses of the child's heart. What counts is love. How much a child loved someone, how emotionally involved and deeply attached he was, determines how much pain he experiences when that person is no longer part of his daily life.

One cold afternoon eight weeks into the programme, the boys seemed especially quiet. Outside, under a steel grey sky, a fierce winter storm raged. The howling wind whistled at the windows and piled drifts of snow across the playground. Darkness was closing in early. Josh stared at the sombre scene and talked quietly about his father. 'Yeah, I guess I do miss my real dad and get kind of sad that he's gone,' he finally admitted, addressing no one in particular.

Josh's honesty opened the floodgates. One by one, as the afternoon light faded, the boys acknowledged being lonely. They remembered the times that they had felt scared and insecure. Each one owned up to problems dealing with friends and relatives. 'People always feel sorry for me,' Josh said. 'I don't want their pity.'

31

At every session that followed, the conversation quickly moved to a deeper, more heartfelt level. One day, Mark, who was usually polite and reserved, became visibly agitated. Flushed with anger, the young boy stridently denounced his father, who had died from lung cancer, for not having taken better care of his health. He'd hardly finished talking when Brian began to rail about his mother's 'stupidity'. The others sat quietly, heads nodding in solemn recognition of the constant gnawing anger that they all felt.

As time went by, the boys' attitudes and demeanours altered. Jeff and Brian seemed more relaxed. Mark became less haughty. Josh interrupted less often and grew more attentive to the others. He told me happily that he was getting better marks in school. Each of the youths smiled more readily. John's transformation was most pronounced. After several weeks with the group, he began to display the softer, sweet side to his personality. He became more open, less defensive. Ultimately, John cut his straggly hair and stopped dressing exclusively in black.

The last session with the group was very profound for me. The boys were talking about the forthcoming prizegiving ceremonies at their school. Under the circumstances, their losses weighed heavily. It really hurt, Mark told the others, to realize that his father wouldn't be at his prizegiving day or the sports award ceremony. 'Yeah, mine neither,' John said. 'I can't even send him an invitation. I don't know his address.' Jeff shook his head. 'My dad's never been to a school event in my whole life.'

As the boys conversed, they again found different ways to come to terms with their situations. Mark decided that his dad was watching over and would 'really' be there that day. John said he was going to save his certificates, pictures and awards — all the memorabilia connected with the big day. 'Someday, I'll find my dad and show them to him,' he said. Jeff liked that idea and said he would save everything, too. All through this discussion, Brian had been sitting quietly, lost in thought. 'You know, guys,' he said finally. 'My mum's going to be released from jail in a couple of years. I'm going to put away my stuff for her. When we're together again, I'll tell her *everything*.'

Once more, the boys had shared their individual pain. And again, from their perspective, no one's heartache was deeper or more intense than any other's. The precipitating events varied, but the grief was equally intense. The boys knew it. I had just learned it, from them.

What Triggers Grief

Some experts argue that only death results in grief. I believe that any traumatic change that results in loss overwhelms children and teenagers with powerful emotions and leads to grief of varying degrees. These events include:

Death. A person's life has ended. Someone we love is gone. It is especially difficult for young children, who have no concept of finite time, to understand the finality of death.

Divorce. A marriage ends. A family unit is for ever altered. Divorce represents the end of a nuclear family's existence. Often, there is ongoing conflict and tension. For example, two years after her parents divorced, Christine told me they are still fighting. Now all the arguments centre on her — late child support payments, when she should be picked up or dropped off, with whom she should spend her birthday. The bickering is constant, said Christine, and makes her feel like she exists in a war zone.

Abandonment. Someone we love or want to love has left us. In RAIN-BOWS, we have seen that even single-parent children who have never known their fathers feel they have been deserted by their dads and endure the agony of great emptiness.

Illness or disability. Well-being has ceased to exist. An 8-year-old girl who had recently been diagnosed with diabetes was referred to a child psychiatrist at her local hospital because she deliberately flouted doctors' orders and often took risks with her diet and lifestyle. In a special RAIN-BOWS group on the children's unit of the hospital, the quiet young patient

33

DEATH AND DIVORCE: CHILDREN'S PERSPECTIVES

Grief counsellors and hospice workers often take exception to my view that divorce can have as great an impact (and sometimes a more long-term and detrimental effect) on a child or teenager as a parent's death. In fact, while there are similarities and differences between them, both losses can be overwhelming. Here are what I have found to be the immediate and long-term effects and reactions described by youngsters who have experienced such events.

Similarities between Death and Divorce

Sadness

Anger

Blame

Shame

Memories revered

Guilt

Worry

Parent dating

Family life different

Economic changes/problems

Fear of losing other parent

Regrets

Changes in lifestyle

Future unknown

Differences between Death and Divorce

Death	Divorce
Corpse	No body
Public acknowledgement	No public acknowledgement
Part of life cycle	Embarrassment
Will never see person again	Caught in middle
	Bitterness
	Ongoing conflict
	Hope of reconciliation

admitted that she was upset because she wasn't 'like the other girls any more'. Disease had robbed her of a normal childhood and she mourned the loss.

Incarceration of a parent or sibling. In this case, children are deprived of a loved one's daily presence. Patrick was 11 when his father, a banker, was found guilty of mismanaging money at his job and sent to prison for three years. Overnight, Patrick's world collapsed. The boy wrote to his father weekly, but his dad refused to allow him to visit the prison. Relatives and friends stopped calling. Patrick's mother went to work full time. Pressed for funds, she sold their spacious house and rented a tiny two bedroom apartment. At first, Patrick steadfastly proclaimed his father's innocence; after a while, he stopped talking about him altogether.

Other types of loss. Children may grieve for a home and treasures lost in a fire, flood or other devastating disaster. They may grieve the death of a beloved pet. A child may grieve for the friends or school left behind when her family has relocated to a new city or town. Even the loss of a parent's job can deeply affect a child. For instance, when Amelia's father was made redundant, there never seemed to be enough money to pay the mortgage and the other bills. One night, Amelia took an overdose of sleeping pills. 'With one less person to feed, you'll be able to make it,' the distressed 12-year-old wrote in a note to her parents.

The overall traumatic impact of each loss event depends on the child's relationship with and how much she values the person or thing that is lost. Every loss is painful. The only difference is degree.

Grief is difficult to watch in children and adolescents. We want to spare them the pain and protect them from the heartache. So we assure ourselves that children, especially very young children, are not really affected by loss. But they are — more than we may care to acknowledge.

A loss event becomes part of a child's personal history for ever. It alters a child's deepest feelings and affects his view of life. In some intrinsic way, loss changes children. For example, it makes them more or less cautious, more or less aggressive and determined, or more or less outgoing.

Loss cannot be erased. Grief cannot be wished away.

What Children Want You to Understand

Children express their grief in a multitude of ways. Their actions reflect their ages and personalities, the intensity of their feelings, and their family situations. Each of the following stories carries a message to you from a bereaved child.

'I HAVE SAD ATTACKS'

Children's grief is profoundly different from adults'. Children and teenagers grieve in their own way and in their own time. One minute a child may be happily playing tag in the school playground; the next, he may be leaning against a tree, looking profoundly sad. Moments later, he may be back playing tag. Adults, because of their emotional maturity, usually grieve in a continuum. I have seen it in myself and others; after a painful loss, we are thrust into grief, a time of anguish and despair. Even for adults who work daily on their grief, it still takes months before they feel like smiling again. And then it is years before they genuinely re-embrace life. Grieving adults seem to follow an almost visible path as they slowly move away from their great sadness.

For children, the grieving process is different. Minutes after they have been told a loved one has died, or their parents are getting a divorce, they run outside to play. It isn't because children are not feeling deep sorrow about the news they just heard, but rather because they are only able to grieve for short periods. Their lack of emotional maturity simply doesn't allow them to sustain intense pain for long periods. I call these intermittent bouts of grief 'sad attacks'.

Sad attacks are spontaneous. They come without warning and cannot be prevented. Anything that reminds children of the people who are missing from their lives can trigger a sad attack. A bereaved child can be in the midst of playing a game, doing the washing-up, or even watching television, when an advert, song or image washes over him with memories of the past. If the child is working through his grief, sad attacks occur with less frequency over time, although they never cease entirely. Years later, a memory or event can trigger a quick bout of sadness.

Sad attacks are healthy. They give the grieving child time to reflect on and revisit his grief. They help him assess how far he has come and also help move him forward in the work of healing.

'I'M NOT TOO YOUNG TO MISS MY DADDY'

Grief is the normal, natural human reaction to a significant loss or change in our lives. When love is removed, when a loved person or object is taken from our lives, we are filled with poignant sorrow. Grief, then, is an expression of love. It is a consequence of loving.

Anyone who is capable of loving is capable of grieving. Age doesn't matter. 'A person is a person no matter how small,' said Dr Seuss. When a loss occurs, even children too young to articulate what is missing know that something important — a voice, a touch — is no longer part of their lives.

Nicole was 8 months old when her father died from an aneurysm. Initially, Nicky remained a calm, good-natured baby. But after a few weeks, she suddenly became fussy and irritable. She wanted to be held constantly and seemed to only take comfort from a male voice. 'She's just a baby; she doesn't know what's going on,' relatives and friends insisted. The child's mother disagreed. She realized that at some conscious level, the baby was aware of her father's absence and longed for him. After all, he had been an ongoing presence in the little girl's short life. He had talked to Nicole when the baby was still in her mother's womb. When Nicky was born, her dad cut the cord and was the first to hold her. Later, at home, he gave the baby her nightly feeds and watched Sunday afternoon football games with her. When Nicky was only 3 weeks old, he began taking her along on Saturday errands. Now, he was gone. 'Nicky misses her daddy,' her mother told the family.

> If a child is old
> enough to love,
> he is old enough
> to grieve.

'I DON'T KNOW HOW I AM SUPPOSED TO ACT'

Sixteen-year-old Larry knew his older brother Danny was seriously ill. Danny had been diagnosed with leukaemia six months earlier and had been hospitalized for long periods since. The parents openly discussed the treatments Danny had to undergo, but neither ever acknowledged that Danny, 18, might die. Larry thought it was simply a matter of time before his brother was cured and back to normal.

One afternoon, Larry walked in the front door after school. His parents, sister, grandparents and the family minister were seated together around the dining room table. They all looked stricken and sad. When Larry entered the room, his mother burst into tears. 'Danny's dead,' she blurted out.

Larry didn't say one word. He ran from the room, grabbed a basketball from the garage and biked back to school to shoot baskets. Several hours later, he returned home. His parents were upset and angry.

'How could you leave? You should have been here with us,' his father said.

'Aren't you going to cry? Doesn't it matter to you that your brother is dead?' his mother demanded.

Larry slunk away. Later, he came to his parents and admitted that he was confused by and ashamed of his own behaviour. 'I didn't want Danny to die,' he said. 'I never knew anyone who died, and when it happened, I didn't know how to act, what to do or how to feel.'

Stunned by the news of his brother's death, Larry desperately tried to make life seem normal. So he did what he routinely did after school: played basketball. It was, he acknowledged to his parents, a way to deny the truth that he couldn't face and to avoid the horrible sad feelings that were washing over him.

'I'M SO WORRIED'

Children also grieve for reasons that are not always apparent to adults. After his parents divorced, 9-year-old Gary and his younger sister lived with their mother. Marcia had gone back to work and struggled hard to make home life stable for her children. Marcia was surprised when Gary's teacher told her he wasn't doing well in class. 'He's not a discipline problem,' the teacher said. 'But he seems disengaged from the rest of the children. In fact, he spends most of his time staring out of the window.'

Back home, Marcia sat Gary down for a serious talk. 'Nothing's wrong,' he insisted, fidgeting and refusing to catch her eye. Marcia persisted, posing questions about every important activity and person in Gary's life.

Finally, Gary looked up. 'It's Daddy,' he whispered sadly. He was worried, he said, that his father didn't know how to care for himself. 'He can't cook!' the boy exclaimed. 'His place is a mess. He doesn't know how to clean it up.' Gary couldn't imagine his dad living alone. He was afraid for him.

'IF YOU TELL ME WHAT'S GOING ON, I WON'T BE SO UPSET'

Our culture does not prepare children for loss. As a result, feelings of grief are alien to our young people. Many children, especially the very young, don't even know the words to describe their emotions. Often, grief is expressed through misbehaviour or physiological ailments, such as a headache or stomach-ache.

The morning before Tommy's family was to move from their city apartment to a house in the suburbs, the lively 3-year-old woke up unable to walk. His parents found him lying on the floor of his room, crying. Each time the little boy tried to stand, his legs crumpled and he fell to the floor. At the accident and emergency department, doctors could find nothing physically wrong. After talking with the parents, one doctor suggested that the boy might be reacting to the family's move. 'He doesn't understand what any of it means. Fear of the unknown can be terrifying to a child,' the doctor said.

Tommy's parents bundled him up and drove him to the new home. They showed the boy his new bedroom and slowly carried him through the house, explaining what each room was and where the furniture would go.

When they got back to the apartment, Tommy's mum and dad began packing more boxes. But this time they let Tommy 'help'. They handed the toddler a black magic marker and set him down in the middle of the packing cases. As each box was filled, Tommy was to write down the name of the room it was to go in at the new house. The adults knew Tommy couldn't really write, but that didn't matter. They hoped that participating in the move would give their son a sense of control over the situation. And it worked!

The next day as the three of them followed the moving van to the new house, the parents talked to Tommy about the new neighbourhood. When they arrived, Tommy's mother carried him in and sat him down on the floor of the living room so he could watch all the activity. For a while, Tommy sat quietly. Then, without saying a word, he jumped up and started telling the movers where the boxes went and why.

If loss occurs and no one talks to children about how family life might change, they are left to create their own fantasies about the situation.

And though some of these fantasies can seem absurd to adults, to children they are very real — and very scary. Consider the case of a 6-year-old who refused to board his school bus for home one afternoon. Sobbing, he told his teacher that his parents had been forced to sell the family farm. 'Yesterday, when I got off the bus, a truck was there taking away the pigs,' he said. 'Today, they're probably going to take me away.'

As children mature into adolescence, they learn how to express their feelings verbally and should be better equipped to cope with loss. Rarely, however, do adults talk to them about what has happened. I have had teenagers say to me, 'If these terrible feelings are a normal reaction to loss, then how come not one adult has ever talked to me about them? After all, they talk to me about all the other stuff I should know about, like driving, drinking and dating.'

Grieving teenagers are left thinking that their feelings are weird and unacceptable. Worse, they may lose their grip on reality.

Lucy, a 17-year-old overweight girl, convinced herself that if she starved herself, her mother, who had died from a brain haemorrhage, would come back to life. 'My weight problem was the only thing we ever argued about,' she said. 'I thought if I was thin, it would change everything and Mum would come back.'

'WHAT'S GOING TO HAPPEN TO ME?'

Little blonde, blue-eyed Chris was only 2 years old when his identical twin brother Alex died. Not wanting to upset Chris, his parents sent him off to live with relatives for a number of weeks. They did not allow him to see them crying or attend any of the funeral services. They never talked to Chris about Alex. Two years passed. One day, when Chris was 4 years old, he pointed to a photo in the living room that showed him and Alex together as smiling toddlers splashing about in a paddling pool. 'Am I going to disappear like the other boy in the picture?' Chris asked.

Grief is such a small, unassuming word, yet it collapses even the strongest adults. Perhaps this is why so many people are afraid of it and hesitate to talk to children about loss. When we think of grief, we think only of pain and suffering. And, yes, these are the initial very real associations we have with loss. But if we learn to look at grief as a process that moves us from one place in life to another, from one level of personal development to a higher level of existence, it becomes possible to take a more positive look at grief and present that view to our children.

'I FEEL TERRIBLE INSIDE – PLEASE, LET ME TALK ABOUT IT'

Late one hot summer night, a 6-year-old girl named Fayeesha awoke to find her dad and uncle arguing in the kitchen. The two exchanged angry words and began shoving each other around the cramped room. Then, while Fayeesha watched helplessly, her uncle grabbed a knife off the kitchen counter and plunged it into her father's chest. The police were at the scene in minutes. Soon afterwards, a social worker came and took Fayeesha into temporary care in a children's home, while the authorities searched for her mother or other relatives.

Although Fayeesha's shoulder-length black hair had been hastily brushed into two uneven pigtails, she was still wearing her pyjamas and slippers when she arrived at the home. Breakfast was being served, and Fayeesha was hurriedly seated at a table with several noisy children. Exhausted and in shock, Fayeesha slumped down in the chair and stared at her fingers.

Soon a staff worker arrived with a plate of food and began serving the other children. 'What's wrong, honey?' the woman asked the frightened child.

The little girl looked up, eyes brimming. 'I saw my daddy get killed last night,' she whispered sadly.

The other children stopped eating and glanced nervously at each other. The staff worker froze in place. There are many things the woman could have said or done to help Fayeesha at that moment. But she was so flustered, so distressed by the child's horrible experience, she could not think of a single appropriate response.

'Here, dear, have some toast,' she said and hurried away. The traumatized little girl was left to a pain-filled silence and the stares of the other children.

Fayeesha needed someone to bear witness to her story, someone willing to take on a tiny portion of her great burden of grief by listening to what she had to say and acknowledging the horror she had witnessed. But instead of a compassionate listener, she got food. Adults do that a lot. We offer the grieving child material goods — ice cream, a second serving of cake, a new dress, better skates, the latest designer jeans — because we don't know what else to offer. We don't know how to respond to pain-filled statements with words; we don't know the questions to ask that will prompt grieving children to share their emotional pain.

Often, grieving youngsters are left to their own inner silence because we, the adults in their lives, won't listen to them. We don't let them talk about the loss event. Uncomfortable with grief, we don't want them to discuss their anxieties. We ignore their feelings and hope that the grief will resolve itself and go away on its own. It doesn't.

'I SAY THAT EVERYTHING'S FINE, BUT IT'S NOT'

Ironically, not all troubled responses are obvious. At the other end of the spectrum are the grieving children and teenagers who carry on without any noticeable change in their personality or lifestyle. It's tempting to breathe a sigh of relief and say, 'Thank goodness, this kid's fine,' when a child moves through a loss experience with what appears to be perfect equanimity. But we shouldn't let ourselves be fooled. These youngsters need help too and, in fact, may be harder to reach than those in open rebellion. That's because rather than dealing with grief and its attendant emotions, they have stuffed their feelings deep inside.

Wayne was a normal, easygoing child. He liked football, computer games and skateboarding. Friday night was video night at Wayne's house. Every week Wayne and his dad rented a film from the local video shop, and then he and his parents ate pizza and watched the film together. When Wayne was 9 years old, his father died suddenly of a heart attack. 'When my mum told me, I couldn't cry or say anything,' he told me. 'I didn't know what to do.'

A few years later, Wayne's mother remarried. Wayne liked his step-father. After his new baby sister was born, Wayne said he felt like part of a real family again. Then everything unravelled. His parents began arguing. One day, Wayne's stepdad left, without even saying goodbye. After this event, Wayne came to RAINBOWS. He told us that he was worried about his sister, but that he was OK. Indeed, he seemed fine. Wayne was well-mannered; he did well in school; he never got into trouble.

Finally, at the seventh meeting, one of the other boys in the group prodded Wayne. 'You lost two fathers! You must be upset about that,' he said. Wayne flushed bright red and slammed his fist against the tabletop. 'You can't say that,' he yelled at the other boy. 'How do you know how I feel? Everything's fine.' Wayne's outburst silenced the other children. He glared at the anxious adolescent faces gathered around the table, daring anyone to challenge him further. Finally, one of the girls spoke up. 'I don't think I'd be OK if that happened to me,' she said gently. The colour drained from Wayne's cheeks. Tears welled in his eyes. As the others waited, Wayne's façade crumbled. 'I get so scared sometimes, I can't even think,' he admitted. His deepest fear, he told them, was that his mother would leave him, too. 'That's why I'm good all of the time, so she won't abandon me like both my fathers did,' he sobbed.

Unless they are able to acknowledge their pain to themselves or to someone else, children like Wayne will never fully work through their grief. It will haunt them throughout their lives.

'I Haven't Finished Grieving Yet'

Monica was 11 years old when her mother died suddenly of a thrombosis. Initially, the teachers and staff at Monica's school comforted her. But three months after the funeral, Monica's teacher lost patience. Monica was failing academically. Often, she sat in the class and stared out of the window. Monica told me she would never forget the day that her teacher snapped at her, 'Your mother has been dead for months ... just forget about it! You can't use her death to excuse your low marks any longer.'

Grieving a serious loss like death or divorce takes years to complete. Oddly, the first year is usually the easiest. The grieving child is numbed by her loss, and family, teachers and friends tend to be the most understanding and supportive during this time (though there are exceptions, like Monica's teacher). The magnitude of the loss usually sets in during the second year. Just about the time that everyone assumes the child has finished grieving, she is really just beginning. It usually takes three years after the loss for the intensity of the pain to diminish enough to allow the grieving child to begin reconstructing a new life. By the fifth year, the child is usually able to experience happiness and promise once again.

Grieving cannot be hurried.

By not allowing children time to grieve, adults prolong the process for them. Monica's teacher is not alone in her efforts to 'hurry along' her charge. All too often, well-meaning parents, grandparents and teachers tell grieving children to 'be strong for their parent', 'behave' or 'keep up those grades'. Translated to a child or an adolescent, this well-intentioned advice means 'don't talk or think about your loss'. Rather than dealing with their feelings

GRIEF GOES TO SCHOOL: WARNING SIGNS

I have been in classrooms where 50 per cent or more of the children have lost a parent to either death or divorce. Children don't leave their grief at the school door; it comes into the classroom with them. Sometimes, concerns that children suppress at home show up at school.

One day during her first-lesson maths class, Larissa, a lanky 12-year-old, jumped up from her desk and burst into tears in front of her startled classmates. Then the distraught child turned and ran out of the room. The teacher, a wise and compassionate woman, followed Larissa into the corridor. She found the girl curled up on the floor in the girls' toilets. The teacher knelt down, put her arms around the sobbing child and comforted her as she cried. Finally, the girl's sobs began to subside. 'What's wrong?' the teacher asked. Larissa looked up, her freckled face strained and lined with tears. 'Right this minute my mum and dad are in court fighting to see who gets custody of me,' she said. 'Maths doesn't seem very important. Nothing does, compared to this?'

Teachers tell me that they can often predict as much as a year before the event when a student's parents are getting divorced or when there is some other family trauma occurring.

or needs, grieving children bury or deny their emotions. Consequently, the grief may linger beneath the surface for years.

Children's grief should never be ignored. The consequences are too great. When children and teenagers suppress the powerful emotions of grief — really disclaiming or ignoring them — they use an incredible amount of energy to obscure the painful feelings. This energy is diverted away from school, sports, hobbies, jobs and other positive opportunities in their lives. It is part of their potential, and it is lost for ever.

Their divination, they admit, has nothing to do with extrasensory perception. It is based solely on changes in the child. Here are some of the warning signs that teachers have observed that signal a student might be experiencing turmoil at home. The child or teenager:

❋ Often leaves lunch, gym clothes or homework at home and wants to phone home almost as soon as he arrives at school.

❋ Has difficulty concentrating. Her homework and tests are incomplete. Grades decline.

❋ Is very emotional or cries easily.

❋ Acts out his feelings, becoming the class clown, truant or developing a discipline problem.

❋ Daydreams. She is preoccupied and often forgets homework, sports match dates and so on.

❋ Has an untidy locker or desk or hands in messy homework. The external messiness seems to coincide with his internal confused, 'messed up' feelings.

❋ Withdraws from school activities and social activities or sports.

Repressed grief does not dissipate. It simmers within. Sometimes it is expressed through chronic health problems. Invariably, it subtly shapes and influences the child as she grows up and becomes an adult. Submersed grief colours her outlook on life. At work or with friends, she tends to be cynical and treat even weighty matters like a joke. There is an edge to her. She maintains a careful, calculated distance. Fear of intimacy keeps her from serious commitments and makes her wary of establishing lasting relationships.

When the painful emotions of grief are disavowed or withheld, all other feelings are repressed as well. It's impossible to deny some feelings and express others. When grief is suppressed, anger is buried along with it, as are joy and love. Over time, suppressed grief invades every facet of a child's life: academics, activities, relationships, emotional and physical health, and dreams.

What's Normal

When Samuel was 10, he went to stay with his grandparents for two weeks during the summer holidays. One day, the outgoing, energetic boy sat on the garage floor while his grandfather, a hearty 72-year-old retired mechanic, tinkered with an old car he was trying to get going. The vehicle rested precariously on a slender, modern jack. Sam's grandfather lay under the car. Without warning, the jack slipped and fell, trapping the boy's grandfather underneath.

Horror-stricken, Sam rushed into the house. He called the paramedics, and then he and his grandmother stood by helplessly as the rescue squad lifted his grandfather into the ambulance. Despite several operations, the elderly gentleman never regained the use of his legs. He came home in a wheelchair.

By then, Sam had returned home and was back at school. He didn't tell any of his friends what had happened; at home, he never mentioned the accident and neither did his parents.

On the surface, everything continued normally. The family plunged into a hectic autumn schedule. Sam had plenty of homework and a full line-up of sports activities to keep him busy after school and on weekends.

But for Sam, life had inexplicably changed. Nothing held his interest. His grades fell; he became sullen and withdrawn. He dropped out of the football team. In October, for Sam's birthday, his parents bought him a mountain bike, which he had long coveted. Sam rode the bike several times, then he parked it in the garden shed and ignored it. 'It's just a phase,' the boy's mother said. His teachers agreed. Family and friends tried to cheer Sam up, but without success. Finally, in spring, the vicar from the family's church talked to Sam. 'What's wrong?' he asked. It was the first time anyone had put the question to the child.

Struggling to hold back his tears, Sam recalled what had happened to his grandfather. 'I think about it all of the time,' Sam explained. 'I can't help it; I feel so terrible about that morning. I didn't do anything to help, and now he's never going to get better.'

Most of us recognize the more obvious symptoms of grief, such as crying and sadness. But what about when a grieving 7-year-old throws frequent temper tantrums or a straight-A school student refuses to do her homework? These responses are also signs of grieving.

Although it may seem surprising, most behaviour changes in grieving children are normal reactions to a significant loss. Unable to express their feelings and emotions, grieving children and teenagers act them out. This can be frustrating for the adults in the youngster's life, but it can also provide insight into the child's emotions. Dramatic shifts in attitude can indicate unresolved issues of grief and anger and should be viewed and handled in that context. Behavioural changes may appear immediately after a loss, but more often they don't surface until several months later. In some instances, it can even take years.

Here are telltale signs of normal behaviour changes for different age groups.

BIRTH TO 2 YEARS OLD

Agitation and inability to follow the normal routine. Darren was 6 months old when his father, who was in the Navy, left for a three-month tour of duty at sea. Almost immediately, the baby boy became inconsolable. He fussed at bedtime, refused his bottle and cried constantly until someone picked him up.

Like Darren, infants from birth to 24 months of age require consistency in their environment. They are upset by sudden change and often respond by becoming lethargic and/or clingy. Sleep and eating habits change.

Fear and regressive behaviour. Amanda was 2 years old when her family relocated to the other side of the country. Her parents thought that Amanda wouldn't notice the change. They were stunned when the normally happy, calm toddler became fussy and miserable. For three months after the move, Amanda cried whenever she was taken from her bedroom. She would eat only while sitting in her cot.

Frightened by change, toddlers seek security and cling to their mother, father, or other main nurturing figure. Their behaviour regresses. They suck their thumbs. Toilet-trained 2- and 3-year-olds may lose bowel and bladder control. They may be afraid of being left alone or refuse to sleep in the dark.

3 TO 6 YEARS OLD

Fantasizing about a return to the status quo. Alicia's parents separated in late winter and finalized their divorce before summer ended. During the week, Alicia lived with her mother. She spent most weekends with her father at his new flat. Five-year-old Alicia didn't seem overly upset by the arrangement. One day in early December, Alicia's aunt took her Christmas shopping. To the woman's dismay, Alicia insisted on buying a joint present for her parents. 'Daddy's coming back home,' the little girl explained. 'But don't tell Mummy. It's a surprise.' In fact, Alicia's parents had never discussed reconciliation.

Like Alicia, young children aged 3 to 6 often fantasize about the non-custodial or deceased parent's return.

Bedwetting, thumb-sucking and other regressive behaviour is common. Outwardly, these children are often aggressive and hostile towards other children.

7 TO 10 YEARS OLD

Fear of abandonment. Neal was 8 years old when his parents divorced. A year later, his mother started dating. Every time she left the house on a date, the young boy worried that, like his father, she might not come back. On his mother's date nights, Neal clutched a can of soup to his chest when he went to bed. 'It's the only thing I know how to cook,' he said.

From the ages of 7 to 10, children fear abandonment. They're deeply saddened by family loss. They often withdraw from peers and pick fights with friends and siblings. They complain of headaches, do poorly in school and can't concentrate.

11 TO 14 YEARS OLD

Mood shifts. Jessica was the oldest of three girls. When her father deserted the family, her mother struggled to make ends meet financially. Jessica had to shop at secondhand and charity shops and take over some of the chores that their former cleaning woman had handled. Pizzas and trips to the cinema became rare luxuries. Although Jessica never complained, she became withdrawn and sombre. She stopped hanging out with her old friends and started spending her evenings at the computer, visiting Internet chat rooms.

Struggle for identity. When the family structure or status changes, young adolescents often become angry and ashamed of being different. Their emerging sense of identity may blur. Their moods shift dramatically. They're distracted at school and their marks go down. Seeking to stabilize their lives, they often seek friendships with other adults, such as a teacher, coach or neighbour.

15 TO 20 YEARS OLD

Bravado disguising fear. For the four years since their parents divorced, 15-year-old Dean and his 17-year-old brother Gerald had insisted to their mother that the divorce wasn't a problem for them. 'That's between you and Dad,' they said. 'We've got our friends. We're fine.' Then, their mother was diagnosed with an aneurysm and sent for a series of tests. The boys went to the hospital with her. Gerald hovered nearby as his mum lay on a trolley waiting to be taken for the tests. Just days earlier, the teenage football fan had assured her that he was an adult and soon would be on his own. Suddenly, Gerald leaned over his mother and in an anxious whisper said, 'Mum, who will take care of us if anything happens to you?'

Teenagers and young adults from the ages of 15 to 20 often respond to grief by rebelling against family norms. They become negative and cynical. Their moods shift abruptly. They become angry. Often, they try to satisfy their emotional hunger with material goods. They demand better stereos and expensive clothes. But underneath the bravado, they're like Gerald, still children at heart. They're alarmed at the thought of losing their parents and frightened by the prospect of being left alone.

What's Not Normal

Erik was 9 years old when his parents divorced, and for a long time afterwards he seemed the perfect child. He earned straight A's in school, was a great defender in football and was active in his Scout troop. Erik's parents were well-educated and affluent. Although the boy lived with his father, he saw his mother regularly. By all accounts, Erik wasn't at all affected by the divorce. Then, at 13, Erik turned rebellious. His bedroom became a hovel; he dropped out of football and started playing truant. He let his neatly cropped hair grow into long, stringy locks.

One day, Erik bought a secondhand black leather jacket. On the back, he spelled out the word 'Help' with safety pins he had carefully strung together. No matter what the weather, Erik wore the jacket. His friends thought it was cool. Parents and teachers assumed that Erik was going through a phase and would eventually outgrow it. Incredibly, no one asked the boy what he needed help with. Certainly, no one linked Erik's behaviour with his parents' divorce. That seemed like ancient history. The only person aware of the enormous turmoil seething inside Erik was the mother of one of his best friends. Once a week, she said, Erik sat in her kitchen and pounded his fist against the table, as he raged against his father. 'I'm so angry with my dad. I want to kill him,' he said. The friend's mother didn't take him seriously.

But one day, when he was 16, Erik made good his threat. Using a hunting rifle from the garage, the teenager shot his father in their garden. Erik's dad died, and Erik's story made national news. Listening to the news report, I was overwhelmed with sorrow. It seems that both the boy and his father were victims — victims of anger never acknowledged, never discussed, never diffused.

Extreme behaviour changes, like those belatedly exhibited by Erik, indicate serious problems. Not all grieving children and teenagers will exhibit extreme behaviour changes, but all are at risk for them.

Here are some troubled responses to loss for different age groups.

BIRTH TO 6 YEARS OLD

Strong resistance to forming new attachments. Alastair was at nursery school when his mother died and 7 years old when his father remarried. The boy insisted that he liked his stepmother, but his actions towards her were always cold and distant. Every June, he forgot her birthday. He never gave her a card or present at Christmas. When Alastair turned 18, his stepmother finally suggested that they should talk honestly about their relationship. It was only then that the young man admitted his fear that she would die just like his mother had. 'I never want to hurt like that again,' he said. Fear of loss and the subsequent pain also were the reasons that he'd never had a girlfriend.

Exaggerated clinging. Four-year-old Emily loved nursery school. Every morning, she'd kiss her mother goodbye and skip into the room. Then the little girl's parents divorced. Now Emily arrives at school agitated and anxious. She begs her mother not to leave; once her mum is gone, Emily cries and misbehaves for 10 or 15 minutes every morning.

7 TO 13 YEARS OLD

Anxiety or preoccupation with further loss. Brandon was 8 years old when his 24-year-old Aunt Mary died suddenly. After the funeral, Brandon kept asking to go to the graveyard. While his parents waited nearby, he sat on Mary's grave and 'talked' to her until his mum and dad coaxed him to leave. Brandon became fixated on death. He talked about it nightly at bedtime. He begged his mother to assure him that no-one else he loved would die.

Persistent fears of catastrophe. Any crisis or natural disaster — such as a fatal plane crash, hurricane, or terrorist attack — can cause intense, ongoing fears that disrupt normal activity and recovery for children and teenagers.

14 TO 20 YEARS OLD

Sexual activity. Pre-adolescents and teenagers use sex as a substitute for the parental love that is lost through divorce, separation, abandonment or death. Hungry for affection, they're apt to become involved with anyone, unaware or unconcerned that promiscuity exposes them to sexually transmitted disease. Many girls even get pregnant deliberately; they want a baby so they'll have someone to love them exclusively.

Drug and alcohol abuse. Grieving children and teenagers may use drugs or alcohol to numb the intense pain they're feeling. With these readily available substances, they find temporary relief from their emotional distress.

Gang activity or other trouble with the law. Following her parents' divorce, Kelly began stealing earrings from a local department store. She was 14 and a 'good girl'. When her parents found out, they were shocked; unprepared for this kind of behaviour from their daughter. The reasons grieving children get into trouble are as varied as the children themselves. They could be shouting for attention because their previous, more subtle, attempts weren't noticed; they could be so numb from the pain that they choose risky behaviour to stimulate some internal response; they might feel so angry and wronged that they want to get even; or, in the case of gangs, they might desperately be trying to find somewhere they feel they belong.

Talk of suicide. Any mention or hint of suicide is truly a cry for help and must be taken seriously. At a RAINBOWS session, a 15-year-old boy was distressed because his mother was soon to be released from a mental institution. The child, who had lived happily with his grandparents for several years, worried that 'everything was going to change' when his mum moved in with them. 'I just want to die,' he said. Uncertain if the boy understood the gravity of his words, the RAINBOWS facilitator asked how he thought that might happen. 'My grandfather's an artist,' the boy responded. 'I'll use his craft knife to cut my wrists.' Alarmed, the facilitator immediately telephoned the grandparents and the social services department. Within 2 hours, the boy was in counselling.

Depression. Sadness is a visible sign of depression and can be witnessed in even the youngest of children. Depressed teenagers daydream constantly, play too many video or computer games, sleep excessively and pull back from their friends.

It is important to understand that these troubled behaviour patterns are not rigidly tied to age. I have heard of teenagers who wet the bed and 5-year-olds describing in detail how they were going to commit suicide. Any

NORMAL VERSUS TROUBLED RESPONSES TO LOSS

Here, at a glance, is a list of how normal responses to loss compare with troubled ones.

Normal	Troubled
Decreased ability to function, apathy	Isolation, withdrawal, depression
Loss of appetite	Change in eating habits, eating disorder
Restless sleep	Refuses to sleep alone, nightmares
Irritable, crabby	Physical aggression, violence
Stomach-aches, headaches	Psychosomatic illness, accident-prone
Shock	Total denial of loss event
Decline in school marks	Drops out of school or is expelled

troubled behaviour warrants immediate attention and shouldn't be ignored as 'just a phase'.

The Special Needs of Teenagers

Adolescence tends to be a complicated, difficult period. Most teenagers feel insecure. They fear rejection and often mask their real feelings. Many teenagers find it hard to believe that they are accepted and worthwhile; often they feel they are not loved.

Here's what is going on during *normal* teenage years.

• Physical: the adolescent often experiences a clumsy, awkward period of growth spurts, bodily changes and hormonal imbalances.

- Sexual: teenagers experience sexual awakenings and aren't sure how to deal with them properly.

- Familial: adolescents receive mixed messages from parents and other adults. They're told 'You're too old for that' as well as 'You're too young for that'. At the same time, teenagers are beginning the parent-child separation process. Friends start becoming more important than family.

- Social: the adolescent craves and needs acceptance from his peers. Friendships fluctuate. Peer pressure is intense. A young adult desperately needs to belong to a peer group and struggles to relate to members of the opposite sex.

- Academic: the teenager's grades fluctuate as rapidly as her moods, relationships and self-esteem.

- Emotional: the adolescent seems to cry or explode for no apparent reason. He is outgoing and friendly in the morning, sullen and withdrawn after lunch.

When a loss occurs during the teenage years, the adolescent must cope with many additional burdens at an already challenging time. For the grieving teenager, life can seem almost unbearable.

THE STRUGGLE FOR IDENTITY

When Dennis was 16, his mother told him and his sister that, five years after her divorce from their dad, she was getting remarried. Dennis's initial reaction was light and joking. 'It's about time,' he teased his mum. A few moments later, Dennis asked his mother if she intended to take her new husband's name. 'Yes, of course,' she replied. Dennis hung his head. 'Then I won't be linked to you any more,' he said quietly.

Although the teenager is struggling to establish his own separate identity, his self-image is still strongly linked to his family. If the family unit disintegrates or is substantially changed during these formative years, the teenager is left adrift. He may assure himself that the loss doesn't matter because he is an 'adult', but in his heart, he yearns for a 'real' family.

GROWING UP TOO FAST

If divorce, death, or some other type of loss occurs during adolescence, the teenager is often pushed into an adult role as her parent's confidant or replacement spouse. Single parents may take their teenage children along as their 'dates' to a social occasion or a work-related employee/spouse outing. The teenager might even be asked to serve as her parent's spokesperson or to assume a part of the financial responsibility for the family.

Marguerite had just turned 12 when her mother died. After the funeral, many of the family's friends and relatives told the petite young girl that 'she was the woman of the house now'. They told her it was her job to 'take care of her dad and brothers'.

Grief needs a voice.

Marguerite was in a state of near panic. She knew how to prepare a few simple dishes, put clothes into the washing machine and clean the house. But there was so much her mother hadn't taught her yet — how to change the sheets, make lunches, and iron the shirts her dad and brothers wore.

Determined to live up to the expectations others had for her, Marguerite withdrew from her friends and school activities and became an efficient young homemaker. But she began to change in other ways as well. Her style of dress became more adult; she started wearing make-up. Once a sweet, innocent girl, Marguerite suddenly looked 18.

When she was 15, Marguerite started not coming home after school and not phoning, either. Once, after a loud argument with her father, she stormed out the door and stayed away for several days. When Marguerite finally came home, her arms were badly bruised as if she'd been beaten and her breath smelled of beer. Her father looked at her sadly, trying to find

WHAT CHILDREN HAVE TAUGHT ME ABOUT GRIEF

In my many years of working with bereaved children and teenagers, I have gained an intimate insight into grief. The greatest source of my knowledge has been the children themselves. From them I have learned that:

* Grief is normal.

* Children and teenagers who experience loss are wise beyond their years.

* Grieving children and adolescents are frightened and overwhelmed by their feelings.

* Both children and teenagers need adults to protect them and guide them through the grief process.

* Grieving youngsters need to be reassured that they can survive the crisis.

* Children want to talk about the loss event but hesitate to initiate the conversation.

some vestige of his little girl in the hardened teenager who stood before him, defiant and prematurely 'grown up'.

Good Grief ...

Mark Twain once said that grief can take care of itself. As much as I admire Twain's witty, common-sense observations and comments about life, I beg to differ with him on this statement.

Grief rises from the heart. Children cannot wish away the emotions that result from it.

Grief demands understanding, guidance, and time. Grief acknowledges and honours the love of someone or something that is now absent from our lives.

Grief's pain is deep. It is unlike any other suffering we endure. It carries its own unique agony.

When we help children deal with grief in appropriate and life-giving ways, we teach them to be resilient. We provide them with invaluable lessons for life and prepare them for the other life-changing losses they will inevitably encounter in future years. Children and teenagers who learn how to grieve will not be overwhelmed by the pain of loss that strikes later in life. They will understand it and know that they need to experience it in order to move through the process of grief.

Grief hurts.
It requires healing.

That's why it is so important that we do not leave grief to chance. It is tempting — but foolhardy — to hope that grief will take care of itself. We wouldn't leave a broken bone to heal by itself and expect the fracture to mend properly. Just as a broken bone heals stronger at the fracture site if properly set, loss can be a life-giving, not life-threatening, experience — when it is approached and dealt with appropriately.

Chapter 2

Grief's Tangled Web: the Complex Phases of Children's Grief

A NUMBER OF YEARS AGO, I received a telephone call from a grandmother whose eldest granddaughter, Sara, 16, had been killed in a snowmobile accident the previous winter. 'Sara had been told not to go out riding that day, but she deliberately disobeyed,' the grandmother said brusquely, as if this fact were important. She went on to say that although the family was devastated, they had faced the tragedy stoically. They had finished with their grieving and moved on, she said, all except Sara's 14-year-old sister, Lisa, who wasn't coping well and whose behaviour was distressing everyone else.

I asked what the girl was doing that was upsetting her family. The grandmother explained that Lisa cried often and spent hours looking through Sara's photo album, reliving the stories that went with the pictures. Lisa was doing poorly in school and had stopped socializing with her friends. At least once a day, she went outside and pounded on the garage door where the snowmobile had been stored. Lisa, the grandmother contended, was wallowing in emotion and doing nothing to help herself.

I thanked the woman for her concern as a loving grandmother and then explained that Lisa's actions were appropriate and that she obviously needed to grieve. I also asked if the grandmother could find someone — a family member, friend, or teacher — to listen to Lisa's concerns on an ongoing basis and guide her in the healing process.

The grandmother was taken aback by my response and suggestions. Like many people, the well-intentioned matriarch assumed that following a death in the family, the surviving children would grieve for an 'appropriate' amount of time and then get on with their daily routines, much as she was able to do. The grandmother felt that something was wrong because Lisa's grief was so obvious, and so different from her own.

THE VOCABULARY OF LOSS

Adults often use the words bereavement, grief and mourning interchangeably, but the terms define three distinct human conditions, and children experience them all.

Bereavement is the state of being deprived. Something we value is gone. Anyone in this state is likely to feel 'torn apart' and children and young people will have special needs after a loss.

Grief encompasses the emotions felt as a result of being deprived. Grief is precipitated by an external event, but it is felt inside. Grieving is a process of working through loss. It is not a specific emotion, such as sadness, but rather a constellation of often-conflicting emotions, beliefs and actions. When we grieve, we use our entire selves. That is why it is so exhausting.

Mourning is the expression of the grief emotions. This is the time when all of the emotions inside come tumbling out; it is a shared social response to loss.

Grief is like that. Personal. Individual. Defiant of all logic. Each child's grief experience is universal, yet it remains as unique as her fingerprints.

In RAINBOWS, we have identified 10 different phases that grieving youngsters experience. While many experts in the study of adult grief divide the grieving process into five or six stages, I've found this categorization too limited to describe the chaotic cyclone of emotions and events that affect grieving children and teenagers. It may seem logical to apply adult standards of grief to youngsters who have experienced loss, but my work has convinced me that this approach is simply not adequate. Children's grief is different; it plunges deeper and spreads wider than that of adults. To understand grieving children, we need to confront the entire painful picture.

Like Lisa's grandmother, most of us would probably prefer a tidy, clearly delineated roadmap to guide us through the morass of children's grief. Unfortunately, grieving is not a neat and orderly procedure. Although the 10 intervals of grief identified through RAINBOWS sessions are presented below in a loose chronological order, it's important to remember that the phases can as easily follow a different pattern. Similarly, we must accept that there is no 'correct' or appropriate amount of time that grieving youngsters should spend in each phase. One child may remain mired in a particular stage for months or even years; another will move quickly from one to another and then hopscotch back through the entire emotional menu. Many of the stages are revisited again and again. Ultimately, each phase or step must be acknowledged, wrestled with, spoken out loud and then finally let go.

Here is a description of each of the 10 phases of grief in children and adolescents.

Denial: 'It's Not True!'

On a rainy Saturday morning in late November, Zach's parents called him away from his computer and asked him to come into the living room for a family conference. Zach, 12, took the stairs two-by-two down from his second-floor bedroom; he wasn't worried. His grades were good; he hadn't forgotten any chores. 'What's up?' the energetic lad asked cheerfully. 'Sit down, darling,' his mother urged. Curious, Zach dropped into a nearby chair and waited. He thought that perhaps his parents wanted to talk about holiday plans. Instead, as calmly as possible, Zach's mum and dad told him that they had decided to divorce. In fact, the boy's father would be moving out that afternoon.

The colour drained from Zach's face. His shoulders slumped, and he seemed to shrink into himself. Then, suddenly, Zach leapt up. 'No!' he shouted frantically as he began to pace back and forth. Zach's parents tried to calm him. His mother assured him that things would be OK. His father talked about his new apartment and how often his son would get to see him. Zach covered his ears. 'I'm not going to listen to this. I can't hear you,' he screamed. When the bewildered adults finally stopped talking, the boy ran back up the stairs to his bedroom. A few minutes later, he rushed back into the living room with his camera. As tears streamed down his face, Zach begged his mother and father to sit next to each other on the sofa so he could take their picture together. Despite everything that he'd been told, Zach was determined to produce concrete proof that what his parents had said was not true. The photograph would capture them the way they should be, the only way he could imagine them — together. The picture would make a lie of what they had just told him. His mother and father were not splitting up. 'Look, here they are,' just like he wanted them to be.

'What about Christmas?' Zach demanded finally. 'We'll still have Christmas here, won't we, just like always?'

When the truth is too much to bear, children turn away. They deny that the loss has occurred. They refuse to listen to the very words they are being told. 'This is *not happening*.' 'Parents, siblings or loved ones don't die.' 'My parents won't divorce.'

Denial is a buffer; it creates a safety zone where the child can escape from reality until he's ready to absorb the painful truth of what has happened. Denial is a protective shield. In most instances, it makes no logical sense. Jonathan was 14 when his dad was killed in an car accident. It took nearly a year for Jonathan to accept his father's death intellectually. At the emotional level, where the feelings of grief reside, the reality had not taken root. Jonathan's father always jingled his keys on his way to and from the car, and every time Jonathan heard the familiar sound, he 'knew' it was his dad walking into the room. Often, even years after the funeral, he would turn, expecting to see his dad smiling at him.

To avoid confronting their loss, children and teenagers frequently use denial statements, such as, 'My dad's a pilot. He's away now, but he'll be back soon' or 'Mum's a little angry, but she's not gone. She'll be back.' Often a child will shift suddenly from one dimension to the other, one minute accepting the loss event, and denying it the next.

Denial shapes behaviour and is a normal response to loss. Here are some telltale signs of denial.

* The child feels numb or is in shock. She appears robot-like and usually exhibits a general lack of any emotion.

* After a death, the child refuses to go to the cemetery.

* The child fantasizes about conversations with the absent or deceased person.

* The child may experience emotional or physical health problems.

* The child appears to be unaffected. No tears, no talk about what has happened. Even though life at home has been permanently altered, the child's behaviour, actions, grades and activities are exactly as they were before the loss occurred. Often the child is exceptionally enthusiastic about wanting to help out. In most instances, though, emotional turmoil seethes beneath the 'cool' exterior.

Bargaining: 'I'll Behave, I Promise!'

Late one night, a friend called me from the local accident and emergency department. Could I get there immediately? Tania, her 11-year-old daughter, had swallowed a handful of aspirin and had to be rushed to the hospital to have her stomach pumped. My friend was shaking and distraught. She had just called her husband, who was away on business, and told him what had happened. He was taking the next flight back. The two had recently separated and were beginning divorce proceedings.

When Tania was finally transferred upstairs to a children's ward and resting quietly, I went in to see her. She was thin and pale, her fine blonde hair

DO RAINBOWS' METHODS WORK?

Two research studies substantiate the positive changes that we witness regularly at Rainbows.

The first study, conducted by six child development experts at Loyola University in Chicago, began with 140 children from four schools in the Chicago area. Each child had experienced their parents' divorce or the death of a loved one and was participating in RAINBOWS for the first time. Noting that numerous previous studies had revealed negative self-image as a common characteristic of children affected by loss, the researchers conducted in-depth before and after interviews with the subjects to determine if RAINBOWS had any effect on their self-esteem. Eight months after the study began, the results were in. Not only did the children, who ranged in age from 7 to 13, demonstrate notable, positive change in self-concept, but teachers also reported noticing 'significantly higher self-esteem' among them. Academic performance improved as well. Based on the study results, says chief investigator Jack A Kavanagh, PhD, 'It is evident that RAINBOWS is successfully meeting a growing need in today's society.'

A second study completed in 2000 by researchers at the University of Illinois looked at the short-term impact the RAINBOWS fanned out like a halo on the pillow. Seeing me, she bit her lip and clutched at the covers. We talked quietly for a while. Then I asked her what had happened. She told me exactly what she had done. 'Did you know it could hurt you?' I asked. Tania nodded her head. 'Did you want to die?' I went on. 'No,' she whispered, and turned away. I waited patiently. Finally, Tania looked back at me. In a voice that was even quieter than before, she said, 'I thought if I was really ill and my parents were both here worrying about me that they would somehow love each other again.'

When the family is threatened by a life-altering event, children will do anything to make things 'right' again. They think that they have the power to change or stop what is happening and will bargain with God or

programme had on children of divorced parents. The subjects were 124 children aged 9, 10 and 11 from 28 different schools. Of these, 82 per cent said RAINBOWS helped them to better understand their feelings; 80 per cent said the programme taught them new ways to solve problems. Interestingly, 98 per cent said they would recommend RAINBOWS to their peers.

Parents gave the programme high marks as well: 71 per cent said their children were less likely to get into trouble after completing the programme; 70 per cent said their children's behaviour improved; and 60 per cent said their children's sadness and depression decreased. Eighty-three per cent said their communication with their children had improved; 75 per cent reported that their youngsters were more optimistic about the future; and 66 per cent said their children were more cooperative at home.

In addition, parents credited RAINBOWS with teaching children to control anger and with improving their behaviour, attitude and academic performance. The researchers themselves described the programme as both effective and beloved.

anyone whom they feel has the power to affect what is happening. They'll play whatever youthful chips they have to offer. Some telltale signs of bargaining are:

• The child hopes to reconcile the parents or to heal an ailing loved one by promising to be exceptionally well-behaved, keep her room neat, help with chores, study harder and do better in school. The offers are sincere and heartfelt because children truly believe that they possess the power to stave off the pending loss.

• The child uses phrases such as 'what if' or 'if only' in his conversations.

Guilt: 'It's My Fault'

When Kyle was 2 years old, his father went out to buy a loaf of bread at the local convenience store, where he was shot and killed in a robbery. At 12, Kyle, a tall, hulking boy, was convinced his father's death was his fault. 'I should have stopped my dad from going out that night,' he insisted. What Kyle didn't know was that he was asleep when his father left the house. He couldn't have stopped his dad from leaving, even if he had wanted to.

In RAINBOWS sessions over the years, we have consistently found that at least 90 per cent of the children and teenagers in each group feel some responsibility for family crises. Many, like Kyle, assume the entire burden of guilt. Developmentally, children view themselves as the force that sends the world spinning. In their perspective, everything they do has an impact on those around them. Children and teenagers honestly believe that if they had behaved differently, received better grades in school, not quarrelled with their brothers or sisters, or done their chores more readily, Mum and Dad would not have divorced or their loved ones would not have died.

One day, I was talking about loss with a classroom full of students, many of whom had recently experienced a divorce or death in the family.

'How many of you think you were responsible for what happened?' I asked. Almost every hand came up. 'It's my fault that my parents got divorced,' 8-year-old Grace confided to me at the close of the session. I asked why she thought that. She hung her head and explained that her mother always said that her dad spent so much time with the kids, he didn't have time for her. 'I shouldn't have asked my dad to go swimming or to take me for ice cream,' Grace insisted. 'If it wasn't for me, my parents would still be married.'

If parents aren't honest about problems and loss events, children make up their own scenarios. The fantasies that grieving youngsters create are often more frightening than the truth and usually have the children playing a major role in the drama.

Feeling responsible for a family tragedy is an overwhelming burden to carry. Guilt hammers away at a child's self-esteem. It creates a self-imposed emotional tyranny that burrows deep into the heart and can cause an ache that lasts a lifetime. After a death, even children who don't assume responsibility for the loss event may feel guilty about things done or not done.

'I always talked back to my mum and didn't have a chance to say I'm sorry.'

'I never said thanks to my dad for teaching me how to throw a cricket ball.'

'I never told my grandmother "I love you".'

Some telltale signs of guilt are:

- The child verbalizes regrets, such as 'I wish I had ...' or 'I am sorry that ...'

- The child's self-esteem plummets.

- The child tends to take the blame for anything and everything or to blame someone else for what has happened. Either approach is an attempt to absolve himself.

- The child is hostile or aggressive.

Fear: 'What About Me? What's Going to Happen to Me?'

When Operation Desert Storm started in the autumn of 1990, thousands of parents of young children were sent overseas on active military duty. In many instances, these children watched real battle scenes broadcast on TV and were understandably traumatized. Teachers from schools everywhere called RAINBOWS asking for help in dealing with students' concerns. Many of the children and teenagers in their classrooms were worried that their parents would be injured or killed. The youngsters wanted to know who would take care of them while their parents were gone.

Closer to home, a neighbour's daughter received word that she'd been accepted by a top university. Alexis had always been a model student and daughter. Both she and her parents were thrilled. It was a dream come true for the family.

Suddenly, two months before Alexis was to leave home, she completely changed. Once cooperative and obedient, she became unruly and wilful. She started drinking, ignored her curfew and refused to clean her room. 'I don't even recognize this girl any more,' her exasperated father said one day. Neither he nor his wife understood Alexis's negative, defiant behaviour. They repeatedly asked her what was wrong, but she always shrugged off their concern. One week before Alexis was scheduled to leave for college, she sat at the dinner table with her parents.

Over dessert, her father started talking about his experiences leaving home for the first time. 'We're really going to miss you when you go off to university,' her mother said. Then she asked Alexis: 'How do you feel about going away?' For the first time, Alexis admitted that she was terrified by the prospect. 'I've never been away from home. I don't know what to expect. What if no one likes me? What if I fail?' she wailed. On and on, she spilled out a list of fears.

Adults rely on a long string of accumulated life experiences to prepare for new circumstances. Children don't have that crutch. They're facing life events for the first time. More often than not, they really don't know what to expect. It's understandable, then, that new situations evoke feelings of fear and nervousness about how they'll cope and if they'll be able to get through the situation successfully.

> Grief originates from the heart. It is not linked to age, life experience, or understanding.

Craig was 6 years old when his parents divorced. Two years later, his father was transferred to the other side of the country. Each summer, Craig spent a week with him there, enjoying every minute of his visit. But one year, the schedule was different. Craig was asked to come and stay with his father for three weeks. During that time, his dad was getting married again. Craig would be meeting and living with a new stepmother and stepbrother. Craig's mother thought he was looking forward to the extended visit, but her son was scared. 'I don't know what it will be like. I don't know what I'm supposed to do or if you'll be OK with me gone that long,' he told her.

Then there are situations that even adults are ill-prepared to confront. Since his father had died, 10-year-old Martin went to incredible lengths to avoid spending time at home. He absolutely refused to be left alone in the house and would not step into the living room even if the rest of the family was sitting there together. He was afraid to go in there, he told his teacher one day, because his father's ashes were kept in an urn on the mantelpiece.

Often, children's anxieties and fears stem from emotional neglect. During times of family crisis, even the most attentive, dedicated parents may overlook their children's emotional needs. Emotionally distraught parents may reprimand inappropriately or discipline irrationally. They may be quick to anger or become reclusive. Their actions aren't intentional, but the parents may be so torn themselves, so overwhelmed, so consumed by their own pain, or so worried about finances, that they simply can't cope with the full roster of duties and parental obligations they once handled with ease. It is all too much. In some instances, adults are simply unaware of children's emotional pain. A relief worker told me that if children aren't hurt in a natural disaster, parents assume everything's OK, forgetting how lost and scared children feel when living in a shelter surrounded by strangers and without the comfort of their personal belongings.

When a loss occurs, we may become so consumed by our own grief and fears that it seems impossible to console others, even our own children. But if we're honest about the loss and our own profound sadness, we can help children work through their emotions and fear. Consider the case of Ryan. Loud pounding at the front door woke the 5-year-old in the middle of the night. Half asleep, the timid little boy stumbled from bed and huddled at the top of the stairs. Maybe his father had returned home early from his business trip, he thought. Instead, Ryan saw his mother talking to two police officers at the door. The boy knew something horrible had happened but couldn't bring himself to go downstairs. Instead, he crept back to bed and waited for his mother to come and talk to him. But she didn't. Upstairs, Ryan spent an anxious, restless night imagining the worst.

The next morning, several aunts and uncles arrived. They hugged him and shook their heads, regarding him sadly. Then they surrounded his mother and whispered quietly among themselves, ignoring Ryan's questions. A conspiracy of silence had descended upon the house. Everyone knew the secret but him. Eventually Ryan slunk away.

That night, Ryan's mother finally told him that his father had been killed in a train crash. Sobbing, she tried to pull her son into her arms, but Ryan broke away. His mother grew more distraught. 'I only wanted to protect you from this great sadness,' she cried. Ryan ran from the room.

We'd like to think that a single episode of emotional neglect couldn't harm children for the long term. But sometimes the ramifications can be far reaching. For Ryan, this one incident planted seeds of distrust and alienation that grew stronger over time. Once a quiet, well-behaved child, he became bad-tempered and unruly after his father's funeral. When Ryan was 11 years old, he started sniffing glue to get high. 'I don't care about anything,' he told his cousin. 'Why should I? I don't count.'

After a loss event, children may be physically neglected as well. Not being well cared for makes children fearful and anxious. Parents forget to buy groceries, and the hungry child finds nothing to eat in the house. They may not be interested in making dinner, and suddenly the usual nutritious, tranquil meal is a thrown-together affair or something picked up last minute at the nearest fast food restaurant. Parents may forget to do laundry or to sign forms or permission slips for school activities. They may not have the time or energy to clean the house, and so children accustomed to a well-organized household are forced to live in chaos.

One September, three young siblings started attending RAINBOWS sessions at a church on the outskirts of a large town. The children — two boys aged 9 and 11, and a 4-year-old girl — were new to the community. The staff knew nothing about them. Each week when they arrived for RAINBOWS, the trio simply showed up at the front door. Although the children were well-behaved, they were distracted, restless and obviously not well cared for. The youngsters often came with dirty hands and faces. Their hair was usually greasy and uncombed. Winter came early that year. Despite heavy snow in November, the three continued wearing lightweight summer clothing. When the RAINBOWS facilitator wanted to report a case of neglect to the social services, I suggested she first learn more about the family structure — especially since it was a grandmother and not a parent who had signed up the children.

The facilitator soon learned that the children's mother had walked out on the family the previous summer. For a while, the children lived with their father and his elderly parents. By autumn, their dad was drinking heavily. One day, he went out on a binge and never came back. The grandparents, who were in their late seventies and in poor health, were left to care for the children. The couple loved the kids dearly and did the best that they could, but they simply didn't have the energy or resources to cope with the ongoing daily needs of the three abandoned youngsters. As a result, the children were left anxious and fearful. Some telltale signs of fear are:

- The child is preoccupied with illness or death.
- The child grows anxious when family or friends argue.
- The child has a constant need to phone home when away.
- The child clings to a parent or caregiver.
- The child reattaches to a favourite teddy bear or blanket that he had as a youngster.
- The child obsesses about food: is there enough in the house and is it food that he knows how to prepare?

Anger: 'I Hate You'

Ewan grew up in a devout Catholic family. At the age of 8, he became an altar boy, one of the youngest in his parish. A quick, bright boy with a ready smile, Ewan seemed so happy when he was in church that his parents thought he might even become a priest when he grew up.

When Ewan was 9 years old, his parents began having serious marital problems. Struggling to save their marriage, they started seeing a counsellor. They told Ewan exactly what was happening. 'Pray for us,' his mother often urged the boy. Ewan got up early and went to mass every day before school. He promised he'd be an altar boy his entire life if God would keep his parents together. 'Please, don't let them get divorced,' Ewan begged as he knelt by his bed at night and prayed.

Shortly after Ewan turned ten, his parents divorced. Today, Ewan sees his father only on rare occasions. Despite his mother's pleas, the young boy refuses to pray and has stopped going to church. 'I'm angry with God. I'm never going to talk to Him again,' Ewan told her.

Many grieving children are angry at the world and nearly everyone in it. They are angry with parents, family, friends, classmates, pets, teachers and even God. Grieving children are angry that the loss event happened to them and their families. This strong emotion usually surfaces once the reality of the loss event has sunk in. Children realize that no amount of denial or bargaining will change the outcome.

Often, the anger seems misplaced, unreasonable and unwarranted. But no matter how adults characterize and perceive this rage, the wrath is very real to the children. The rage erupts at random and is sent in all directions. They are angry with anyone and everyone. Some telltale signs of anger are:

• The child is upset with himself because he thinks he caused 'it'.

• The child blames God for allowing the loss to occur.

• The child accuses teachers of not being fair.

• The child resents classmates for having 'normal' families.

• The child may be angry with the parent who died (for deserting her) or with the parent who is still alive ('Why couldn't it have been you, instead?'). Similarly, in the case of divorce or abandonment, the child or teenager may be angry with the parent who moved out or the parent who stayed.

Anger is a normal reaction to loss. It is integral to the grieving process. Why shouldn't you be enraged that someone or something you loved has been taken from you?

Anger that is not acknowledged and properly channelled intensifies and becomes unmanageable as time passes. My friend Ellen refused to discuss her divorce with her four sons, then aged 10 to 15. 'I can't be honest and vulnerable with my own children,' she said. Once well-behaved, good students, the boys began terrorizing their teachers. At home, they deliberately broke windows and destroyed furniture. Three of the four eventually dropped out of college. Today, all of them use drugs. They are no longer naughty little boys. They are angry young men.

Isolation: 'I Have No One to Talk To'

Eight-year-old David, an introverted child with few friends, told me this story about what happened after his father's funeral.

'We all came home, took off our coats, and went to our own bedrooms. My mother closed her door and my brother did the same. I didn't know what else to do, so I closed the door to my room and talked about my dad to my pet gerbil. There wasn't anyone else.'

A conspiracy of silence often descends on a family following major loss. Families either tell children directly or subtly convey to them the message that they are not to speak about the person who is gone or who has died because it is 'too upsetting'.

Six-year-old Eva adored her father. He called her his angel and shared secrets with her. Just a few months ago, he'd taught her to play the guitar and ride a bike.

When Eva's father walked out after seven years of a contentious marriage, her mother, Clare, announced that his departure was a blessing in disguise. Clare had long been unhappy with her husband. He was a sporadic heavy drinker; he had trouble keeping a job; he was often moody and withdrawn. After he left, Clare forbade Eva to ever talk about her father. 'We're better off without him,' she told the heartbroken child.

Some adults honestly believe that not talking will help children get over trauma faster. According to a study in California, only 10 per cent of children of divorced parents had anyone talk to them about the situation during the time that their parents' marriages were unravelling.

A close friend was away at college when his mother died. Some years later he told me: 'Afterwards everyone asked me, "How's your father?" No one ever asked about me.'

Other factors also contribute to isolation.

• The resident parent has more responsibilities and less time to devote to the child.

- Thinking they are 'protecting' the children, adults deliberately leave kids out of family discussions and decision-making processes.

- Children themselves withdraw as a way of avoiding the changes that loss has imposed on family or personal life.

When children are isolated in their grief and forced to mourn alone, healing becomes a daunting task. Some telltale signs of isolation are:

- The child stays in her room and avoids interacting with the family.

- The child withdraws from school activities, sports, or friends.

- The child becomes immersed in the Internet or in computer games.

- The child constantly watches TV or listens to CDs.

- The child creates imaginary playmates or friends.

Pining: 'I Miss You'

Bobby and his grandfather were inseparable. They did everything together, fishing, hiking and playing hide-and-seek out behind the barn on the farm where they lived with the youngster's parents. The child had even been named Robert in honour of the older man and quickly assumed the nickname 'Little Bobby'. Grandpa, of course, was 'Big Bobby'. The two even looked alike, each tall and lanky, with the same bright blue eyes and unruly sandy hair.

When Little Bobby was 7 years old, his grandfather was hospitalized with a broken hip. That night, the boy took his grandfather's worn green sweater off the back of the rocking chair in the dining room and wrapped it around himself before climbing into bed. Every day that the old gentleman was gone, his grandson slept in the sweater.

Big Bobby's surgery was a success, but pneumonia set in. In the middle of a fine spring day, Big Bobby died. The child was heartbroken. Every day, he trailed around the farm, tracing the path the old man took on his daily round of chores. Often, in the late afternoon, Little Bobby's mother found him asleep in the rocking chair, the sweater clutched tightly to his thin chest.

One day, the boy awoke to find his mother watching him. Little Bobby smiled and rubbed the sweater to his cheek. 'It makes me feel good,' he said. 'It's warm and fuzzy and it smells like Grandpa.'

Children pine for the person or thing missing from their lives. Even children who have never known a parent can experience this craving. Stefan, 13, had grown up as the only child of a single mother, an executive secretary who had provided a good, stable life for him. Still, for years, Stefan wondered who his father was. When he reached his teens, Stefan began demanding information from his mother. 'Is he tall? What colour eyes does he have?' He insisted on having a photo of his father. 'I just want to know what he looks like,' he said.

Even a simple loss can make a child ache for what is missing. Kara, the youngest of three girls, was 8 years old when her family moved from a big city to a small town. In many ways, life in the family's new home promised to be much more exciting for Kara. She had more freedom than she'd ever enjoyed in her urban neighbourhood and a big bedroom that she had helped to design. She even started taking horse-riding lessons, which she'd wanted for years. Still, 14 months after the move, Kara longed for her old home and friends. She often asked her mother: 'When are we moving back?' Some telltale signs of pining are:

- The child longs for objects associated with the absent loved one or thing.

- The child asks repeated questions about the person missing from her daily life and wants to know every detail about them.

- The child wears or keeps an object that belonged to the missing beloved person.

- The child talks about the missing person or thing all the time.

- The child wants to visit the cemetery often.

Confusion: 'I Don't Know Where I Belong'

Children who have suffered loss often face an avalanche of change in their lives. As the landscape shifts around them, they wonder what else will go wrong.

Before my divorce, I was a traditional, full-time, stay-at-home mother. Afterwards, I was absent from the house 90 to 100 hours a week trying to make financial ends meet. At one point, I worked full time in a doctor's office and held down two part-time jobs, one in the evenings and the other on the weekends that I didn't have the children.

For a long while, I was bitter. I suffered agonizing loneliness and was tortured by doubt. I cried whenever I was alone. Though I knew the divorce was the right thing to do, I was joyless, exhausted and angry. Everything depended on me. I was a model example of a bereft single parent.

My children saw it all. My three sons lost not only their father but the mother they knew, too. They had to adjust to their father's absence and to the dramatic changes in me. Even the routines we had established — home-made cakes, parents at their school activities, socializing with family and friends — were no longer present in their daily lives.

From their perspective, everything had changed. The firm foundation of family had been pulled from under their feet, leaving them in emotional free fall. They struggled to determine what their roles in our new family structure would be and to establish new daily routines.

Almost every major family crisis packs a similar double wallop to the children and teenagers. The situation is especially daunting for youngsters who live between two households. They are constantly shifting from one house to another. Their belongings, schoolwork and, often, friends exist in two locations. The more disruptions children experience in their daily lives and the less control they have over relevant circumstances, the higher their levels of anxiety. Even the most protective parent can't shelter a child from the winds of change. Children are profoundly affected, even when things are going 'well'. Consider Olivia. She's 9 years old, the older of two sisters. Her parents recently initiated a trial separation; they've explained the situation to Olivia and her sister and they're both working hard to keep the children's lives as unruffled as possible. When Olivia's father moved out of the family home, he rented an apartment near school. He even arranged his work schedule so he could be home by 3 p.m. Monday to Friday. Every day, Olivia and her sister leave school and walk over to their father's place; they spend 2 hours with him before the babysitter comes to take them home.

This arrangement is much more child-friendly than most separated or divorced parents are able to arrange. Yet Olivia remains sad and withdrawn. Once a happy-go-lucky little girl, she now experiences bouts of anxiety and frequently finds it hard to catch her breath and concentrate in school. 'My thoughts get all mixed up and fly out of my head,' she told her teacher. Often, at break, surrounded by her young, caring friends, Olivia cries. 'I don't know where I belong.' Some telltale signs of confusion include:

• The child's bedroom, desk, or locker is in disarray.

• The child's homework and other projects are messy.

• The child forgets game times, homework, or projects — even social engagements.

Depression and Sadness: 'Why Bother?'

Diane was an energetic teenager who seemed to enjoy an enchanted life. Good grades and friends came easily to the petite, outgoing 15-year-old . She often came top of her class, played tennis and volleyball, and sang in the church choir. Yet the perky adolescent was never too tired or busy to help organize fundraising events for the school or church, or help her younger brother Colin with his homework. Friends dropped by and phoned every hour of the day and evening. Weekend sleepovers were a regular part of the routine for Diane. Then, early in the winter, her brother was diagnosed with a rare kidney disease. For months, he was in and out of the hospital for tests and treatment. All the while, Diane maintained her busy lifestyle and good spirits. 'You're going to be fine,' she told her brother every day. When her friends asked about Colin, she assured them that he was doing really well.

One spring night, Colin died quietly in his sleep. It was as if Diane had died, too. She dropped out of all her school activities. 'Why bother? It's all stupid,' she told one of her teachers two weeks after her brother's funeral. Although Diane maintained her good marks at school, she insisted on studying alone in her room. When her friends rang, she refused to come to the phone. 'Tell them I'm busy,' she instructed her parents. The weekend overnighters ceased entirely. Although Diane's friends continued to call round to the house as they had before, they never stayed long. In early summer, the visits abruptly ended. Diane was distant and rude, the girls later told her bewildered parents, and they felt uncomfortable hanging around when she clearly didn't want them to be there.

Once Diane had been a bouncy, friendly teenager. Grief made her a hermit in her own house.

A significant loss, such as a divorce or death, sends a child's world spinning out of control. Everything he has held as normal or stable shifts and changes. Realizing that he will never recapture what has been lost, the child is filled with sadness. This usually signals that reality is settling in.

As we discussed in chapter 1, because of a lack of emotional maturity, children typically aren't able to grieve for long periods of time. Unlike adults, who may become engulfed in a period of deep despair and mourning, children experience 'sad attacks'. These spontaneous periods of sadness may be triggered by a memory of the lost person or thing and usually end as quickly as they begin.

When a child is experiencing a sad attack, don't try to hurry him through it. It's important that the child works through his feelings of grief, even if the process occurs intermittently over a long period of time.

Acknowledgement of the loss event is a healthy sign as long as the child continues to move forward.

Sometimes, a child feels loss on so many levels that he becomes confused and overwhelmed by his emotions. At this point, the child may experience the intense and consuming sadness of depression. If you believe a child is depressed, it's important to talk him through his feelings of grief, working with a professional counsellor if necessary.

THE MANY LOSSES THAT CHILDREN SUFFER

When family structure is altered by death or divorce, children struggle with a number of losses and obstacles that threaten to confuse and overwhelm them.

Children are robbed of their own childhoods. After their parents divorce or there is a death in the family, children are often encouraged to take on parenting roles and adult housekeeping or decision-making responsibilities. Some are so heavily saddled with adult chores that they have no time to be children. I know of boys and girls as young as 9 or 10 whose daily after-school routine goes like this: pick up younger siblings from the babysitter, go home, clean the house, take care of the little brother or sister, cook dinner for the family, wash the dishes and then do homework.

Sometimes children and teenagers try to assume adult responsibilities on their own.

Shauna lived with her mother and younger sister. The girls' father had never been a part of their lives. When Shauna turned 12, she decided that she should become the family protector. Every night after midnight, she took her pillow and blanket into the living room to sleep by the front door of their apartment. Shauna was worried that someone would break in.

After my divorce, my eldest son Michael appointed himself 'father' to his two younger brothers. He tried to discipline them, demanded that they do their chores, and ordered them to do their homework. Michael's actions were not uncommon, but they were inappropriate. Somewhere in the dismantling of our family, Michael decided that he needed to be in charge.

Children lose a sense of who they are. A child's identity is intrinsically linked to her family. She thinks of herself as being part of the family unit, linked by an emotional umbilical cord. After a divorce, she needs two cords, one tying her to her mother (and probably to her other siblings) and one joining her to her father. This new identity, or new linkage, can't be forged overnight. It takes time and nurturing.

Extenuating circumstances can further weaken a child's identity. A child who thinks of herself as 'Daddy's little girl' may be emotionally lost and adrift when her father dies. For many children, identity begins with their name. They may feel confused and abandoned if, after a divorce, their mother reclaims her maiden name. If she later remarries and assumes her second husband's last name, the children are further removed from her.

Children encounter celebration chaos. Life continues. There are birthdays, anniversaries and seasonal celebrations to observe. With whom does the child celebrate? Who hasn't been invited? I know children who dread Christmas. Why? Because first they have to eat Christmas dinner at Mum's house and then, despite being completely full, they are expected to eat a second big feast at Dad's house.

If a sibling has died and the parents are afloat in their sea of grief, they may not be up to executing a birthday party or celebration. The remaining children feel slighted. This omission compounds their pain.

Children are forced to make painful choices. One Saturday morning last autumn, I visited Molly, 13, and her mother, Roseanne, who had recently got divorced. Roseanne was bitter about the dissolution of her marriage and was still very much in love with her former husband. Molly, a tall, gangly girl, had been talking about the science fair at school. Suddenly, she glanced at the kitchen clock and stood up. 'I'm spending the rest of the weekend with Dad,' Molly said, hesitating, 'and my new stepmother.' Then she raced from the room to get her things. A few minutes later, Molly returned with an overnight bag. She said goodbye, kissed her mother and breezed towards the door. Roseanne hurried after her.

'If you talk to that woman, don't bother to come home,' Roseanne shouted from the front porch. 'She's the reason we got divorced.'

Mid-stride, Molly's face froze and her shoulders slumped. Her steps stiffened as she hurried towards the kerb. Slipping into the waiting car, Molly avoided her mother's angry glare.

What choice does Molly have? In order to obey her mother, she must be rude to her stepmother, thereby engendering her father's anger. If she is civil to her stepmother, she is being disloyal to her mother.

Throughout their lives, children of divorced parents are forced to make painful choices. At a wedding or family celebration they have to decide whom to invite, whom to talk to first, and with whom to sit. Imagine the agony that 13-year-old Angie faced as her school prize day approached. Angie's parents had divorced when she was at nursery school. Each parent had remarried. Now, each of the four important adults in Angie's life wanted to attend her prize day. But the school allowed only three tickets for each student. As Angie saw it, no matter whom she invited, she had to leave out someone and risk hurting someone's feelings.

Even if a parent has died, a child may still feel that he is being disloyal to his deceased parent if he accepts the new people in his life. Nathan has great memories of playing basketball on the driveway every weekend with his dad, who died several years ago. Now that Nathan's mother has remarried, her new husband wants Nathan to play basketball with him. Nathan likes this guy but feels that if he does play, he is betraying his dad's memory. When Nathan sees his stepfather with a basketball in his hand, he wants to turn and run the other way, because he doesn't know what to do.

What's more, children like Molly, Angie and Nathan don't experience the pain of their parents' divorce or the death of a loved person just one time. At various stages in life, the feelings of loss may be rekindled or the memory of the event resurrected, triggering a sad attack. This can happen repeatedly as children mature and move into adulthood. It can be a recurring trigger for sadness and depression. Some telltale signs of sadness or depression are:

- The child demonstrates an overall lack of emotion.

- The child withdraws from favourite activities or friends.

- The child describes a 'darkness in his heart'.

- The child is attracted to sad or morbid television programmes, books or films.

- The child dresses almost exclusively in dark colours.

- The child talks about suicide.

Acceptance: 'I'm OK'

Julia, 13, had always been very close to her mother. When her mum died unexpectedly during an operation, Julia struggled to understand and accept what had happened. She comprehended the finality of death but couldn't imagine growing up without a mum. Although the family's strong religious convictions and belief in the afterlife brought some comfort to the young teenager, her own future stretched out in front of her, dark and forbidding. She simply couldn't visualize what every day in her life would be like without her mother. Over and over again, she confided her pain to her father.

One day, he said to her, 'Juli, life will never be the same without Mum with us. But it will be good again.'

His words, honestly spoken, helped Julia put her loss in perspective. Her grief was not diminished, but she was better able to understand its impact and eventually learned to live her life each day without her mum.

Healthy mourning often takes years to complete. It is achieved when the grieving child has successfully moved through the phases of grief and has learned to accept the changes created by loss. Acceptance does not mean that he thinks what has happened is OK; it means that he acknowledges it and is able to assimilate the loss into his daily life. Acceptance is the period of healing that comes after all the pain of loss has been dealt with. Acceptance frees the child from the intense pain of the past and sets him on the road to a strong, healthy future.

Acceptance is the goal of the RAINBOWS programme — a goal that I hope we can help all grieving children achieve. Some signs of acceptance of the loss event are:

• The child is willing to plan for the future.

• The child adjusts to new routines.

• The child talks about the loss event matter-of-factly. ('Yes, this has happened, and ...')

• The child offers to reach out to other children (and even adults) to help them cope with similar situations.

As children experience each phase of grief, they need us — parents, extended family, community workers and other adults — to reach out and guide them on their journey. In Part Two of this book, you will learn how to help your children successfully navigate through the healing process.

Chapter 3

Children and Death

B RIAN, THE GREEN-EYED, dark-haired middle son of a family of five children, was diagnosed with leukaemia. Despite intensive medical treatment, Brian's health deteriorated. In May, five months after diagnosis, 9-year-old Brian slipped into a coma.

'Is Brian going to die?' his 11-year-old sister asked.

'Your brother is very ill,' her mother replied, avoiding the question. 'We need to pray very hard for him.'

One spring day, Brian came home from the hospital. The family lived in an old house on a quiet, tree-lined street near the edge of town. Neighbours stood on their porches and watched silently when the ambulance pulled into the driveway of Brian's house and paramedics carried the boy inside. Earlier a bulky hospital bed had been delivered to the house; too big and unwieldy to be carried upstairs to Brian's room, the bed was installed in the only space large enough to accommodate it: the living room. It was here the medics settled Brian. When they left, the other children immediately gathered around their brother.

'How come Brian can't talk?' the family's 6-year-old demanded.

'He's resting, building his strength back up,' their mother replied and shooed the children outside.

The parents knew otherwise, of course. They understood that their son was terminally ill, but they had agreed not to share this basic truth with the other siblings. 'If we tell the children that Brian is dying, it means that we've given up hope,' they rationalized.

During the summer, Brian never regained consciousness. For three long, hot months, he lay silently in the middle of the living room. Every time Brian's brothers and sisters, aged 6 to 17, went into the kitchen or upstairs to their rooms, they had to walk past their comatose brother. Questions were shushed away. Mum even planned a camping trip that the family would take 'when Brian's better'.

Brian died in the autumn. Since his death and funeral, his siblings have been anxious and depressed. The youngest suffers nightmares. The eldest plays truant regularly. Before, the children often gathered in the living room to watch TV or talk. Now, they refuse to sit there. All of them are in therapy and remain immersed in grief.

We live as if death is uncertain and life is certain. In reality, the opposite is true. Life is uncertain, but death is not.

Eventually everyone is touched by death. Even children. By the age of 18, one in every six children will experience the death of a parent. Parental death creates a continuing sense of emptiness. As the child matures, there is an ongoing need to rethink the role the parent would have assumed in the child's life at each phase of their development. For a child, the death of a mother is especially difficult. It precipitates more changes in daily and family life and is associated with higher levels of anxiety, lower self-esteem and more troubled behaviour than the death of a father.

Children also may endure the death of a sibling, other relative, teacher, classmate or family friend. The death of an important person in a child's life leaves an indelible mark and becomes a life-defining event. In many instances, other significant occasions in his life are dated in his mind before or after the death of a loved one. Having someone die is among the most stressful experiences that a youngster will encounter. For a child or adolescent, death is an incomprehensible event that represents inexplicable emotional pain.

Each Child's Reaction Is Unique

How children cope with death depends on a number of factors: the relationship to the person who has died; the type of death; previous death experiences; the family's ability to communicate with one another; the children's ages and emotional maturity; and the family's social, cultural and religious beliefs. Each of these elements must be taken into consideration when a child experiences the death of a loved one.

Each death will be processed differently. Each death is cloaked in its own unique circumstances and brings its own anguish. Here is how three different children reacted when faced with the death of someone they loved.

'No! No! No!'

Josephine, a quiet, happy child and the eldest in a family of three, was especially close to her Aunt Teresa. The girl was just a toddler when Teresa began taking her to football matches at a nearby park. Later, when Josephine joined the local girl's football league, Teresa, who worked as a regional sales manager for a fitness equipment manufacturer, volunteered as a coach. Though her job took her on the road frequently, she arranged to be in town for her niece's practices and matches. Teresa also taught Josephine how to play draughts and they often went to the cinema together. 'You two,' Josephine's mother would say and shake her head. 'What am I going to do with you?'

One morning, shortly after Josephine's eighth birthday, her Aunt Teresa left on a routine trip. Several hours later, some 200 miles away, a drunk driver lost control of his vehicle and smashed head-on into Teresa's car. She never had a chance.

Josephine was in her room getting ready for a match when her mother entered. Unable to give voice to the terrible news, she collapsed in tears on the bed. 'Where's Auntie Teresa?' Josephine demanded. Her mother lifted her head and murmured, 'She's dead.'

For a moment, the girl regarded her in stunned silence. Then Josephine screamed 'NO!' and flew into a rage. She tore off her football shirt and flung it down. She pulled at her straight black hair and kicked her desk chair against the wall. 'No! No! No!' Josephine darted towards her chest of drawers and with a wide sweep of her arm brushed everything from the top onto the floor. Trophies, pictures and loose change rained down. 'No!' she continued to shout. With her mother close behind, the child raced from one bedroom to the next and, in each, crashed everything on top of the dressing tables and chests of drawers to the floor.

Finally, her fury spent, Josephine sank to the floor. Her mother dropped to her side, wrapped her arms around the child's thin shoulders and held her tightly while she cried.

'IT WAS MY FAULT'

I don't think I'll ever forget Matt. He was 17 when we met at one of the early grief retreats I helped coordinate. Matt was a star football player and one of the most popular boys at his school. He seemed to be the perfect adolescent — polite, articulate and engaging. 'Why had he come for help?' I wondered.

Eventually, Matt told me his story. It began 18 months earlier, on a warm Sunday autumn morning. Matt had attended early morning practice every day for weeks and had planned to sleep late that day. Around 8.30, Matt's father came into his room. 'Time to get up,' he said.

'The lawn needs mowing. It's your job. So get up and do it.' Matt grumbled and rolled over. Matt's dad wasn't about to take no for an answer. He kept on at his son until, finally, the teenager reluctantly got up and went outside. Although Matt mowed the lawn, he resented every minute he worked. Annoyed with his father and determined to have the last word in their dispute, Matt deliberately did a poor job, upsetting his dad even more.

The bad feeling between the two simmered throughout the day. When Matt's dad left for the hospital that afternoon to prepare for a routine procedure the next day, Matt turned his back and refused to say goodbye. The following afternoon, Matt's father had a heart attack and died.

As Matt talked to me, his voice was flat and distant, as if he were relating someone else's experience. When I asked the teenager how he felt about his father's death, he shrugged. 'I'm OK,' he said. I questioned him further: how did he feel about not saying goodbye? Matt collapsed in my arms, sobbing, and I knew there was more going on inside this 'got-it-all-together' boy. Finally, Matt told me that he thought the argument on Sunday had caused his father's fatal heart attack. *Matt really believed he had killed his dad.*

For nearly two years, this boy had kept his shame, guilt and agony hidden. 'How long could he keep this torment buried inside before he exploded?' I wondered. No child, no matter what his age or size, should carry that much pain in his heart. It was crushing him.

'THE DAY ANDREW DIED'

Often, children have very specific reasons for being deeply affected by death.

Alicia was 3 years old when Ted and Andrew bought the house next door and became her new neighbours. The two middle-aged men doted on the child. They gave her biscuits and lemonade in the garden and brought her souvenirs from their holidays. Their first Christmas in the house, they turned up at Alicia's door with a huge stuffed animal. 'Santa left this at our house by mistake,' Andrew said mischievously and handed the patchwork dinosaur to a delighted Alicia.

No one suspected that Andrew, the older of the two men, had a life-threatening cardiovascular disorder. One morning, Andrew went to work as always, but he never came home again. Around noon, he suffered a massive stroke and died instantly.

That evening, Alicia's mum sat on the sofa with the little girl and told her daughter what had happened. The mother expected Alicia to be upset, but she was surprised when the child began to sob. 'Alicia, darling, what's wrong?' she asked. 'Andrew was a nice man, but he wasn't your uncle or cousin or anyone related to the family.'

Her face etched with despair, Alicia looked at her mother. 'He's the only person I ever knew well who died,' she said simply and continued crying inconsolably.

Ted has long since moved and a new couple occupies the house, but Alicia, at 16, still occasionally talks about 'the day Andrew died'. Clearly, this man's death is imprinted in her store of childhood memories.

Explaining Death to a Child

Our society does not like to talk about death. We pretend it doesn't exist until, of course, someone we love dies and we are faced with it head-on. When this happens, we are overwhelmed and in such great emotional distress that we are often rendered speechless. We can barely help ourselves, much less offer guidance to the children who also have been touched by the event. As adults who care about children, ours and those of others, we must become comfortable with the topic. Death is the last stage of life; we are going to die, and our beloved ones are going to die. Avoiding the subject does not keep death away.

When we talk with children and teenagers, the information we give them about death and dying should be conveyed as directly as possible. Clear, undeniable language is best. Softening the phrase doesn't soften the blow. And it can cause confusion. We help children understand and accept death when we use the words *die*, *dying* and *buried*. We blur the issue when we use words like *lost*, *departed* or *laid to rest*.

> Helping children understand death doesn't lessen their pain, but it does diminish their fear.

Elizabeth was a toddler when her father suddenly disappeared from her life. She remembers being told when she was a little girl that her daddy had died, but she wasn't sure what that meant. Later, whenever Lizzie asked about her dad, her mum said: 'You lost your father when you were three.' Well, the little girl understood what that meant, because she had once lost a pair of mittens, only to find them again a few days later. 'I lost my daddy,' Lizzie thought. 'I have to find him.'

When I met Elizabeth, she was a 28-year-old teacher. One day after I'd presented a seminar on grief, she told me the story and how, subsequently, she had spent many painful years searching for her father. 'It made sense to me because of the lost mittens,' she explained.

'I thought that if I looked hard enough and long enough, I'd eventually find my father, too.' With tears in her eyes, Lizzie admitted that she was well into her teens before she stopped looking for her dad!

How much information about death should you share? Let the child guide you. She will let you know what she wants to know and how much she can handle. When their aunt was diagnosed with terminal cancer, Cindy, who was 9 years old at the time, only wanted to know the name of the disease. Her 14-year-old sister Joanna asked why the doctors hadn't recommended surgery and weren't offering chemotherapy or radiation treatment options. The children's mother gave each daughter as much information as requested. No more, but no less either.

WHAT IS HEAVEN?

Many families have a faith tradition that clearly emphasizes the existence of heaven and a life after death. Heaven is usually described as a place above us in the sky with winged angels resting on fluffy clouds, great joy and pure love. The descriptions are plentiful.

While it is one thing to explain your family's beliefs about the hereafter, it is probably also wise to remember that no living adult knows exactly what heaven is like. If we describe this wonderful, peaceful, magical place, the child may want to go there NOW and be with his or her loved one.

The easiest and best approach is to ask the children what they think heaven is like. They may share your beliefs or have some of their own. They may even believe that there is no heaven. Our role is not to impose our beliefs on them but to support and honour theirs, remembering that as children mature, their concepts of heaven will probably change.

Most importantly, let the child talk. We think that our role as adult is to *tell* children what to think or believe. In fact, we need to *listen* to what they want to share with us. A few specific questions can open up the dialogue.

For example, you might ask:

• 'What do you think death is like?'

• 'Why do you think _____ died?'

• 'Do you think that there is a heaven?' (Our individual religious beliefs determine how we approach the discussion of the soul or afterlife.)

WHAT YOUR CHILD NEEDS TO HEAR FROM YOU

There are certain truths about death that, though they are difficult to accept, children need to learn. It is best if they hear them from you.

Death is natural. Birth is the beginning of life. Death is the end of life. We only need to look at nature and our ancestors to understand the cycle.

Trees, flowers, animals and humans are born and at some time they die. What is in the centre of these momentous events is life itself. Once we accept this truth, we can fully embrace each day and not be afraid of death.

Death is inevitable. My friend Carolyn went to visit her mother the day her mother had been diagnosed with Stage 4 pancreatic cancer. Doctors had explained to both the patient and her family that the tumour was inoperable. Because the cancer had already metastasized to the liver, the physicians ruled out any additional therapy. Radiation and chemotherapy would cause additional suffering without affecting the eventual outcome. On her long drive to the hospital, Carolyn agonized over what to say to her mum. Ultimately, it was her mother who spoke the most meaningful words to her.

'Remember,' she said as they sat together in the visitors' lounge, 'no one lives for ever.' Carolyn nodded. She had heard her mum say this before. 'And,' her mother added softly, 'I'm old enough to die. I have had a good life.'

A sense of comfort settled over Carolyn. Her mother's simple statement did not decrease her sadness at the impending death. But it conveyed a profound message that helped her accept the inevitable.

That evening, Carolyn told her 15-year-old daughter Shannon about Nana's illness. As simply as possible, she explained the prognosis. Finally, she told Shannon what her grandmother had said. Carolyn smiled. 'I tried to think of the right thing to say to Nana, but she was the one who was strong for me, strong for all of us.'

Death is final. Very young children are easily confused when confronted with death. They can see the body of the loved one but they cannot interact. The personality, the spirit, has disappeared. In this sense, death is like a glove without a hand in it; or like a building with no people inside. To a child, understanding death is like putting together a puzzle blindfolded. They've never seen the pieces, can't imagine how they fit together, and have no idea what the final, completed picture is supposed to look like.

Lindsey was 5 years old when her big sister Pam died of leukaemia. Her parents had spent lots of loving time with Lindsey explaining cancer and

HOW DO OUR CHILDREN LEARN ABOUT DEATH?

In a society that is uncomfortable talking about death, it is unfair to expect children to fully comprehend a concept that is so apparently distant from and at odds with daily experience. The lessons we need to teach about death are the opposite of what children absorb from the world around them.

Between the ages of 8 and 13, children spend nearly 7 hours a day with some form of media – television, radio, music, video games, computers, films, books and magazines. For a quarter of children, television alone takes up 5 hours a day of their time. A recent study on TV violence found that very young children witness around 8,000 murders on TV before they start nursery school. On the ubiquitous screen, children are treated to wholesale death that is usually violent and represented in a manner that has little connection with real life and real death.

From TV and other media, children learn that death is:

﹡ Temporary: someone dies on Tuesday night and reappears alive and well on another programme 6 days later.

﹡ Glamorous or easy to handle: on one popular prime time animated programme, kids laugh at death. Video games award points for every 'kill' or death the player executes. Rarely is death associated with evident emotional pain.

her sister's death. They were confident that Lindsey understood and accepted what had happened. But one morning, three months later, Lindsey came bouncing into the family room, looking wide-eyed and innocent, and said: 'Mummy, I really miss Pam! When is she coming home?'

We can help even young children like Lindsey understand death by talking about what it does to the body.

• The lungs don't breathe.

• The heart does not pump blood.

※ For villains only: death descends on the corrupt; the representatives of good triumph – and live.

Our communities are not much better teachers. Death is rarely discussed openly. Rather, it is cloaked in denial and euphemism. When someone dies, we hurry and rush to get things over with. When there's a death in the family, our fast-paced world allows us 2 or 3 days off from work or school to deal with the final services. The implication is that when someone dies, you go through the rituals, thereby accepting your loss; rein in your emotions; and get back to the job or the classroom (and the demands of daily routines) within a week.

Even as individual adults, most of us do a poor job of imparting the truth about death. Mostly, we prefer to avoid the topic. Think of the many books a toddler has read to him or that he receives as gifts. Do any of them deal with death? Probably not. Our excuse: it would be too morbid or upsetting. Thus we make an unconscious decision not to teach a child about an inevitable life experience and leave the child completely unprepared to encounter death.

Death teaches us to appreciate and cherish life. Why wouldn't we want to teach this valuable lesson as early as possible?

- The hair stops growing.

- The body will never be hungry again.

- The person who dies will no longer walk, dance, talk, feel or think.

These kinds of concrete examples provide points of reference for a child. Children can visualize all these things happening, just as they can recall the image of a dead pet or a bird found in the garden. It's very important never to compare death to sleeping. Children interpret our words literally; they fear that by going to bed or to sleep, they, too, will die. Even older children who haven't yet experienced the death of a family member or friend may have trouble understanding the finality of the event. Faced with terminal illness or even death itself, they may ask: 'Isn't there *something* the doctors can do?'

Superstitions do not cause death. When death occurs, children — like Matt who thought arguing had killed his father — face their own self-imposed guilt. Too often, well-meaning adults add to the burden with mindless folk tales and nonsense beliefs about death.

Kristen and her aunt were standing on a street corner one autumn morning, waiting to cross at the light. The two were heading for the local coffee shop for a Saturday morning breakfast together, a monthly ritual they both enjoyed. Kris, 14, wore jeans and a red twinset; her youthful, middle-aged aunt was similarly dressed. Kris was talking about the championship match her volleyball team was to play in that weekend, when a funeral entourage came down the street and passed directly in front of them. The long line of cars moved slowly; Kris fell silent and stepped back from the kerb. She was surprised when her aunt reached over and caught her by the elbow.

'Grab a button or someone you know will die,' Kris's aunt whispered urgently.

Kristen laughed. Her aunt's demeanour and remark were so out of character, the young teenager thought she was teasing. 'Go ahead, grab a button,' her aunt insisted.

Kristen pulled away. 'That's silly,' she scoffed.

Less than a week later, Kris's father died suddenly from a massive stroke.

For years, Kris was haunted by the events of that morning and her aunt's warning. 'In my head, I knew that what my aunt had said was nonsense. But in my heart, I wondered if she weren't right and if I had only grabbed the button on my sweater that day my father might not have died.'

There are no secrets. The kindest approach is the truth, no matter how dreadful — even if the death is the result of suicide or murder. What does make a difference is what grieving youngsters are told and by whom.

We should never lie to children about the cause of death. However, the facts should be presented in a context that is appropriate for the child. For example, if an adult in the family takes her own life:

• A 2-year-old niece need only be told: 'Auntie Lydia died.'

• For a 9-year-old nephew, the explanation would be: 'Auntie Lydia died by taking her own life. This is called suicide.' (Provide more details only if the boy asks questions.)

• Lydia's own child, who is 15, would be told: 'Suicide is a permanent solution to a temporary problem. When we're struggling, we need to ask for help. Your mother must have been very sad and confused to take her own life.' (Teenagers and older children may ask how the death occurred. To such questions, it's best to provide a concrete explanation — 'She hanged herself.' 'She used a gun.' 'She asphyxiated herself in the garage with fumes from the car.' — with no embellishment or judgemental comments.)

> When children are told the truth, they develop the inner strength that they need to cope with life.

For children, no matter what their age, the most important aspect of death is that a special person is gone from their lives. Initially, they wonder how this absence will affect them. This doesn't mean that they're unkind or selfish. Children know instinctively that they can't take care of themselves; they depend on family members and friends, and now one of the people they need is gone.

Children and teenagers perceive themselves as immortal. They can't process death quickly. As they mature, they will revisit the event many times, trying to grasp what is meant by dying. Only when they move into young adulthood do the circumstances surrounding the event become important.

'SHH ... DON'T BOTHER YOUR DAD NOW'

When a parent dies, family and friends often try to keep the children away from the surviving spouse. Their intentions are noble – they want to provide the grieving adult with privacy and time for solace. But for children, the result can be devastating. 'Leave your dad alone right now – he is upset.' Imagine how this sounds to a child whose mother has just died. The message the child hears is quite clear: your feelings aren't important; only those of the grown-ups are. Don't bother anyone.

If death resulted from suicide or murder, they will need to reprocess the *whys* — the reasons — for what happened and will probably experience many of the stages of grief again before moving to acceptance.

All questions deserve answers. One evening in a suburb of a large city, a 12-year-old boy named Max was struck and killed in a hit-and-run accident. His body was thrown into a densely overgrown wooded area and not discovered until the following morning. It was a brutal, awful experience for the parents. When they told their other children, 6-year-old Samantha turned to them wide-eyed and asked, 'Did the deer lick Max's face during the night?'

The heartbroken mother replied as honestly as she could, 'I don't know,' she told the little girl. 'What do you think?'

'I think that they did because deer are kind animals, and they would want to keep Max warm since it was so cold the night that he died.'

In the midst of their overwhelming pain, the parents had the wisdom to consider their daughter's strange question, rather than dismiss it as nonsense or disrespectful. Children mean no harm by their questions. Faced with death, they may be curious; they may be struggling to comprehend what to them appears an inconceivable event.

All of the questions that children pose deserve answers. Most kids, especially younger children, are satisfied with general information. Older children usually ask for specific details.

Sometimes, children may ask the same query over and over again. This does not mean that your initial answer wasn't helpful. Rather, it indicates that they have tried to process the information but haven't been successful yet.

If children ask a question that leaves you stumped, admit that you don't know the answer and assure them that you will do your best to find out. Then follow through and tell them what you've learned as soon as possible. If you tried and were unsuccessful, tell them you gave it your best but couldn't find the answer to the question.

Helping a child through one death experience equips her to face and cope with other eventual losses as well. It really is never too early to start.

Children and Funerals

When Bridget's grandfather, 'Pop Pop', drowned in a boating accident, her parents were at odds over how to handle the situation. Greg, Bridget's father, didn't want his daughter involved in the funeral in any way. 'She's too young,' he insisted. Greg's mother, Sharon, sided with him and even went a step further, contending that Bridget shouldn't be told about the accident and death. 'Being killed like that was just too horrible. It would break my heart to see my little granddaughter so sad,' she said. On the other hand, Susan, Bridget's mother, felt strongly that the little girl should participate. After all, it was Susan's father who had died and she felt that it was important that everyone in the family be part of the farewell to her dad.

After several very emotional discussions, Sharon — who had been a close personal friend of mine for years — called and asked my advice.

HELPFUL STRATEGIES

A child will cope with the death of a loved one most easily if:

※ She is told about the death as soon as possible.

※ She is told the truth.

※ The news is conveyed by a trusted adult.

※ Adults reassure the child that she will be cared for and loved.

※ The child's family and caregivers maintain normal routines, such as mealtimes and bedtime, as well as expected behaviour and consequences. Continuity conveys a sense of normality and actually mitigates some of the child's fears.

※ The child's family and other caring adults make additional time to spend with the child to answer questions and provide companionship. The child must not feel isolated from the other members of the family as they mourn and grieve the loss in her life.

'Indeed, this is going to be difficult for everyone, especially Bridget,' I acknowledged. 'To begin with,' I said, 'Bridget must be told that Pop Pop has died. She knows that people don't just disappear from our lives without a reason.' Then I asked Sharon how she thought Bridget would feel, as she got older, eventually learning about the accident and realizing that she hadn't been included in the final services. 'Well, it won't be an easy thing for her to deal with,' Sharon admitted.

Next, Greg called. From him I learned the details of the accident. And it was awful. 'Bridget doesn't need the step-by-step specifics,' I told him. 'But she needs to be told that there was an accident, and she needs to have you or her mother explain what death means and how everyone in the family is going to say their final goodbyes.'

'You're sure it's better that way?' he asked.

'Yes.'

'OK,' he said reluctantly, 'but Bridget shouldn't come to the wake or funeral. Those are times to be respectful and solemn. She's just a child — what if she runs around or giggles at something?'

'Do you think her grandfather would mind?' I asked him gently. 'If he had anything to say about it, what would be more important to him and his memory — that Bridget was perfectly behaved or that she had been there for him?'

Greg was silent for a long time. 'Pop Pop adored Bridget,' he said finally. 'He would want her there.' After a while, Greg began to ask very specific kinds of questions: what words should they use in telling Bridget about Pop Pop; how should they describe the wake and funeral; what options should they give her?

Several days later, Sharon called again to tell me that Bridget had chosen to attend both her grandfather's wake and funeral. 'She wanted to say good-bye, too,' Sharon said. Had it been a sad occasion? Yes, very much so. But affirming, too. 'Especially everyone being together,' she said. 'I'm glad that Bridget was there.'

As apprehensive as we are about discussing death with children for fear of upsetting them or not explaining it properly, we are equally wary about having children participate in funerals. A funeral is a poignant ritual for letting go of a loved one or friend. It entails a series of traditions that bring meaning to the deceased's life and help surviving family and friends face the reality of this special person's death. Funerals are powerful and important experiences. There are no steadfast rules of etiquette governing the ceremony; in fact, today, final rituals increasingly reflect the family's wishes, character, and needs.

When a loved one dies, children should not be forgotten or left out, but they should also not be expected to act like adults. Instead, special consideration should be given to their specific needs, among them the appropriateness of children attending the funeral; the specific details of how to

HOW TO PREPARE A CHILD FOR THE DEATH OF A LOVED ONE

Unfortunately, there is no blueprint for guiding a child safely through the experience of losing a loved one to death. Each child is unique, and each will have specific concerns and fears. Below, though, are some suggestions to help ease the process as much as possible.

* If possible, take the child to a cemetery and funeral home *before* a death occurs. Talk with the child during this entire excursion, asking him frequently about his understanding of what you are showing him.

* Tell the child as soon as possible after a death occurs. Explain what has happened in words that are appropriate to her age. Children are literal. Discuss death as a biological event. Death is final and not reversible.

* Ask the child about his thoughts on death. Don't deny his beliefs in spite of how different they are from yours.

* Ask the child if she would like to participate in the funeral arrangements.

* Answer the child's questions honestly, but do not elaborate.

prepare children for a funeral service; and finally, how to help them partici-pate in the final farewell, whether or not they attend the funeral.

DECIDING IF CHILDREN SHOULD ATTEND A FUNERAL

When a death occurs in the family, one question is invariably asked: 'Should the children attend the funeral?' My response is always the same: only if they want to, and only if everything that is going to happen has been explained to them. As you talk with your children about an forthcoming funeral, bear in mind that if they have never been to a wake or funeral,

❋ Assure the child that she did not cause the death.

❋ Permit yourself to cry. Children benefit from seeing family members cry. Tears validate the child's deep emotions and give her permission to cry, too.

❋ Don't expect a child to sustain her periods of grief. She will have sad attacks. Watch for and respond to these moments.

❋ Do not assume a child is handling the death 'just fine' if he doesn't talk about it. It is in the talking out of feelings that healing occurs.

❋ Ask the child to share her feelings, fears and questions with you. Then listen – and affirm.

❋ Don't promise the child that you'll never die. Assure him that it will probably be a long while before this happens to you.

❋ Be attentive and patient with children affected by death. Allow them the gift of time for healing.

❋ Encourage counselling or support groups for family members.

they will have no idea what to expect. They are not familiar with the rituals and don't understand their significance. They cannot decide whether or not to participate unless they have a clear understanding of what will take place.

PREPARING A CHILD FOR A FUNERAL

The first and possibly most important step in preparing children for a funeral is to discuss what is going to happen and why. Take them through the process step-by-step, explaining the rituals the family will include in the funeral service. There may be a wake in a funeral home where family and friends come to pay their last respects. Some families, however, extend an invitation to the wake only to immediate family members. Extended family and friends pay their respects at the family home after the burial. In many families, a religious service follows the wake. Usually, the last part of the ritual is cremation or burial.

Once the family has determined specific plans, the children should be told what will be taking place. Walk them through each part of it; at each phase, explain what will be happening and why, who will be present, and how people may react. It is perfectly OK to prepare the children to see adults crying or being visibly upset.

Funerals are not the same for every family. What matters is that children understand what final rites will occur for their loved one and the purpose for each.

Once the children understand the various rituals that will occur over the next few days, ask them to decide if and how they want to participate. They may choose to join in one part and not another. For example, the children may want to be present at the wake but not want to approach the coffin. Or they may join the family in saying a prayer at the coffin but absolutely refuse to touch the body. Give them time to think about the situation and to make up their own minds. Let the children take the lead. They know their own comfort levels.

Often, children turn to adults for guidance. Youngsters may ask: 'Do you think I should go to the wake (or funeral)?' Or they'll wonder: 'What do the adults want me to do?' We can ease the struggle by simply asking the children what it is they would feel comfortable doing and assuring them that we have no preference.

I think the best response to questions about funerals and farewell rites is to talk about how various aspects might affect them. On the one hand, funerals make us feel sad. On the other hand, funerals let us honour the deceased and say one last goodbye.

THE MOST COMMON FUNERAL RITUALS

Various cultures and religious faiths use different rituals in responding to death, but all of them help us say our last farewells. Generally:

* The wake is the social goodbye, the time to share tears, stories, and even laughter with those who knew and cared about the deceased.

* The religious ceremony or service represents the spiritual goodbye, when we pray for the deceased.

* The burial or cremation is the physical goodbye, the time of letting go of the body.

For children and teenagers, just as for adults, all three steps are important. All are difficult. All are necessary to begin the grieving process.

Finally, make sure that you let children and adolescents know beforehand that they can make a quiet exit any time they feel the situation is more than they can manage. This reassurance alone makes such a difference in their decision making. Remember: children are apprehensive of the unknown.

AT THE FUNERAL: GUIDING A CHILD THROUGH THE RITUALS

When her great-grandmother died, 3-year-old Rose attended the wake and saw the body in the coffin at the funeral parlour. The next day, before the church service, the little girl was present when the top of the coffin was closed on the body. Later, after mass, she went to the cemetery with her family.

As the pallbearers carried the coffin over the half-frozen ground, Rose walked hand in hand with her mother towards the grave site. Suddenly the child stopped and pointed at the entourage. 'What's in the box?' she chirped.

'Great-grandma,' her mother whispered fiercely.

'Oh.' Rose kicked at a pile of snow and then began walking forward again.

Shouldn't Rose have remembered? Perhaps. Was her question out of bounds? Her choice of words inappropriate? No. She's a child. She had never seen a coffin before that weekend. In her world, *things*, not *people*, were put in boxes. Everything connected to the death and funeral of Rose's great-grandmother was new and unfamiliar, and she was simply curious.

If a child decides to participate in the funeral rituals, make sure that a trusted adult accompanies him. A parent or close relative is the most obvious person to fill this role, but usually they are too caught up in their own grief to properly look after the needs of a bewildered, curious child. Someone who is able to put the child first during every step of the service could assume this very important role. The person should have enough emotional distance from the deceased to be able to observe the child carefully and know or anticipate his feelings and needs.

Often, a close neighbour or family friend makes an ideal companion for the child. When Chareese and Sonja's grandmother died unexpectedly, the girls, who were aged 8 and 13, didn't know what to expect. They had never experienced the death of a loved one. Their mother was so devastated by the loss that she couldn't talk to them without weeping. Nancy, a close family friend, offered to 'be there' for the girls. On the first day of the funeral rituals, Nancy arrived at the funeral home shortly after the wake began and for the next six hours tended to the girls' needs. When Chareese and Sonja weren't with their parents or talking with relatives, Nancy sat and chatted with them about school, their activities and, yes, memories of their grandmother. Later, she took them out for dinner. After they returned to the wake, she helped the girls serve coffee and cake to visitors. The next day, Nancy sat behind the girls at the funeral; along with their parents, she

---

'NO ONE TOLD ME WHAT TO EXPECT'

Several times a year, I present grief workshops to teachers, parents and counsellors. As part of the programme, I ask the participants to recall their first encounter with death. Listening to them is a heart-rending experience. Invariably, the memories shared deal with events that occurred when these adults were children or teenagers. Here's what they remember.

* No adult told them what really happened.

* No adult told them what to expect.

* No adult sat close to them during the service.

* No adult ever asked afterwards if they had any questions.

* No adult asked if they wanted to talk about the death of this loved person – ever.

---

was another reassuring presence. She stayed nearby at the cemetery. At the luncheon, the girls' parents shared a table with the grandmother's surviving sisters. Nancy, Sonja and Chareese sat at the next table with other family members. For two days, Nancy was truly a compassionate companion to the grieving youngsters.

During the funeral service, some families adhere strictly to established rites, while others allow and even encourage children to create their own farewell rituals. A child can make a card or draw a picture for the deceased, or she can give up a special keepsake — a small stuffed animal, for example — that she or someone else can put in the coffin for her. One young girl wrote a private message to her aunt who had died. She attached the message to a balloon that she released at the cemetery.

Adolescents may want to speak at the funeral to say their farewells or share the relationship that they had with the deceased. Or they may write a poem that they read aloud or simply place in the coffin.

For any child, simply being present at the memorial services can often provide a valuable and tangible way to begin the grieving process. All families have rituals for marking significant events in their personal lives and in the family's history. The death of a loved member of the family is the most meaningful. How could we ever think of not inviting everyone to participate in the final celebration of someone's life?

Sometimes children *do* giggle or run around in the funeral home. These actions don't signal disrespect. Chances are the children are nervous, hungry, tired by the long day, or stressed by the heavy air of solemnity that settles on such proceedings. Please try not to say 'You shouldn't do that' or 'That isn't appropriate'. Such reprimands only pile guilt on top of the grief they are feeling. Instead, find someone to take them outdoors for a short walk or to get a bite to eat nearby.

Some children will walk up to the coffin and reach out to feel the body of the deceased. Why shouldn't they? This person is their loved one, too.

IF A CHILD DOESN'T ATTEND THE FUNERAL

A child or teenager may decide not to attend the funeral services. Do not be upset or try to convince her to do otherwise. Above all, do not use guilt! Avoid phrases like, 'What will your grandmother think?' 'What will the neighbours say?' 'Your little cousin is going; if she can handle it, so can you!' This is a time to try to understand the child's concerns and respect the child's wishes.

Children still need a way to say goodbye. Perhaps they can write a poem or draw a picture that expresses their feelings. The chapter on Activities and Rituals for Healing describes several other activities you can do with children to assist them in letting go of their loved ones.

AFTER THE FUNERAL: KEEPING THE LINES OF COMMUNICATION OPEN

When the funeral services are concluded, make an effort to spend some time alone with the children who attended the rituals. You can do this as a group or individually. You can spend 10 minutes or 2 hours. The most important thing is that you are comfortable talking about the events of the last few days. The purpose of this time together is to answer any questions that the children may have about the services; to revisit the purpose of the rituals they have just experienced; and lastly, and most crucially, to get the children to talk about how they are feeling.

A few weeks later, do it again. Remember, children cannot take in and process events of this magnitude in one sitting. They are bound to be confused; most helpful for them are conversations linked together over time. By demonstrating that you are always available to answer any questions the children may have or simply to listen to their thoughts, worries and fears, you will be a reassuring source of strength to them at one of the most tumultuous periods in their lives.

Chapter 4

Children
and Divorce

KEN WAS 10 when his parents gathered him and his two younger siblings around the kitchen table one sunny afternoon for a family talk. 'Your mother and I have something to tell you,' his father began. And thus unfolded the news of the divorce. While the two younger children seemed confused by the information being presented, Ken asked a few questions and dutifully nodded at the explanations. After a while, he asked if he could go to play with his friends. Ken walked out of the kitchen seemingly undisturbed by the conversation.

By the end of the week, Ken's father had packed his clothes and piled boxes of his belongings in the hall. On Saturday morning, a removal van arrived and the workers began carrying the boxes and a few pieces of furniture from the house. Ken watched for a few minutes and then disappeared. His dad found him in the basement.

'What's up? Why are you down here alone?' his father asked.

Ken ignored the questions. 'Why is that van here?' he demanded. 'What's in the boxes?'

'Remember, we talked about this last weekend?' Ken's dad answered. He sat down next to the boy and went over the facts and concerns of the divorce. Ken blinked back tears. His father stayed with him until every one of his questions was answered, assuring his son that the divorce was not his fault. Once again, Ken's dad said, 'Your mum and I worked hard at staying married, but this divorce really is going to be the best for everyone.' Ken turned away.

Throughout adolescence, Ken was haunted by the divorce. For seven years, he was literally cloaked in black: his clothes, mood and attitudes all seemed coloured by that one event. Ken was a bright student who didn't do well in school and a natural athlete with no interest in sports. Growing up, he embraced music with harsh, brutal lyrics. He hung out with a gang who always seemed to be on the verge of getting into serious trouble. Ken was a constant worry to his parents. They weren't certain if his behaviour represented a struggle with adolescence or was a repercussion from the divorce.

Love is the most complex of all emotions that human beings share. Despite the books, poems and songs written about love, no one really understands this feeling. Not only can love fill us with joy, it can painfully break our hearts.

When Ken was 17, he and his stepmother were talking about the divorce. At one point, she asked directly, 'Did you ever feel responsible?'

'Absolutely,' he said, without skipping a beat.

'Didn't your mum or dad talk to you about the divorce?'

'Yeah,' he said. 'But still …'

'Ken, what do you think you did to cause your parents' divorce?' she asked.

'I'm not sure,' Ken replied. 'I just know I should have been able to fix it.' For years and years, he said, he'd tried to figure out what had gone wrong and felt he had failed the family because he couldn't make it whole again.

Children naturally assume that they will be growing up within a family — that their parents will always be living with them, providing protection and keeping them healthy and emotionally secure. As newborns, children enter the world fearing abandonment. The terror of being left alone gradually diminishes as the child's parents fulfil the infant's needs for nourishment, physical well-being and unconditional love. As the child grows both physically and emotionally, her parents become her first teachers — coaxing her first word, guiding her first step, and allowing her to feel secure and loved. All this time, the child views everything — herself and the world around her — through the eyes of her family. Family gives her strength and shapes her personality. It is her jumping-off point into the world.

So what does a couple do when their marriage is in disrepair? Should they stay together for the sake of the children? Many organizations, authors and researchers believe the answer is yes, since divorce can be detrimental to the children in the family. Certainly, for this reason alone, any couple that is contemplating divorce should put every possible effort into saving the marriage. Having said that, however, I must also state that I firmly believe that it is far better for a child to come from a divorced family than to live *in* one. To grow up in a home where there is abuse or constant arguing or where there is no love is far worse for the child.

How Children Experience Divorce

Children absorb what's going on around them. Long before the divorce is made official, they are affected by the arguments, tension and general disruption in their lives of two parents feuding. And long after the ink is dry on the divorce papers, children mourn the loss of the family life they once knew. Let's take a look at each stage in the process and explore how divorce is perceived from a child's viewpoint.

> Love is the foundation upon which marriages are formed and families are created. Strange as it is, marriage is also the first step towards divorce.

BEFORE IT'S OFFICIAL

Maya had always been a playful, happy, healthy little girl. Shortly after she turned 5 years old and started school, Maya began complaining of headaches and persistent stomach pains. At first, her mum and dad thought she had picked up a bug at school. But weeks later, Maya was still miserable; by then, the stomach-aches were so severe that they often brought tears to her eyes.

Maya's doctor found nothing wrong. After a second visit, the doctor sent the little girl for a battery of tests. The results came back with the same diagnosis — no medical cause for the abdominal pain. Maya's parents were increasingly frustrated and concerned.

Outwardly, Maya's mum and dad seemed to be the ideal married couple. In public, they were always pleasant and friendly; both were hard-working and successful professionals who were well respected and liked in the community. In reality, the two had been unhappy and struggling with their marriage for several years. Recently, after months in counselling, they had initiated divorce proceedings. While they worked through the details with their lawyers, the two also grappled with how to break the news to family members, friends, colleagues and, especially, to Maya. The situation left them both stressed and with little additional energy or time to take their daughter to more doctors for additional medical opinions.

Eventually, the divorce was finalized, and Maya was told what had happened. The news came as a shock to the child. However, dismayed as Maya was at the breakup of her parents' marriage, she also began to feel better physically — soon the stomach-aches disappeared.

Children are perceptive. They have ears that hear their parents' conversations and eyes that see their parents' facial expressions. As much as adults try to hide their relationship problems, children are aware of sub-surface tensions, camouflaged sadness and suppressed anger. They sense that something terrible is happening around them and wonder why no one will talk to them about the situation. Being kept in the dark makes children and teenagers feel precariously vulnerable. Frightened by what they can't explain and don't understand, many try to fill in the gaps with their own imagined scenarios. Other youngsters internalize their fears and concerns; these suppressed worries often are displayed through illnesses, changed behaviour and social or academic problems.

Telling the Children

After a workshop about single parenting, a woman came up to me with a question about her impending divorce. After 18 years of a difficult relationship, she said, she and her husband had decided to end the marriage. For the past 14 months, they had been working out arrangements for the care of their four children and the division of their property and savings.

Divorce terminates the family unit. It rips apart all that children need and hold sacred.

When I asked her how the children were handling the divorce, she admitted that they had not been told. 'We don't know how to break the news to them,' she confided.

'When is your husband going to move out?' I asked.

The woman flushed. 'Tomorrow!' she said.

The answer left me nearly speechless. In 24 hours, the lives of four children would be dramatically altered, and they were being given no time to prepare.

The parents had had months, perhaps years, to get ready. Those four youngsters had hours.

Usually a separation or divorce is preceded by months or even years of tension, arguments or apathy. Still, parents often delay telling their children about a pending divorce. For one, they instinctively want to protect their kids from the potentially painful news. For another, they are coping with their own intense emotions about the event and would prefer to avoid having to discuss or explain their decisions and actions. I clearly remember believing that if I waited until the last possible minute to tell my sons that their father and I were getting a divorce, the news would hurt that much less. I reasoned that it was sort of like pulling off a bandage quickly — fast and precise — and would therefore hurt for just a second. How very wrong I was!

Talking with children is probably the single most painful event in the divorce process.

Children and teenagers are not capable of quickly processing information about the demise of their parents' marriage. They need time to hear the news, mull it over, ask questions about the decision and begin comprehending what the event will mean.

Children's Reactions

Initially, the children will want to know the particulars of the divorce: where will everyone be living; what about birthday presents; what will happen at Christmas and holidays; how often will they see the parent they won't be with daily? This emphasis on the practical doesn't mean that they are heartless or don't care about the divorce or their parents, but rather that they are trying to shore up their crumbling foundation of security.

Beyond these practical issues, though, are three questions — often unasked — that children of all ages have when their parents divorce.

'Did I cause this?' Even though you have already assured the children that this event is not their fault, they may feel a nagging sense of guilt for a

HOW TO PREPARE CHILDREN AND ADOLESCENTS FOR A SEPARATION OR DIVORCE

No matter how you do it, telling the children about your impending divorce will be difficult for all of you. The following pointers, though, will help to make the process a bit less painful.

﹡ Tell the children as soon as the decision has been made and some of the details have been worked out.

﹡ Ideally, parents should present the news together. If only one parent is able to talk with the children, the burden is heavier for that parent. If someone else must convey the news, the conversation becomes even more complex.

﹡ Choose a familiar setting that is free from distractions.

﹡ Begin by talking about events that the children may have already noticed, such as arguments, tears, and sleeping in separate rooms. 'Undoubtedly, you've heard Mum and Dad argue a lot. We have tried to make our marriage be successful, but ...' This approach helps children connect to what they are being told.

﹡ Remember that physical touch is comforting – an arm around a shoulder, touching hands, holding young children on your lap.

long time. Children want to believe that their parents are perfect. This allows them to edit out Mum's or Dad's failings or mistakes and blame themselves for the problems that led to the divorce.

'Who will keep me safe?' From an early age, children sense the security that comes from having two people taking care of them. Now there will be only one. Worse, they worry that the remaining parent will leave them, too. Children fear that everything upon which they depend will crumple. This is a fundamental anxiety of all children, especially adolescents. While

✳ Assure the children that the separation or divorce is an adult issue. Make sure they understand that they are not responsible. Adults marry. Adults divorce. But everyone hurts.

✳ Tell the children again and again that their mum and dad will always love them. The bond between child and parent cannot be broken. This is a major concern!

✳ Ask: 'What do you need during this difficult time?'

✳ Encourage the children to ask questions.

✳ Answer all questions without accusations or negative comments. Most children will want to know *why*. A truthful, impartial response can be: 'Mum and Dad have grown in different directions, and living together is too difficult.' If there is a question that is too personal or painful to answer, honestly say that to them. Refrain from answering questions about each other's motives or plans. If there has been a history of abuse, addiction, or other turmoil in the marriage, those facts need to be told in a caring way. Keep in mind that the children love their mum and dad and do not want anyone saying negative things about them.

teenagers seemingly are pulling away from their families, they still want to know they have a protective haven to return to when the world gets too frightening or a problem arises.

'Is this going to happen to me, too?' Children worry that history will repeat itself when they grow up and marry. They envisage a future clouded by the inherent pain of separation and divorce. They wonder if every marriage leads to divorce. As parents and caregivers, we can use our life experiences as a teaching tool to assist our children in becoming discerning adults.

119

Telling the stories of our lives and love relationships to our children can help them realize that we all stumble and try again; our hearts get broken and we fall in love another time; we make wise choices and reap the benefits; we make wrong decisions and suffer the consequences. Through it all, though, we learn and become better people.

When children, and especially teenagers, make disparaging remarks about marriage, turn the conversation into a positive discussion about marriage. Explain that marriage means much more than simply falling in love, that it is an ongoing commitment between two separate individuals who have joined their family histories, their values, and their spiritual beliefs. Tell them that this is the reason why it's so important for them to know themselves and their personal goals well before they choose a spouse. This is also a good time to remind children that although 50 per cent of marriages fail, the other 50 per cent function very well.

Ultimately, no matter how well prepared you are, no matter how gently you present news of the divorce, most children will be hurt deeply. Mum and Dad are the two people the children love most in the world — and for them it is incomprehensible that their parents no longer love one another.

Unfortunately, for some children, news of divorce comes as a relief. These children live in families marked by abuse, arguments, or tension. They are eager for a peaceful life and hope that divorce will offer them a respite. For them, the pain comes years later when they look back upon their childhoods and wonder 'What if ...?'

DURING DIVORCE PROCEEDINGS

Brad was 6 when his mother walked out, leaving three young children solely in her husband's care. Brad's father, Winston, had no warning; one day he came home from work and found the children with a babysitter. A note on his pillow simply said that he would be hearing from a lawyer about the divorce. Winston was devastated and angry. As best he could, he kept things going with the children — meals, housekeeping, an occasional treat. But he never talked about his wife. Young as Brad was, he understood without being told that he shouldn't mention his mother and made sure his younger siblings knew this as well.

Christmas came, and Winston hauled the lights and ornaments from the attic. That year, he announced, they were getting an artificial tree. 'Less hassle,' he explained. The children all seemed OK with the plan.

As in years past, there was a fire in the fireplace and hot chocolate for the children as they began decorating the tree. Suddenly, Brad said, 'Dad, do you remember, before Mum left, we always chopped our tree down on the first of December and ...' Winston turned on the boy, snapping, 'Don't you ever mention your mother in this house again!'

During the divorce, parents often are so involved in the day-to-day details of their lives and dealing with their own anger and pain that they do things they wouldn't normally do. The most loving and doting parents can become so obsessed with the dismantling of the marriage that they use their children as weapons for getting even or being heard. They may pit the children against the other parent, deliberately stonewall the process of working out a reasonable parenting agreement, or persuade the children to take sides.

Many parents abandon their responsibilities to their children. Youngsters may be emotionally ignored. They may be shouted at inappropriately or disciplined irrationally. The resident parent may be quiet, withdrawn or depressed. Conversely, the parent may be seething with anger and ready to lash out at the mere mention of the spouse's name.

Throughout this highly charged period, children may be physically neglected as well. For example, meals may not be prepared, laundry may not be done, the house may not be cleaned, and the children may be left unattended for long periods of time. I remember all too well barely having the strength in the morning to pull the covers back and start another new day. I did not want to face another 24 hours in such intense emotional pain.

Children and the Courts

Unfortunately, the legal system offers little refuge for children of divorced parents. While some courts are beginning to be more 'child-friendly', most of them still focus their time and attention on the feuding adults. The court-room is controlled by adults supervising other adults who cannot manage their personal lives. The divorce is all about them — their need to 'get even' and their insistence on getting a 'fair share'. The children who were born from the union are ignored, essentially rendered voiceless. Others are put in untenable situations.

One Tuesday morning during an English lesson, Simone, 13, and her classmates were taking it in turns to read aloud from the play they were studying. When Simone had finished reading her part, she burst into tears and ran into the corridor. Her teacher followed her and caught up with her near a bank of lockers where Simone was leaning. The teacher put her arms around the girl's shoulders and held her while she sobbed. After a while, the tears subsided. 'What's wrong, dear?' the caring woman asked. Simone sighed. 'My parents told me last night that they're getting divorced,' she said, 'and I have until this weekend to decide which one I want to live with!'

Sometimes a divorce may take years to wend its way through the courts. Until all of the details are finalized, the parents remain in limbo, unable to *feel* their loss and help children cope with their own issues. In the worst-case scenario, the final resolution leaves one of the adults claiming unfair treatment, and the wounds of the breakup are opened yet again — not only for the squabbling parents but also for the children.

THE AFTERMATH

Damon dreads the weekends. Every Saturday, the 8-year-old boy wakes up with a stomach-ache and lies in bed trying to remember if this is his weekend with Dad. If it is, Damon's discomfort intensifies.

Don't misunderstand. Damon wants to see his father. Unfortunately, the father-son visits every other weekend are so predictably stressful, they make the boy ill. Here's what happens: ten minutes before Damon's dad is scheduled to arrive, Damon's mum stations herself at the front door with a small clock in hand. If her former husband is late, she gloats and criticizes. If he's early, she refuses to allow him inside to wait for his son or to let Damon run out to the car. She permits no contact between the two until the clock reads exactly 9.30 a.m. — the court-appointed time for the visit to begin.

Adding to the situation, when Damon's parents finally come face-to-face at the front door, they invariably get into an argument. Usually, the two quarrel about money — Damon's mum wants more, and his dad says she is a spendthrift milking him dry. But any topic — family celebrations, school activities, holiday plans — is potential grist for their verbal bashing mill. No matter what they argue about, Damon is literally in the middle, with the nasty accusations and retorts flying over his shaggy blonde head.

Divorce often leaves a child feeling abandoned, angry, betrayed, different from his peers and guilty. Children of divorced parents feel a loss of self-worth and identity, and they mourn the lost daily contact they had with each parent, the established traditions, and the future they had envisaged with their family that will now be altered.

Before a divorce, parents usually argue behind closed doors. Once the divorce is final, arguments are out in the open and usually about topics like child support and visiting rights. So why wouldn't the children feel guilty and think the divorce was really about them?

Many elements affect a child's experience of — and ultimate adjustment to — divorce. Some factors we can change, easing the burden our children must bear. Unfortunately, other factors we simply can't.

What You Can't Change

A child's age, gender and temperament — fixed elements at the time of the divorce — affect his adjustment to the dissolution of the nuclear family.

Age. No one really agrees on an age at which children are best able to handle their parents' divorce. How can anyone ever determine when the pain of divorce will hurt the least? As with other significant events, the impact depends on the emotional and physical maturity of the child, the family's ability to communicate, and the event itself. Here are some specific concerns for various ages.

Birth to 5 years old: children can't comprehend what a divorce really is. They seem to recover quickly, because they have fewer memories of their birth family.

6 to 12 years old: divorce often generates intense anger and reverberates through every facet of the child's life, affecting academic performance, behaviour, and ability to communicate.

13 to 18 years old: adolescence is a difficult time in its own right. Teenagers are trying to separate from the family but at the same time desperately need the security the family structure provides. Their reactions to divorce are mixed and complex and usually simmer just below the surface.

Gender. Studies have found that boys usually experience a severe initial impact to divorce. And in many instances, the effect is prolonged. Young girls, on the other hand, seem to recover quickly. As they reach adolescence, however, their emotional reactions resurface and often result in precocious sexual activity.

In both instances, I sincerely believe that these responses are influenced by the often-diminished role the father plays in a child's life after divorce. Too often, both the mother and the legal system minimize Dad's involvement with the children.

Temperament. The easygoing child who seems to adjust to change readily — new babysitters, starting school, and so on — also tends to adjust well to the changes a divorce brings, such as the back and forth between families, seeing their parents date, and having Mum going back to work. On the other hand, the child who needs a stable routine and advance notice of a change in plans or who has difficulty relating to new surroundings has more problems adjusting to the often ongoing changes associated with divorce.

Obviously, a child's age at the time of the divorce, gender and temperament cannot be altered. For that reason, it is essential that caregivers, family members and parents be attuned to each individual child and how best to help him process the divorce.

What You Can Change

Data from studies about the impact of divorce on children spans the entire continuum from 'rosy' to 'dark'. At one end of the spectrum, a noted psychologist says that children are for ever damaged by divorce. At the other extreme, another expert argues that most children escape largely unscathed. Findings can vary from one population to another and be influenced by the investigator's personal perspective or experience. What I know to be true, and what researchers also agree with, is that children's success in growing through their parents' divorce is influenced by the levels of ongoing conflict, the parents' levels of distress and ability to function emotionally, the child's lingering sense of guilt, parental abandonment, the family's socio-economic status, and the amount of support from extended family and the community.

Ongoing conflict. Georgia's parents divorced when she was 11 years old. She is now 34. To this day, her mum and dad cannot be in the same room together, not at weddings, grandchildren's baptisms or birthdays, or a single Christmas. Neither times of joy nor solemnity. Can you imagine the tensions Georgia and her four siblings live with daily? Absolutely every celebration any one of them could have is marred by their parents' inability to let go of the hostility.

It is not the divorce itself that destroys the children but rather how the parents divorce, and how they rebuild the two new family units.

125

Unlike other losses, divorce usually results in ongoing conflict. Whether overt or submerged, the continual back-and-forth antagonism is the single most damaging consequence of divorce. It is the endless bickering — the family civil war — that destroys and ultimately dooms the children. In a 10-year follow-up study of divorced families, researchers found that half of the women and one-third of the men remained intensely angry with their former spouses. This anger haunts and diminishes the children. It is a constant, dominant force in their lives.

For former spouses, ongoing conflict becomes a contest, a game of wits or revenge that ends up putting the children in harm's way.

Here are some of the more common ways adults involve children in their conflicts.

Negative message carrier. Children are forced to carry negative messages from one parent to the other. The messages always concern adult issues: child support, visiting rights, boyfriends or girlfriends, parenting issues, and so on.

What children hear:

'Tell your father I never got the child support.'

'Tell your mother she is out too much during the week.'

'Tell your dad he has to make better meals.'

'Tell your mum she spends my money on herself instead of you.'

Shooting poison-laced arrows. Children are exposed to negative comments about a parent or extended family members. The criticisms are expressed in certain statements or phrases or conveyed by the rolling of eyes or tone of voice. Each negative comment is a poison-laced arrow that goes right through the heart of the child.

What children hear:

'You are as irresponsible as your grandmother.'

'Your dad and uncle are so lazy.'

'Your mum has no common sense.'

'You are acting as stupid as your dad.'

'Your dad gives you too many presents.'

'Your mum hurt me with her affairs, so she is not welcome in this house, not even to pick you up. I never want to see her again.'

Choosing sides. When divorced parents and their families and friends take sides, children are caught in the middle and forced to align themselves with or defend one parent or faction against the other. This isn't the role of a child. This is the role of an adult referee, and children — no matter what their ages — are not equipped for it.

What children hear:

'Let me tell you what your dad just did ...'

'Your mum never loved us — that's why she left.'

'Your dad is the real reason for the divorce; let me tell you why.'

'If you talk to your mum's new husband, don't bother to come home. He is the reason we are divorced.'

'Your dad doesn't even give me enough money to buy groceries.'

'If you invite your mother to the awards ceremony, I won't come.'

Parent protector. Children are placed in situations where one parent assumes the role of or is perceived as the victim, or where both parents try to use the children as allies against one another. Children feel obligated to 'protect' the wronged parent.

What children hear:

'Your mum is struggling. That's why Grandpa and I help her out so much.'

'I'm too sad to even get out of bed.'

'I don't have any friends now. Will you come with me to see a film?'

At the age of 6, Steven was pretty excited about his dad getting remarried. He liked Sandra, his stepmother-to-be, because she was fun to play with. Steven wished he could see his father more often, but he understood that his mum and dad lived quite far apart and that this was the only arrangement possible. Still, Steven couldn't understand why each time his dad picked him up, he'd ask why the boy hadn't returned his phone calls. 'I called at least twice a week since my last visit,' his dad said.

Each time, Steven would swallow hard and say: 'Oh, I was just busy.' The boy hated lying to his father but felt he'd be betraying his mother if he admitted that she hadn't given him the messages. At the same time, he didn't know how to ask his mum why she did this. Steven always felt confused — how could the two people he loved most in the world despise each other so much?

Divided equally. The child must spend 'equal' time with each parent or the parent's family. What children hear:

'You spend more time with your dad than with us.'

'Every holiday is with your mum's family.'

'No, I won't switch weekends with your mother; that would mean she would have you kids two weekends in a row.'

'No, I won't let you go with your father earlier. You're *my* child. I don't care if you will be late for your day out. He gets you only from 8 a.m. to 6 p.m.!'

The more positive, loving time a child spends with *all* family members, the stronger the child's self-esteem. The best-adjusted children of divorce have lots of time with both parents and extended family and friends — time when they don't have to curtail their actions or monitor what comes out of their mouths; when they can move freely from family to family; when their moments together aren't timed or inventoried.

WHAT CHILDREN LEARN FROM FEUDING ADULTS:

When parents quarrel, they unwittingly teach their children inappropriate lessons about the proper way to interact with others. Among them:

❋ Every problem leads to an argument.

❋ Disagreeing means calling the other person names and raising your voice.

❋ Other people's opinions don't merit respect.

❋ It's OK to be dishonest or to withhold information from one or the other parent.

❋ People and situations can be manipulated and used to their advantage, as in:

'Dad, Mum always let me watch this show on television.'

'Mum, Dad says when I turn 16 he will buy me a car.'

'Grandma, my parents said I am old enough to stay out until ...'

'If you don't let me ... , I am going to go and live with ...'

The parents' levels of distress and ability to function emotionally. How well the parents are coping emotionally has a direct impact on the children's ability to handle divorce. After a divorce, a parent usually feels anxious, angry, depleted, depressed, rejected, guilty and less socially competent. Intertwine those emotions with the powerful feelings of grief most divorced parents feel, and you can certainly understand why adults who have divorced do not function well initially. They may make fewer maturity demands on their children. They tend to be less affectionate and communicative; their parenting is inconsistent and often fluctuates between spoil and strict modes.

Complicating the parents' grief recovery is the fact that their children also are grieving. Unfortunately, the parents and children are rarely at the same emotional level. So while one is sad, the other is angry. When we are grieving, there is little left to offer to anyone else. This is why it's important to get your children the support of other concerned, trustworthy adults who can guide and nurture them through the difficult grieving process even as you are struggling to accept your new circumstances.

Eventually, as parents are swept up into rebuilding their lives, their children again may feel relegated to the margins. As parents take on new jobs, lovers or spouses, their children lose the focused attention they may once have had with their mother or father. Children of divorced parents usually end up moving to different homes, neighbourhoods and communities — often more than once. They lose their friends, schools, faith communities, parks and other favourite places. Some may spend less time with extended family and family friends.

The child's lingering sense of guilt. Scott, 16, worked at the garage where I had my car serviced. He was always friendly, but after he found out about my job and RAINBOWS, our rapport quickly strengthened. One day in late autumn, Scott seemed very preoccupied. His dad had moved out that day, he said, for the fourth time in six years!

'Before, he always came back after a few months, but this time I don't know. It just seems different,' Scott explained. 'You know what he said as he left the house? "Scott, it's your fault that your mum's kicking me out".'

The boy's eyes filled with tears and he looked soulfully at me. 'What did I do?' he said in a low voice. 'I didn't mean to be the reason they split up.'

As calmly as possible, I explained that his father was probably angry and hurt. And since Scott was standing at the door, he lashed out at him. I emphasized that there was nothing Scott could ever do that would cause adults to divorce.

Scott was right; his father didn't come back that time. Instead, he moved into an apartment and only occasionally visited his son. Whenever I saw

Scott, we'd talk about his dad and his parting words. Each time, I reassured Scott that his father must have been terribly upset. And again I reiterated that there was no possible way that Scott could ever cause a divorce.

In all honesty, though, whose voice do you think he kept hearing — mine or his dad's?

It is imperative that we remind children again and again that a divorce is an adult problem. There is nothing a child or teenager could ever say or do that would cause his parents to divorce.

Parental abandonment. Aleysha was 15 when I first met her. She was a beautiful girl with long curly brown hair and large blue eyes, but what really struck me was how alarmingly thin she was. I didn't think it appropriate to say anything at the time, so I waited. During the next few months, Aleysha and I became friends. One night over dinner, she began telling me her story.

Aleysha wasn't totally sure her parents had ever been married; if so, they'd divorced when she was an infant. Growing up, she spent almost every weekend with her dad. She hated saying goodbye on Sunday night, but she was always thrilled by the routine. Invariably, as he drove away, her dad would roll down the car window and yell out 'Aleysha, I love you. I am proud that you are my daughter. Be a good girl.'

Four years ago, everything changed, she said. One Sunday night in July, her dad pulled away from the kerb without a word. She couldn't believe it! 'I stood on the lawn and waited, thinking it was a joke, that he'd drive around the block and toot the horn and call out his usual farewell. But he didn't.' Aleysha has not seen or heard from her father since. Months later, she tried calling him, but there was no answer. Since then, she's discovered that he has moved, and she doesn't know how to find him.

'I must have done something terribly wrong for him to leave like that and not come back,' Aleysha said to me.

Soon afterwards, I asked the teenager why she was so thin. At first she shrugged off the question — it was no big deal, all her friends were. Then, in a whisper, Aleysha said, 'Maybe if I'm really skinny, Daddy will find out and come back to help me.'

When a parent disappears from a child's life after a divorce, the child is absolutely devastated. Every day, she wonders why her mum or dad doesn't love her enough to phone or spend time with her regularly. Unfortunately, situations like Aleysha's are not isolated incidents. After a divorce, nearly half of the children don't see their fathers. Sadly, nearly every child or teenager I have spoken with who has had a parent disappear from her life blames herself.

Except for instances where a parent's behaviour is potentially harmful, children need to have both their mother and father active in their lives after a divorce. In fact, studies prove that children benefit from the role modelling, love and guidance that each parent provides when both share in the parenting responsibilities after divorce.

The family's socio-economic status. Socio-economic stability can have a large impact on a child's post-divorce well-being. While the family does not necessarily have to live at the same financial level as before, it is important that children are assured adequate care, food, housing, clothing, and the opportunity for higher education.

Parents have financial obligations that extend beyond the divorce. Unfortunately, mothers who have the custody of their children often end up at the poverty level and may have to return to work or take on second jobs just to get by. If family and friends are supportive of these changes, the custodial parent and the children feel less isolated. This reinforcement encourages them to rebuild and recover.

Offering to help the beleaguered parent by occasionally assisting with child care, chauffeuring the children to and from places, or inviting them for a home-cooked dinner can be one of the greatest gifts that you can give. There may be situations when you can offer some financial support as well. When doing so, just be careful not to insult the parent or stop her from feeling competent and becoming self-sufficient.

The amount of support from the extended family and the community. Siblings Anne, Amy and Aidan were budding thespians. They not only had roles in all of the school plays but also joined the community theatre guild. Yet despite their talent and enthusiasm for acting, each performance became a tension-filled event — because of Grandma. The children's parents were divorced, and while Mum and Dad had no problem attending the same show, their maternal grandmother refused to come if their father was going to be in the audience. Nana was adamant and really nasty. It didn't matter if the theatre held 500 people or 2,000. It was always up to Dad to juggle his schedule or sometimes completely miss a performance so his former mother-in-law would attend.

Combative, sniping behaviour on the part of family members equates to psychological abuse of the children. Such bickering threatens children's security, self-worth, happiness, social confidence and belief in unconditional love. Why? Because the child is some of each parent. His self-esteem is rooted in his family tree. When you negate the value of a parent or grandparent, you tear at the fabric of the child's being. That's why children will defend and protect their parents, often to an extreme. They are protecting themselves as well.

Grandparents, aunts, uncles and family friends are often equally guilty about sending negative messages. They need to refocus their thinking on the best interests of the child. Whenever the child is present, their actions, words, behaviour and responses must be compassionate, kind and supportive — even when the situation seems unfair or the children are being troublesome.

Grandparents are in an especially difficult spot. They, too, are grieving their adult child's divorce. At the same time that they are distressed and feeling protective towards their own son or daughter, they may still harbour feelings of love for the now ex-son-in-law or ex-daughter-in-law. No etiquette book has been written yet that addresses this complicated situation.

For all concerned, the golden rule 'Do as you would be done by' has never had a better opportunity to be used than in a divorced family!

Children at Risk, but Not Doomed

For adults who divorce, the event is a conclusion. For the children, divorce is often a beginning — of unfinished business, of uncertainty. The child's mind is brimming with questions: Where will I live? How often will I see my other parent? Will my dad's girlfriend leave him? Will my mum marry her boyfriend? Will my parents ever get along?

Adults like to think that children go through a *period* of sadness immediately following a divorce and then simply bounce back to the way they were pre-divorce. Often, that seems to be true. Most children do go on with their daily routines — school, sports, clubs, lessons, computer games and sleepovers. But just because a child appears 'fine' on the outside doesn't mean that all is well on the inside. If children have not grieved the change in their families and have not been given the attention they need to fully comprehend why their parents divorced, their grief and emotional issues end up being buried very much alive and someday will need to be dealt with.

For them, life is an ongoing struggle with:

Nagging questions and unresolved issues. As young children, they may have asked: 'Why did Mummy and Daddy divorce?' As adolescents, they wonder, 'What is love, really? Are commitments supposed to be for ever? Just why did my parents get married — they seem such an unlikely couple?'

Tensions and transitions. At each important milestone in a child's life — awards ceremonies, graduations, weddings and even funerals — her family situation is highlighted again. If the divorce has not come to a healthy resolution, the pain is revisited.

Anger. For many children, anger is the strongest, most long lasting, and most complex emotion they struggle with after their parents divorce. If they also feel protective towards their parents, they suppress their rage, which usually resurfaces later and is often misdirected.

Loneliness. With parents dating or getting remarried, the children feel that they have no one who cares for them exclusively. They feel that they lack an advocate in the world.

Flashbacks. As children mature, their own dating experiences, serious relationships and, especially, potential marriage and parenthood rekindle memories of their parents' divorce.

My son Michael was 25 when I remarried. He was a college graduate living at home to save money to do his master's degree when his stepfather, Marty, and I had our first real argument. Both of us raised our voices. Suddenly, Mike stormed out of his room and rushed out of the house, tears streaming down his face. Marty and I looked at each other and nodded, and I ran after Mike. I found him standing on the driveway, crying almost uncontrollably. 'You just got married, and you're going to get a divorce!' he shouted at me. 'Just like before.' I was stunned. The ghosts had re-emerged and momentarily transformed my accomplished, adult son into a frightened 10-year-old who was reliving the awful times his father and I had argued before the end of our marriage.

'Divorce is a painful solution to an otherwise unsolvable problem.'

T J, aged 15, whose parents divorced when he was 10

To some extent, all these factors — the unresolved issues, tensions, anger, loneliness and flashbacks of divorce — remain viable for years. They are intense, real and ongoing by-products of divorce. Taken together, they put children of divorce at risk of both immediate and long-term physical and emotional problems that can negatively affect their personal happiness as well as their social and work relationships.

But divorce does not have to equate with doom for children. Many children and teenagers who have survived the breakup of their family are stronger for their losses. They have turned their pain into possibilities. These youngsters are much more mature than their peers who have not had this experience. In some instances, they had to care for one or both of their parents and siblings; they have had to take on added responsibilities; they understand financial struggles and independence; and they revere a good family life.

RAINBOWS has worked with hundreds of thousands of children of divorced parents. We have dealt with families from every walk of life, with children of all ages, and with every imaginable situation and problem. We find that two key elements influence a child's ultimate success: the family's ability to rebuild, and the children having and exercising the opportunity to work through their grief and reconcile the loss into their daily lives.

If divorced parents put forth the effort to work through their grief and accept that the divorce has happened, they will eventually let go of their anger and hurt. Then and only then will they be able to put their children first. When the children are allowed to grieve the loss of the family they once knew, there can be hope for the future. With your support and nurturing, children of divorce can once again feel joy.

Chapter 5

Children and Crisis

C ELINE WAS ADOPTED AS AN INFANT. Now, at 17, she agonizes about her birth mother, uncertain whether to try to locate her.

• Cara's best friend committed suicide earlier in the week.

• Mario's father has been in prison since the 10-year-old boy first started school.

• Gracie's mother has multiple sclerosis and is confined to bed.

• Nick held his dog as the animal was put to sleep by the vet.

• Harrison, a former all-round athletic star, has been paralysed since a hockey accident.

• Allison has grown visibly upset about leaving primary school in a few months' time.

- Andreas, 8, and his family have moved four times because of his father's job.

- Diego's house was destroyed by a fire.

- Beth is worried about her mum because she works in a high-rise office.

- Kirk watched the news every night, hoping to get a glimpse of his father on the battlefields of Afghanistan.

Childhood is filled with multiple seasons of grief. Loss can occur at any time and any age. Children routinely face disappointments and failures; many encounter tragedy when least expected. Some losses are soon forgotten; others transform lives. Some affect children directly; others have an indirect though often still profound effect as children observe the changes going on in the world around them. Children feel every loss — the pocket-sized ones and the full-sized ones. Unlike adults, they lack the life experience to realize that subtle changes in circumstances are insignificant and that better things still lie ahead. For young people, every loss brings vulnerability, if only for a short time. Children really don't understand how long their grief will last or how the change will affect them over time.

The depth of the child's feelings of loss and the amount of time he needs to recover are in direct proportion to his emotional investment in what is now gone. Still, whether feelings of grief linger or are sorted out quickly, the emotions surrounding loss are always significant to a child.

Personal Loss Events

A child's family serves as the lens through which she views herself. Even as children grow and naturally begin to assert their independence and individuality, they still form their opinions about the world based on the perspective that they have as a member of a unique, highly individualized family unit. A child's identity is both shaped by and a product of her family. When that family structure is fractured, changed, or revealed to be something different from what the child imagined (as in the case of a teenager who is told for the first time that she was adopted), the child feels the change as a threat to her very identity.

FAMILY STRUCTURE

Increasingly in today's society, traditional nuclear families are in the minority. Three factors — adoption, foster placement, and the increasing number of children born by either chance or choice to single women and men — contribute to the continuing escalation of non-traditional families in contemporary society. In some instances, these families evolve out of painful situations; others are created from a bounty of love. But at the core of each, there is a child touched by loss.

Adoption

Hugh's family was small. It was just him, his sister, and his mum and dad. However, many relatives lived not only in the same street but also in surrounding communities. Each family celebration brought everyone together — grandparents, aunts, uncles and cousins. Hugh was always happy on these festive occasions.

Probably since the family was so close, Hugh never wondered why he and his sister bore no resemblance to their relatives. They were just his family. When Hugh was a young married adult, his much-loved father died suddenly. Hugh's mother was understandably distraught, so, as the eldest, he took it upon himself to handle the family's financial matters. The day after his father's death, Hugh went to the bank to find the safety deposit box for his dad's will. Sitting in a small, quiet room, Hugh shuffled through pages of carefully sorted and labelled legal documents. At the bottom of the pile, he found an unmarked envelope. Inside, Hugh discovered his own adoption papers!

Each year, thousands of children are adopted by relatives or strangers. For any of a multitude of reasons, these children will not be living with their biological parents. Babies are adopted. Adolescents are adopted. Infants have no voice in the decision, but the older children are involved in the process. Each adopted child comes with a genetic history and a personal story. Each one is an ordinary child who runs, skips, watches television, deliberately walks through muddy puddles and wants to be loved.

Adoption has evolved from a secretive process where all birth information was permanently sealed from public view to an 'open' procedure. Today, the birth mother can choose the adoptive family and have a lifelong relationship with her birth child if both she and the adoptive parents consent to the arrangement. Modern adoptive parents — whether a married couple or a single person — are given instructions on how early to talk with a child about adoption as well as guidelines on how to broach the topic. The bottom line, though, is that children *must* be told that they were adopted so that they can begin to heal from the discovery and be assured that they are wanted, valuable members of their families.

All too often, however, adoptive parents prefer to make the discussion of their child's adoption a one-time-only event. They hesitate to periodically talk to an adopted child about her birth parents and worry that raising the issue will:

• Prompt the adopted child to ask some tough questions.

• Hurt the child's feelings.

• Make the child resentful.

• Lead the child to reject them.

The truth is that the adoption is already on the child's mind and in his heart. Avoiding the subject only forces the child to swallow his questions, concerns and feelings and to bury them inside. The child may believe that your silence on the topic is a signal that any discussion he initiates or questions he asks would make you uncomfortable or angry, or that there is additional birth information you are withholding that is too painful to talk about.

Understanding and accepting adoption is a process. Keep in mind that children respond differently at different ages. Young ones listen and thoroughly enjoy hearing their birth story; to them, it is a personal fairy tale with a happy ending. Feelings of grief usually don't surface until the pre-teenage years, when adoption takes on a deeper meaning. The happy ending — that their adoptive parents 'choose' them — is balanced by the harsh realization that their biological mum or dad 'gave them away'. Children must come to terms with this very daunting emotional fact of their personal history.

Make sure that adopted children know they can discuss the topic with you at any time. And realize that that time *will* come, whether it's now or a few years from now. How easily a child approaches the topic depends on her personality and comfort level. If she has heard the adoption story from early on, and the topic is kept alive — presented in a matter-of-fact manner, like the colour of her eyes — then, when the deeper issues surface, she will not hesitate to talk about them.

Of course, that doesn't mean that there won't be times when an adopted child will be angry or feel rejected and abandoned. We cannot take away the sentiments an adopted child experiences when he thinks about his birth parent relinquishing him. All our reassurances — 'But *we* love you' or '*We* wanted you' — will not diminish the child's sadness or confusion. Adopted children need to sort out their emotions; we help by sitting with them, holding them, and acknowledging their feelings. This will not happen in one conversation. As the child matures, more questions and new or deeper responses will emerge. We need to be there at every stage.

At some point, an adopted child might raise the question of finding his birth parents. Statistically, girls are more interested than boys in doing this. Be aware that sometimes, adopted children feel that they must reject the adoptive parent in order to find their birth parent. In other cases, they may become hostile and nasty to the adoptive family, testing to see if you will give them up, too. On these occasions, we must assure them of our unconditional love and our commitment to ride with them through the turbulent times. If they choose to look for their birth family, it's best to assist them in the quest.

The adoptive child needs:

- His birth story to be celebrated and remembered; this can be done through birth announcements, a baby book filled with early stories and photos, and a photo album of his growing-up years.

- A network of adopted friends and families so she, too, will feel connected, just as other non-adopted children are to their friends and families. Work closely with the adoption agency for support and guidance.

- The family to be comfortable with the adoption story and the child's history.

- The confidence and freedom to discuss the adoption when it is on his mind and in his heart.

- To have her questions answered honestly and comfortably.

- His feelings listened to and acknowledged.

- Affirmation and support if she chooses to search for her birth parents.

Foster Placement

Talia has not slept through a single night since she was taken from her family. It's been about a week since the local child protection agency, responding to an abuse report, came to the 8-year-old's home and, after assessing the situation, determined that Talia must be taken from her parents. Social workers grabbed some of the child's clothes and toiletries, stuffed them into a carrier bag, and whisked Talia into a waiting car. She was told only that her mum and dad were not taking proper care of her. 'We will keep you safe, so there is no need to be upset,' one of the social workers assured the little girl.

But Talia was distraught. Strangers had yanked her away from all she had ever known — her parents, her home, her belongings — then driven her to an emergency shelter. There they filled out dozens of papers and gave her a bed in a featureless room. Twenty-four hours later, Talia was living with other strangers. During the day, she kept to herself; at night, Talia lay awake, anxious and lonely. She had never slept without the beloved, tattered teddy bear that had been left behind on her bed. She had never been separated from her parents. Even though her mummy and daddy sometimes hurt her, Talia loved them and couldn't understand why she wasn't at home with them.

In the UK, government statistics show that around 40,000 children were living with foster families in 2003. In 2001–2002, the Australian Institute of Health and Welfare found that around 12,840 children were admitted to out-of-home care. Children are removed from their birth families because of emotional maltreatment, physical or sexual abuse, neglect, abandonment or the death or imprisonment of a parent. They are placed in foster care out of concern for their well-being.

The proces itself imposes multiple losses upon the child: loss of parents, family and friends; loss of home and school; and loss of normal daily life.

Foster children may be placed with a family that is racially or ethnically different from their own or a family concerned only with collecting the fee paid for their care. Tragically, some children are abused by their foster families. Many children are rotated through a series of placements, which only compounds the trauma. Remember, children don't understand the concept of time. To a young child, there is no such thing as a *temporary* situation. Everything is permanent.

It's little wonder, then, that a disproportionately high number of foster children have academic difficulties, developmental delays, attachment issues, impaired social relationships and medical problems. Some may have other special needs as well.

I believe that good foster care entails both short-term objectives and long-term goals. The immediate challenge is to place foster children in nurturing families. At the same time, their emotional issues must be faced. Clinicians rarely ask children how they feel about the traumatic event that propelled them into foster care or about the subsequent losses they may have endured. And there can be so many. Each new family and change of surroundings represents a loss and must be grieved. Case workers and social workers can't always take on the responsibility of nurturing the child through each of these changes. Every foster child needs at least one person whom he can confide in and whom he feels is truly his personal advocate.

Children in foster care need:

- A personal, private place to put their belongings: a drawer, cupboard, box, or a corner of a room.

- A special possession that makes them feel safe, such as a teddy bear that has been with them through their many placements. If you cannot retrieve it from their last family, maybe you can buy one as a surprise or go to the shop to choose one with them.

- Routine, stability and the confidence that they have adults whom they can depend on and trust; this might include their foster parents, teacher or social worker; school can be the best place to offer this stability.

- To have people get to know them — their preferred foods, television shows, sports, music groups, colour, favourite birthday cake and special traditions — then be able to experience these things again and again.

- Understanding of their emotional developmental delay and their apprehension to bond.

- An inordinate amount of patience and love.

- Overt actions of affirmation: verbal praise, pats on the back, encouragement.

- Private times to talk about their feelings, confusion and questions.

- Affirmation, compassion and honesty.

Single Parents

An article in a newspaper told the story of a 2-year-old boy, the son of a single mother, who would run up to strange men at the local park and ask, 'Are you my daddy?' Later, still desperate for someone to fill the role of father in his life, the child took to calling his uncle 'Daddy'. In fact, the child was conceived through artificial insemination. He will never know his father.

The number of children born to single parents is on the increase. Most are born to single mothers pregnant by chance. But an increasingly large number are children raised by single women and men who by choice have conceived or adopted children outside of marriage.

In RAINBOWS, we have worked with thousands of children whose mothers don't know the fathers' identities or who were abandoned before or at birth by one of their parents, usually the father. These children grow up feeling a great loss for the absent parent. With half their heritage missing, they experience an emptiness that can overshadow their lives. Many are left with grief as palpable as that they would have experienced if they had actually witnessed their parent walking out the door.

What about babies who are born outside of marriage by choice? We simply don't know yet how these children will fare as they grow into adulthood. Certainly, they will be loved by the parent they know. But, as with the little boy in the park, it is likely that many will long for a two-parent household. Will they grow up wondering about the unknown person who is an essential part of their personal histories? Given human nature, this possibility seems inevitable. Will they also resent the manner in which they were conceived? Perhaps.

Based on the RAINBOWS experience, I think it likely that they, too, will face issues of grief and loss as they move through childhood. Issues that, if not resolved, will follow them for life.

Single-parent children need:

• To have their never-married parent understand that they will ask questions about their conception and other parent; this is intrinsic to their nature as human beings.

• Their birth story to be celebrated and remembered; this can be done through birth announcements, a baby book filled with early stories and photos, and a photo album of their growing-up years.

• A network of friends and families with similar family histories so they, too, will feel like they 'fit in'. Work closely with agencies and organizations for support and guidance.

• To have adult members of the opposite sex be present in their lives and act as role models.

• Private times to talk about their feelings, confusion and questions.

• To have their questions answered honestly and comfortably.

• Affirmation, compassion and honesty.

• Their families to be comfortable with their birth stories and family histories.

• The confidence and freedom to discuss their conception and family history when it is on their minds and in their hearts.

LOVED ONES IN PRISON

Years ago, I met with two young children whose father had been sentenced to life imprisonment. During his trial, prosecutors presented irrefutable evidence that this man was at the top level of the criminal operation and solely responsible for the crimes he was accused of committing. But to his son and daughter, he was *Daddy*. The children knew their father as a man who went to work every day, provided for them and played with them — coaching their sports teams, taking them on holiday and sitting through long games of Monopoly. At the end of the day when he walked in the door, they ran to him to be scooped up in his arms to get wonderful, comforting 'daddy squeezes'.

With their dad gone, the children were bereft and inconsolable.

In the UK, the Prison Reform Trust estimates around 140,000 children are affected by having a parent in prison (1.2 per cent of the minor population). In Australia, there are no national figures, but the Children of Prisoners Support Group estimates that in New South Wales alone approximately 15,000 children are affected by parental imprisonment (1.1 per cent).

Prison – even an overnight stay in jail – causes the entire family disbelief, embarrassment and disgrace. The shame that accompanies the incarceration is especially hard for children to bear. They become secondary victims.

When a family member is imprisoned, children need to be told the truth, in terms they can comprehend. To help them to understand, remind them of family rules and consequences. Explain that society has rules, too, and that when someone breaks the rules, they must accept the punishment or consequence.

Children usually respond in one of the following two ways. Many children are so ashamed that they will not have anything to do with this beloved person. They won't discuss him with anyone; they refuse to write a letter or talk to him on the phone. For them, it is almost as if this person has died. And maybe, subconsciously, they wish he had. Children need to be told that they can still love this person, in spite of his wrongdoing, and that they can forgive him for his mistake. Other children refuse to accept the fact that their loved one did anything wrong. They see the jailed person as the victim and blame law enforcement officers or the judge for 'picking on' their family member. Rather than face the truth, the children steadfastly defend their loved one's honour.

Either response is problematical and needs to be addressed. If you can, gently coax the child to see the balance — essentially that a good person can make a mistake. Over time, the grieving child will experience many feelings — both love and hate, both loyalty to and embarrassment for the parent in prison — that you can help her confront and work through.

Children who have an incarcerated loved one need:

- To know the circumstances of what happened: provide them with the big picture, not necessarily the details.

- To be placed in a loving family member's home, if at all possible, while the parent is in prison.

- To have some communication with their loved one — letters, drawings or pictures regularly sent and received; phone calls; personal visits.

- The confidence and freedom to discuss the loved one in prison when it is on their minds and in their hearts.

- To have their questions answered honestly and comfortably.

- To have their feelings listened to and acknowledged.

- Affirmation and support of their response to their incarcerated loved one.

A CHRONICALLY ILL FAMILY MEMBER

Alana's parents had always adhered to traditional roles. Dad worked and Mum stayed home with the children. Then Alana's father was diagnosed with multiple sclerosis. Sitting together on the old living room sofa, her parents explained the disease to Alana and her two siblings. 'Dad's not going to die. He'll be with us for a long, long time. But other things around here will have to change,' her mother said.

In fact, the changes were quick and dramatic. Alana's father cut back his workload immediately. Her mother took a full-time job. When the children came home from school, they found Dad resting quietly in the living room. In the kitchen, the worktop was bare — no more homemade cakes or biscuits waiting for them as an afternoon snack. Instead, they found a list of chores that they had to complete before they could start their homework or go out to play. Alana, the eldest, was expected to start dinner. She hated what had happened to her family. 'I liked having my mum chaperone field trips for our class and wait for me after school. We always did fun things together. Now we don't do anything,' she said.

Initially, Alana was angry with her dad because he had this disease. When he was confined to a wheelchair and forced to quit his job, she became depressed. All Alana wanted was to have her family return to the way it had been before.

Monumental shifts in family roles are especially distressing for children and adolescents. They cannot imagine family life transformed. What will the future look and feel like? They are largely unequipped to cope with the clashing emotions and needs that cram into each new day. As parents take on new roles, family life shifts in many frightening ways.

• Children assume new responsibilities.

• Children's after-school schedules change, sometimes dramatically.

• The person who is ill needs and receives extra attention.

• The sick person's needs supersede those of other family members.

As often happens, the adults in this type of situation have resources — social workers, therapists, counsellors — that assist them through these turbulent times. Meanwhile, the children in the family are left to figure out how to cope and manage on their own.

Children with a chronically ill family member need:

• To have their loved one's illness explained to them — what has happened, how the illness will progress and how the family will be responding now and in the future.

• The confidence and freedom to discuss the questions and concerns that are on their minds and in their hearts.

• To have their questions answered honestly and comfortably.

- To have their feelings listened to and acknowledged.

- To have special times set aside for them when they are the centre of attention.

- To have some stability and routine in their daily lives.

- Affirmation and support of their lives; this means having other family members attend their activities and special events.

WHEN YOUR CHILD'S PET DIES …

For many children, the death of a cherished pet is the youngster's first encounter with permanent loss and feelings of grief. As such, pets provide us with a unique opportunity to teach children about life, love, commitment, and death.

When Chad was 11 years old, his dog, Coach, was struck and killed by a car. Chad's mum found the dog lying on the street. She thought of asking the vet to dispose of the body, but something held her back. Instead, she wrapped Coach in an old blanket and laid him in the garage. Later, she drove to school to pick up Chad. When they were sitting alone in the car, she broke the news as gently as possible. After a few minutes of trying to comprehend what he'd been told, Chad started to sob. Later, driving home, he reminisced about the funny things Coach used to do. When the boy walked in the back door and realized that Coach was no longer there to 'attack' him with kisses, the reality of the dog's death hit him full force.

Chad insisted on burying Coach in the garden near a willow tree. When the boy's father came home that night, the three of them dug a hole and gently placed Coach into it. Chad said some prayers and then put a stick into the earth as a marker. Chad's parents left him alone with his thoughts, his feelings and his tears. That evening, Chad boxed up all of Coach's belongings – collar, tags, lead and toys. To this day, that box is tucked away on a shelf in his wardrobe.

MILESTONES, TRANSITIONS AND CHANGES

Clarissa was eager to graduate from university and finally begin her life as an independent young adult. For months, she talked of nothing but her first job and first apartment. No more classes and no more papers to write. Her CV had been sent to many prospective employers. As graduation day approached, Clarissa became irritable, withdrawn and depressed. No one

---

Chad's next pet was a parakeet named Mistletoe. For two years, the bird's cage sat on the top of the boy's chest of drawers. One morning, Chad lifted up Mistletoe's cover. He couldn't believe it – the bird was dead. Chad ran to his parents to tell them what happened. 'You go to school. We'll take care of it,' his mum replied. 'No,' the boy begged. 'Leave him be until I get home.'

That afternoon, Chad buried Mistletoe in the garden, next to Coach. Three years later, when Chad was 15, he told me that the space on his chest of drawers where the birdcage had sat was still empty, sort of a memorial to his 'friend'.

Like Chad, all children need time to grieve the loss of a beloved pet. Often, seeking to protect the child from the pain of loss, adults hide the evidence: flush the goldfish, put the bird in the dustbin, immediately replace the dog with a new puppy. But by doing this, we dismiss the child's feelings of love and loss. We send a message that loved things can just disappear or be effortlessly replaced. We fail to teach the child to value and respect life.

As adults, we can take this opportunity to gently teach the child about the cycle of life. There is a beginning – birth; a middle – life; and an ending – death. We can explain that death always occurs for a reason: an accident, old age, or illness. And we can show the child that mourning the lost pet and remembering his life with joy are both appropriate and brave things to do.

---

could understand it. Late one night, the young woman confided to her best friend that she was frightened of growing up. Leaving university meant leaving her childhood. The independence Clarissa had so ardently sought terrified her.

Children thrive on stability. Yet change is inevitable in life. Every major milestone represents both a beginning and an ending to one of life's phases. Whether a child is moving from nursery school to primary school, primary to secondary school, or changing school systems altogether, the transition is upsetting. Her familiar circle of friends disbands. Everything changes — classroom routines and expectations, teachers, lockers, bus route.

In our mobile society, the average child moves four times before he turns 18. Each shift to a new location brings additional challenges. When children move to a different neighbourhood or town, they feel like they have landed in a strange land. Young children struggle to learn their new address and phone number and to be able to find their way home from a number of community locations.

Children who have experienced transitions, milestones or changes need:

• To be told that change brings opportunity.

• To be taught how to flourish in their new environment.

• To be given opportunities to make new friends.

• The opportunity to learn new coping strategies and skills.

• The confidence and freedom to discuss their questions and concerns when they are on their minds and hearts.

• To have their questions answered honestly and comfortably.

• Their feelings listened to and acknowledged.

• To have special times set aside for them when they are the centre of attention.

• Affirmation and support of their lives; this means having family members attend their activities and special events.

- To have newly created stability and routine in their daily lives.

- To have others acknowledge their grief over what is lost.

Community Crisis

One Sunday, after breakfast, Chloe and her family went off to her brother's football match. At half-time, the sky filled with dark thunder clouds. Lightning flashed and the referee blew the final whistle. Everyone hurried home as fast as they could.

At home, Chloe's dad turned on the TV and learned that the region was under a hurricane alert. There didn't seem to be too much to worry about, and no one was overly concerned — until the local fire siren blared. Suddenly, everyone seemed to panic.

'Get in the basement. Quick!' Chloe's mum shouted.

'Hurry. Run!' her dad yelled.

Downstairs, they huddled together, wrapped in blankets. They listened as the world seemed to tear itself apart overhead. Chloe sobbed uncontrollably.

When the all-clear sounded, the family slowly walked upstairs. They opened the door and stepped into what should have been the kitchen. Instead, they were standing in the open air. Most of the house was gone. All that remained were the remains of a few walls, the sink and the cooker. The rest of the structure had been destroyed by the storm.

And it wasn't just them! The entire neighbourhood had been decimated. As emergency sirens screamed, they saw their dazed neighbours stumbling through the mounds of rubble that dotted the street. Chloe started shaking. Desperate to be held and comforted, she ran to her father, but he was too stunned and overwhelmed to respond. Suddenly, it began raining. Chloe shivered and hugged herself trying to keep warm. 'Mum, what do we do?' she cried. Her mother shook her head and turned away.

Moments later, police, firefighters and other emergency workers arrived. Residents were ordered to move to the local school, where a temporary shelter had been established for those left homeless by the storm. Cold, wet and numb, Chloe plodded along with her parents and brother. Less than two hours ago, life had been normal; now her whole world was destroyed.

In addition to natural disasters such as hurricanes, floods and earthquakes, consider the following other types of crises that can also affect an entire community.

- A gas explosion demolishes homes on a local street.
- A train accident kills seven children riding home on a school bus.
- A beloved teacher suffers a fatal heart attack while on holiday.

A community crisis has a broad reach that touches many people. Some are directly affected by the tragedy. Others watch and share in the suffering of people they know and care about.

In responding to large-scale crises, communities typically go through three stages. Children are affected by each phase.

- **Immediate aftermath:** there is often widespread panic, shock and hysteria. Concern for physical safety is paramount. Youngsters are ordered to stay out of the way. Rarely does anyone talk to them about what just happened. Children are left wrapped in fear and silence.

- **Short-term response:** parents and adults try to assuage children's fears. Rarely, however, are children asked how they feel about the crisis, and grief counsellors may be available for only a few hours or days.

- **Long-term response:** parents, other adults and community leaders focus on preventive steps for the future. As long as the children haven't been physically harmed, adults assume they have 'got over it'.

As the adult members of the community move through these

responses, they also need to bear in mind that the children of the community are looking to them for comfort, support and reassurance. Here are a few things to remember.

• Children react strongly to non-verbal signals. Watching how adults respond to the emergency tells them how to react. Adult horror and panic — which can't always be avoided — infuse children with fear and anxiety. A calm, measured response decreases the sense of terror children feel.

• Children embrace the truth. After the immediate danger is over or the initial shock has subsided, children and teenagers must be tended to — sat with, cuddled, and given an honest and manageable description of what is happening.

• Children grow anxious when their daily routines are disrupted. Events such as natural disasters, which may affect an entire community, can turn life upside-down. Youngsters need new routines as quickly as possible — school, mealtimes, even the assurance that they will have a bed to sleep in that night. Talking with children about the many changes they are enduring validates their experiences and decreases their concerns.

• Children worry, 'What if another emergency occurs?' Who should they contact? What phone number do they give? Older children living in emergency shelters or relatives' homes should be taught basic emergency information: family members to contact, mobile phone numbers, the address and phone number of their temporary home. Younger children should be given the information on a card that is tucked into a pocket or secured on a chain they can wear around their necks.

Local child killings especially amplify children's fears and sense of vulnerability. Children may know and identify not only with the victims but also with the perpetrators. Every child and adolescent in the community feels that his safety zone has been invaded and defiled. Together, they grieve the loss of life and innocence. They agonize over their role: 'What could I have done to prevent this?' They project to the future: 'Can it happen again?'

A FAMILY DISASTER PLAN

To help children feel empowered after a natural disaster or other community crisis, work with them to create a Family Disaster Plan.

After it's completed, practise using it so that everyone feels sure of what he or she should do. The plan can include:

1. The contact numbers of the emergency services in your community, and possibly the Red Cross, and a designated place in the house where the numbers are kept.

2. Detailed information on what to do during a specific emergency, such as a fire or hurricane.

3. A list of warning signals and what to do for each; these signs include:

    ❋ Screeching smoke or carbon monoxide detectors.

    ❋ Emergency warnings on the television or radio.

4. A designated room or area of the house where the family meets in an emergency: store blankets, battery operated radios, torches, water and other emergency supplies in this location.

Indeed, any crisis involving death raises harsh issues: that life is tentative and insecure; that people we value can die unexpectedly, cruelly, or too young. Children know what happened. They feel the loss either directly or indirectly. Trying to shield them from reality does not help them. Telling them to accept the loss conveys the wrong message entirely; children think they are supposed to just 'let go' or 'forget' what happened. They cannot do that, nor should they try. There has been a death, and it must be grappled with. The complex issues of mortality must be faced.

Fortunately, in many ways, a crisis brings out the best that the community has to offer. Residents pull together to support one another, rebuild, and heal. As the adults, it is our responsibility to make sure that the new-found sense of support and unity extends to the younger members of our communities as well.

National Crisis

Ethan, 10, was at school on Tuesday, 11 September 2001, when the head teacher interrupted class and announced over the PA system that the country was experiencing a crisis. 'We will have a normal day of school,' she went on, 'but many parents will be picking up their children at the end of the day.'

At 3 p.m., Ethan saw his mum and dad standing in the hall by his locker. They hugged him for a long time before they headed for home. Ethan's teenage brother was already there. They found him in the living room, watching events unfold on the television. Ethan and his parents sat down, too, and for a very long time no one said a word. The boys' questions came later at the dinner table. 'Why? Who? What does it mean? Can it happen again?' The parents answered the questions as best they could, even if sometimes the response was little more than a shake of the head and a quiet 'I don't know'. Neither child had homework that night, but their mother urged them to read quietly in their rooms before bedtime. Later, she spent a few minutes alone with each of the boys.

Around midnight, Ethan's dad looked in on the younger boy and found him fast asleep, with his arms wrapped around an old stuffed animal named Bunny. The fuzzy rabbit had been a gift to Ethan when he was born. For seven years, the two had been inseparable; wherever Ethan went, Bunny went. Then one day, Ethan propped up Bunny on a corner of his desk and walked out of his room without his longtime companion. A few months later, Ethan moved the bedraggled stuffed animal to a shelf over his bed. But the night of 11 September, Bunny was off the shelf and into Ethan's arms once again.

The next morning — and every day for weeks after — Bunny appeared at the breakfast table. Every day, Bunny waited on the living room sofa for Ethan to return from school.

For Ethan, Bunny represented something the boy desperately hoped to reclaim — a time when life was secure.

INFORMATION OVERLOAD

Media and Internet access give young people uncensored information 24 hours a day about natural disasters, catastrophic events, crimes and crises. The information is often speculative and explicit; it is continually updated, often repeated every few minutes, and may be broadcast live from the scene. Children, especially younger ones, cannot decipher whether a news event is unfolding in real time or is a replay of something that happened earlier.

This onslaught of unfiltered information may cause children and teenagers stress, anxiety and unbridled fear. As parents, teachers and caregivers, we need to be alert to when and how much the children are watching the news. Our role is to:

⁜ Allow very young children to watch television only with an adult who is willing to discuss what is being broadcast.

⁜ Limit the amount of viewing time. Repeated exposure to dramatic TV images imbeds the tragedy in the child's mind and frightens him more.

⁜ Spend time alone talking with the child about the event.

⁜ Ask the child to interpret what he has heard or seen.

⁜ Ask if the child has any questions or worries she wants to discuss.

⁜ Reassure the child that he and his family are safe.

⁜ Describe what the government, police, relief workers and others are doing to ensure the child's protection.

The terrorist attacks of 11 September 2001 were a national crisis unprecedented in American history. As horrific as the events of the day were, they were soon followed by other unsettling situations: an anthrax scare, fighting in Afghanistan and a global war against terrorism.

No one knows what the future holds. We do not know if this afternoon, next week or next year additional threats or destruction will occur, with or without warning, in our own country.

When a national crisis occurs, as it has before, children and teenagers need adults to guide them through the harsh reality of what has taken place and to reconstruct normality in their lives. As their caregivers and protectors, it is our obligation to do so. We begin by understanding how children and teenagers respond to such a crisis.

Here are some special concerns to keep in mind about children and crisis.

- Because of their limited life experience, children are unable to comprehend the magnitude of large-scale destruction.

- Initially, most children ask many questions, such as 'Why did this happen?' and 'Why don't those people like us?' Very young children may pose simple questions that are difficult to answer. After 9/11, for example, a 6-year-old asked her mother: 'Will those bad people be punished?' Some children, however, pretend indifference as a defence mechanism.

- As time passes and the full impact of the crisis sinks in, children's concerns will increase. The terrorist attacks of September 2001 made many children grow fearful of flying or entering tall buildings. Others didn't want their parents going to work in high-rise offices or flying on business trips.

Following are some of the issues that you'll want to be aware of when helping an adolescent through crisis.

- Teenagers' questions are often sophisticated and detailed. After the attacks on Washington and New York, they asked: 'How were the terrorists able to hijack the planes? Why did the towers collapse? Were the police and fire-fighters afraid as they entered the building? Did they think that they were going to die? How could they do that willingly?'

- Teenagers are angry with those they believe initiated the crisis and others whom they feel may have been lax in protecting innocent lives.

- Teenagers and young adults worry about the impact on their lives. For the first time, they think about military service and possible war as issues with which they may be directly involved. They have a heightened concern about their nation's vulnerability and their personal security and they may wonder about the advisability of visiting a shopping centre or attending a popular concert or sports event.

- They may rethink or change their career or education goals.

After a national crisis, we must focus on the positive lessons to be gained for the future and show children how to pick up and move forward. In tragedy, we teach our children and each other about inner strength and perseverance.

IMMEDIATE OUTREACH

After a natural disaster or widespread crisis, children are worried that:
- The event will happen again.
- Someone that they know or love will be injured or killed.
- They will be separated from their family members.
- They will be left alone.

A major crisis or disaster can leave the most rock-solid adult visibly shaken. In many instances, children have never seen such signs of distress in their parents or other adults and are frightened because of it. During and after any violent or traumatic event, adults must control their own reactions and intervene immediately to help alleviate children's concerns. Here are the important steps to take.

- Explain the event as well as possible. Use words and descriptions that are age-appropriate. Speak calmly and truthfully. Stress that the disaster or violence occurred in a specific locale.

- Allow the child or teenager to ask questions. Children may ask the same questions repeatedly; this means they haven't yet been able to grasp the full meaning of the event.

- Comfort children — tell them that you love them and will care for them.

- Encourage youngsters to talk about their feelings and fears — allow honest expression of emotions. If a child can't verbalize his thoughts, get him to draw pictures or do some of the activities suggested in the chapter on Activities and Rituals for Healing.

- Listen without judging.

- Don't discount the statement 'I am afraid' by saying 'Don't be'. Ask the child what she is worried about. Talking will comfort the child and allow you to work with her to alleviate her fears.

- Share your feelings, calmly. You can say that you are very sad without crying hysterically.

- Don't bring up anything that the child has not inquired about.

- Permit *temporary* changes in behavioural patterns such as sleeping with siblings or parents for a few nights.

- Don't criticize regressive behaviour.

- Explain what is being done to protect them. But don't promise that the event will never happen again.

- Talk about why the event occurred even if there are no acceptable or comfortable answers. A young child can be told, 'There are bad people in the world, but not everyone is bad.' Older children and teenagers need more detailed information, 'Terrorist or criminal acts are committed by people who are desperate or fanatical about a cause.' Talking openly about a crisis helps to reconcile what has happened (see chapter 8).

• Encourage children to do something physical to help victims. They can pray, make cards for those who are injured, send usable toys to children who have lost theirs in the disaster, serve food, fill sand bags or raise money and send it to a relief agency.

• Acknowledge and validate the child's feelings. Remember that children who live close to the area that was hardest hit or who have friends or family who were directly affected by the event or who have experienced previous traumatic losses may have protracted reactions.

Moving Ahead

As time moves on after a crisis, keep children informed about what is going to happen next. Knowing what to expect comforts children and reduces their anxiety. It may even calm the adults because it forces them to make a plan and begin to think about tomorrow.

Keep the family together. If this is not possible, arrange for children to stay with people they know — teachers, classmates, neighbours or relatives.

When you must leave, inform the children. Tell them where you are going, what you will be doing, and the approximate time you'll be back.

Explain again. Tell the child again what happened, why it happened and what you think will happen next. After a flood, for example, explain that there was too much rain for the sewers and earth to absorb; once the rain stops falling, the river will stop getting higher and slowly the water levels will go down. Until then, the family will stay in a shelter or temporary housing.

Involve children in the recovery activities. Helping and participating gives them a sense of power and control over their lives and what has happened.

SILVER LININGS: A COMMUNITY CRISIS RESPONSE PROGRAMME

Rainbows developed a programme called Silver Linings that may be used in settings with large numbers of children or teenagers who have experienced a life-changing crisis. Silver Linings encourages young people to articulate their feelings, come to grips with their fears, and learn appropriate coping strategies designed to reconcile the crisis into their lives. The programme can be used in a classroom, at a community agency or in a temporary shelter. Silver Linings has three age-level editions and covers six sessions; each edition contains an Instructor's Manual and reproducible Participant Booklet. See page 336 for further information.

Talk with authorities at the child's school or faith community. Ask about their responses to the event. Having family, school and faith communities respond gives a strong message of solidarity and support. However, try to coordinate events so children are not exposed to prolonged discussions or continual memorial services.

Sit with the children daily; ask them how they are feeling. Do they have any new concerns or questions? If a child's feelings of anger, fear or sadness persist or are exceptionally intense or worsen over time, consult a mental health professional.

Remain available, dependable and reassuring as life returns to normal. Every loss or disaster that a child endures — whether it's on a personal, community or national level — needs to be dealt with and processed. These events, tragic as they are, become the scaffolding for surviving the subsequent crises that life will bring. Each reconciled loss builds a child's resilience and ability to face tomorrow.

Part Two
The Healing

Beatitudes for Those Who Comfort

Blessed are those who hear with their hearts,
for they have the gift of empathy.

Blessed are those who in spite of being uncomfortable
step forward to comfort the grieving,
for their presence shows inner strength.

Blessed are those who refrain from giving advice or platitudes,
for their wisdom reminds the bereaved
there are no answers to loss.

Blessed are they who continue to call, visit and
send notes long after others have stopped,
for they are living examples of compassion.

Blessed are those who understand the timetable of grief
and the fragility of bereavement,
for they possess a gentle and loving heart.

Chapter 6

Becoming a Compassionate Companion

MY MIDDLE SON, TOM, had always enjoyed and been good at basketball. When he was 14, he was picked for the school team. Even though his new coach Stan insisted on early morning practices and worked the team hard, Tom never complained and was pleased as his ball-handling skills steadily improved.

During the following year, I noticed that Tom was spending a lot of time at school helping Stan with extra projects. At home, Stan's name popped up frequently in Tom's conversation: 'Stan says this …' or 'Stan thinks I should …' Soon it became obvious that Tom was turning to the coach for advice and direction on more than basketball. Initially, I was hurt that Tom wasn't coming to me for guidance. After all, he was my son. I knew him intimately and always had his best intentions at heart. What was going on, anyway?

One day, I sat down with Tom and shared my concerns. At first, he hesitated, then he said: 'Well, since last year, Stan's always been there for me.' Slowly, the story unfolded. 'The coach always asks, "How's it going?" He asks about the divorce and how I'm dealing with it. Sometimes we just talk, you know, about life.'

I was stunned. The divorce had occurred some eight years earlier; hadn't Tom worked out all these issues? It turns out, he told me, that many things still bothered him, things he couldn't discuss with me or his dad but that he could talk about with Stan. 'He really cares about me,' Tom said. 'He doesn't lecture, he just listens. I know I can trust him.'

As I came to know and trust Stan as well — and to appreciate the important role he played in my son's life — I began to realize that Stan wasn't a threat to my authority: he was an ally. As a responsible adult, he had instinctively reached out to an adolescent struggling with loss issues and had helped guide him through the turbulent teen years. To this day, I am thankful to Stan for his involvement in Tom's life and for teaching me an invaluable lesson.

Healthy grieving requires courage during a most difficult time. Where do children get this courage? Usually from the guidance of caring adults who can accompany them on their difficult and frightening journey. While the most fundamental guidance usually comes from the child's parents, I sincerely believe that the job of nurturing a child through a loss falls to all those who play a part in the child's life — grandparents, uncles, aunts, teachers, coaches, even family friends. These people can serve as what I call 'compassionate companions' to a grieving child, helping the child not only through the immediate aftermath of a loss event but also in the months and — as in the case of coach Stan — sometimes even years following it.

Of course, reaching out to a grieving child or teenager can be intimidating. Many of us may not feel up to the challenge. In reality, though, each of us can do much to help a child cope with loss. We don't need to be therapists or any other type of medical or child care professional. Most of the grieving children in our midst simply need loving, attentive adults to light their path as they walk the journey through grief. Working together, we can build a much-needed safety net for bereaved youngsters.

Many people ask me, 'Isn't the role of compassionate companion a job for the child's parents? Shouldn't they assume responsibility for advising and guiding their children after a loss?' These are reasonable questions. But loss often defies logic. Grief changes the rules.

When great loss or fundamental change strikes a family, there are any number of reasons why parents may not be able to effectively help their children.

• Parents are probably grieving themselves. Even the most loving and caring mothers and fathers have to heal themselves before they can effectively respond to their children.

• Adults and children grieving the same loss may not be at the same emotional phase of grief. One may be sad, another angry. One may be moving forward, the other still in shock.

• By the time the bereaved parent is healed, it may be too late to help the child. By then, he may already have found another, perhaps unsuitable, method of coping.

This is why it is imperative that other caring adults recognize the grieving child's special needs and respond in a meaningful way as compassionate companions.

By acting as compassionate companions and sharing loss experiences with children and teenagers, we help them make sense of the chaos that has happened. We help them avoid behaviour that is harmful to themselves and others. By allowing young people to mourn, we enable them to reconcile their loss into their lives, ensuring that they become healthy, productive members of our communities.

Through the years, I have met many people who cared about the grieving youngsters in their lives and wanted to help them. But they had

CAN YOU HELP A GRIEVING CHILD?

Are you willing to be a compassionate companion to a grieving child or teenager you know, but unsure if you are the right person to take on this responsibility? Ask yourself the following questions.

✳ Have I experienced a recent loss? If you have, you must first take the time to work through your own loss. Be aware that this process could take a couple of years.

✳ Do I feel guilty or anxious because of this loss? If yes, you need to work through your feelings to a healthy resolution before trying to help anyone else. Children need their compassionate companions to be able to listen and support them in an unbiased way, which requires a certain emotional distance from loss.

✳ What are my personal feelings about death or divorce? If you have negative or potentially harmful feelings or attitudes about either of these events, you are not the compassionate companion the child needs.

✳ Am I worried about crying? It's OK to cry with a child; in fact, tears are a healthy response to intense feelings.

✳ Do I have expectations about how the child should respond? It's best to put all of your expectations aside so that you are completely open to listening and guiding the child with her needs.

✳ Am I angry or upset with someone in this child's life? If you cannot put those feelings aside or work through them, then you will not be able to help the child.

no point of reference, no framework to guide their efforts. Many simply didn't know where to start or were uncertain whether they should get involved. Even adults trained to work with youngsters can be stumped when faced with issues of children's grief.

✳ Do I have the family's permission or encouragement to help? It's critical that you let the parents or guardians know you are willing and able to help their child.

✳ Do I have sufficient time to spend with this grieving child or teenager? Every relationship is different, but you will need to make sure you can meet or talk on the phone with the child at regular intervals and be available when he needs you. Try to achieve a balance in your relationship with the child: you don't want him dependent on you, but you do want him to feel that you're someone he can rely on. As he reconciles his loss, he will need you less and less.

✳ Can I establish a rapport with her? Not everyone 'clicks' with a child. Does this child seem comfortable and open with you? If not, help the child find another compassionate companion.

✳ Am I willing to respond to his needs? Compassion for the child and a willingness to make time for him are the two most critical elements of helping a grieving child.

If you're still unsure about getting involved, it might be helpful to talk with a trusting, objective friend or counsellor. If you are satisfied with your comforting capabilities, go ahead and reach out. Elisabeth Kübler Ross, psychiatrist and author of *On Death and Dying*, said: 'You do not need a degree to sit with someone while they grieve.' And it's true. What you do need are ears that listen and a heart that cares.

Recently, I gave a seminar about bereaved youth to teachers and counsellors. These well-educated professionals were eager for whatever information they could gather to better support the children they tend. The need for guidance is echoed in the calls that come in almost daily to RAINBOWS. No matter what the circumstances, the queries always come down to one question: is there anything I can do to help?

The answer is yes: *you can be a compassionate companion to the grieving child.* This chapter is written for the many adults who wish to take on this responsibility. Based on the same successful approach RAINBOWS has implemented in sites around the globe, the chapter provides a basic blueprint for helping children cope with loss, including practical advice for tailoring your approach to the child's age and maturity level.

Adults as Role Models

From birth, children look up to and need adults. Whether we are parents, grandparents, family members, neighbours, teachers, clergy or mentors, it is our job to help children grow up responsibly and resiliently. Children aren't born with these qualities; they learn them as part of healthy maturation. As their role models, we teach by both our words and our actions.

When a child's foundation of security is damaged, such as when his parents divorce or a loved one dies, he looks to the adults in his life for assurance about the future. Though we may not even be aware of it, children watch us to see what we say and do in response to a loss. Among the things they observe are:

• How are we reacting?

• Are we sad?

• Do we talk about our feelings?

- Do we discuss with them what has happened?

- Do we cry?

Tears are a complicated issue. If children are watching us and looking to us for reassurance, is it OK to cry? Often, we are shamed or embarrassed by tears, whether they're our own or someone else's. Yet crying is crucial to the grieving process. Modern research substantiates a direct link between shedding tears and personal well-being. In one study, 85 per cent of women and 73 per cent of men reported feeling better — less sad or less angry — after crying.

How does crying help? According to one expert, tears remove stress-related chemicals from our bodies, a necessary first step in feeling better. Another researcher speculates that tears stimulate the release of endorphins, which are mood-elevating substances in the brain.

Myth: adults shouldn't cry in front of children.

Truth: crying is crucial to the grieving process.

Tears are not a sign of weakness. In fact, the grieving person who cries demonstrates great strength. Tears validate the depth of our feelings, and hiding them from children does not protect them. It harms them.

The 18th-century French writer Voltaire called tears 'the silent language of grief'. Our tears speak volumes to grieving children. They are an outward message that we are deeply moved by their story and their pain.

Responding to Children's Needs and Concerns

An adult who serves in the role of a compassionate companion can respond to the child's fundamental, ongoing needs for nurturing and emotional support as well as tend to the transitions that loss imposes. The sheer volume of tasks is the primary reason it is important to have more than one compassionate companion for a grieving child and also helps explain why parents, who also are grieving, cannot sufficiently take care of their children during such a difficult time.

All of us react to turmoil in our lives. Children are much more transparent. They either express their feelings — usually by acting out — or try to suppress or hide them from the world. Their responses to distress can be as diverse as the children themselves. All reactions deserve our attention. As a compassionate companion, one of your jobs is to help the child or adolescent understand that unsuitable behaviour — especially denying their feelings — will sustain the emotional hurt that comes with loss, while constructive grieving strategies will actually heal the wounds of loss. In other words, *it doesn't need to hurt for ever.*

As a compassionate companion, you have the unique advantage of being able to observe firsthand the coping strategies the child is employing. Take notice of the words the child uses and any unusual behaviour he displays. Remember, your goal is not to criticize or lecture, but to acknowledge the child's pain and loss and to teach him positive and healthy ways of coping. After loss, it's tempting to excuse misbehaviour and moodiness; some adults may even think it's OK to let a child 'act out his feelings', even if those actions are unhealthy. But by doing so, we fall short of fulfilling the role of a caring, compassionate companion.

Instead, we must do two things:

1. Help the grieving child understand the reasons for her feelings and behaviour.

2. Provide alternatives that allow the grieving child to express her feelings in an appropriate rather than destructive manner (see chapter 9 for some specific strategies).

MAKE YOUR RESPONSE AGE-APPROPRIATE

Though each child's grief is unique, children tend to have certain basic needs and reactions to loss depending on their age. The following list details these patterns. Keep in mind that some children display only a few of these reactions; some carry on as if nothing unusual has happened; and others exhibit every response imaginable. Any sustained aberrant behaviour is, without a doubt, a cry for help. We must pay attention to it.

Infants: Birth to 18 Months

Basic Behaviour and Needs

• Nurturing care and protection.

• Close relationship with primary caregivers.

• Stable environment and consistent routines.

How They React to Loss

• Disturbed sleep.

• Changes in eating habits.

• Clinging to caregiver.

• Lethargy.

What You Can Do

• Maintain stable environment and consistent routines.

• Keep atmosphere calm.

• Introduce lifestyle changes gradually.

• Minimize separation from primary caregiver.

Toddlers: 18 Months to 2 Years

Basic Behaviour and Needs

• Fears losing primary caregiver's love.

• Craves stability; copes poorly with multiple changes.

How They React to Loss

• Acts out feelings.

• Becomes irritable, anxious, bewildered.

• Regresses: wets bed, sucks thumb, talks like a baby.

• Has insatiable need for affection and approval.

• Understands that family member is absent following divorce or death.

• Repeatedly asks for absent person.

• Fears separation from parent or caregiver following crisis or natural disaster.

• Becomes physically aggressive: hitting, bullying, pounding.

• Refuses to sleep alone or in a dark room.

What You Can Do

• Nurture abundantly with holding, caressing, cuddling.

• Reassure the child of your love.

• Limit separation from primary caregiver.

• Maintain routines.

• Teach appropriate ways to release hostility and frustration.

• Explain loss in simple terms children can understand; affirm that loss is not their fault.

Young Children: 3 to 6 Years

Basic Behaviour and Needs

• Begins establishing self-identity (separate from parents).

• Believes his actions control others' behaviour.

• Identifies with opposite-sex parent.

• Fears abandonment.

How They React to Loss

• Regresses: wets bed, sucks thumb.

• Becomes irritable, aggressive, hostile.

• Yearns for absent parent following divorce or death.

• Becomes clingy; has fears or anxieties not previously expressed.

• May have headaches or stomach-aches.

• Nightmares.

• Realizes that family is different following divorce, the death of a parent or other crisis that alters family structure.

• Acts as if the deceased person is still alive and will reappear.

What You Can Do

• Be attentive; assure child he is loved.

• Nurture through cuddling and tenderness.

• Explain changes that have occurred in family.

• Teach appropriate ways to release hostility and aggression.

Children: 7 to 10 Years

Basic Behaviour and Needs

• Loyalty, understanding, support, supervision and consistency.

- Friends and self-image are important; defines self in relationship to others.

- Strives for independence.

- Seeks to be treated fairly.

How They React to Loss

- Blames self for loss following divorce or death of loved one.

- Angry with parents after divorce; with government or world after major crisis; with friends who have traditional families; or with God for not preventing the loss.

- School work suffers.

- Disruptive behaviour at home or school.

- Self-image blurs.

- Withdraws from activities or people.

- Sensitive to conflict.

- Concerned about money, food, shelter following divorce or death of parent; fearful about the future following a major crisis or natural disaster.

- Understands differences in family after divorce, the death of a parent, chronic illness or imprisonment; self-conscious about family being different.

- Conflicting loyalties following divorce; wrestles with relationship with parents.

- Fantasizes about parent reconciliation following separation or divorce.

- Insatiable hunger for material goods: bicycles, clothes, money.

What You Can Do

- Provide ongoing reassurance that child is loved and future is secure.

- Maintain consistent routine.

- Discuss family situation with teachers.

- Ask family and friends to give additional support.

Young Teenagers: 11 to 13 Years

Basic Behaviour and Needs

- Wants to be accepted and respected.

- Seeks autonomy; assumes more responsibility for self.

- Struggles to establish a personal identity.

- Self-conscious; fragile sense of self.

- Considers peers more important than adults; seeks greater intimacy with peers.

- Less monitoring by parents and caregivers.

How They React to Loss

- Withdraws from friends and activities; academic decline or indifference.

- Displays range of negative behaviour: lying, stealing, cheating.

- Loss of identity; low self-esteem.

- Feels powerless, insecure, vulnerable.

- Appetite and sleep changes (often excessive fatigue).

- Worries about custody arrangements following divorce.

- Hostile to one parent, empathetic to other parent after separation or divorce.

- Demands explanations from adults.

- Ashamed that family is different or changed because of divorce, the death of a parent, chronic illness or imprisonment.

- Headaches, stomach-aches.

- Extreme anger.

- Depressed, lonely.

What You Can Do

- Encourage communication; set aside special times to talk and listen.

- Answer all his questions.

- Affirm her feelings; teach positive coping methods.

- Encourage healthy adult friendships with teacher, youth-club leader or minister or rabbi.

- Allow more personal freedom.

- Ensure that home setting is comfortable, inviting.

- Seek help from school or religious counsellors or therapists, if needed.

Adolescents/Young Adults: 15 to 20 Years

Basic Behaviour and Needs

- Moody; often expresses negative ideas or feelings as a way of testing their own beliefs and those of others.

- Overwhelmed with additional responsibilities.

- Craves peer approval; prefers friends to family.

- Fears parental illness.

How They React to Loss

- Denies inner turmoil following divorce or separation.

- Conflicting loyalties between custodial and non-custodial parents.

- Sensitive to family tensions.

- Avoids reminders of trauma following natural disaster or major crisis.

- Experiences flashbacks to traumatic event.

- Experiments with drugs and alcohol.

- Drawn to troubled peers and possible gang involvement.

- Experiments with sexual activity.

- Decline in academic performance.

- Depression (often severe); withdraws from family and friends; may think, 'What's the use?' and harbour suicidal thoughts.

- Aggressive behaviour.

- Tests limits.

- Craves material goods to compensate for loss.

What You Can Do

- Reassure the teenager of your love and concern.

- Establish fair limits and expectations.

- Encourage communication; set aside special times to be alone with the teenager.

- Seek additional support from family and friends.

- Seek professional counselling or therapy, if needed.

BE PREPARED FOR POSTPONED GRIEVING

Since she was a toddler, Dara has known that she was adopted. Growing up, she seemed intrigued by the fact that both she and her older sister, who is the biological child of their parents, had the same blonde-coloured hair and blue eyes and pleased that she had been 'specially chosen' by her parents. As Dara approached adolescence, her parents became concerned about teenage identity issues and offered to help their younger daughter locate her birth mother, if that was what she wished. Dara gave the matter careful thought and decided against it. 'You're my real parents,' she said. 'I don't need to know anything about my birth mother.' For several years, Dara's mum and dad periodically raised the matter, but Dara always demurred. 'I'm fine,' she insisted.

When Dara turned 16, her older sister went away to college, and the teenager suddenly found herself adrift. High school friends and activities no longer interested her. The once outgoing, happy girl became sullen and withdrawn. She missed meals, began dressing entirely in black and started dating a local troublemaker. Her parents reached out to her repeatedly, but their overtures were ignored. Finally, Dara's mother took the girl to the family doctor, a woman they had known and trusted for many years. As Dara sat alone with the doctor on her second visit, the doctor asked, 'What's going on?' Dara scuffed at the floor and said she hated herself because she didn't deserve the life her adoptive parents had given her. She hated her birth mother for giving her away. 'Why did she abandon me?' Dara wailed. 'Why didn't she love me?'

Often, children try to ignore or deny the pain of loss, rather than admit to and deal with it. They usually do so for one or more of the following three reasons.

- They are determined to be strong. Therefore they 'stuff' their pain and feelings inside, put on a stoic face and stalwartly go on with life, much to the relief of family and friends.

- They are simply too afraid of these unfamiliar feelings to say them out loud.

- No one has asked the child how she is feeling. Subsequently, she thinks there's something wrong with herself and tries to push away or deny her feelings.

Unfortunately, these 'coping' responses only delay a child's healing and his return to feeling better.

In the 25 years I have worked with grieving young people, I have lost count of the number of parents, doctors and educators who insisted that a child who had experienced a recent devastating loss event was doing 'just fine' or 'handling it well', because the child was performing well in school and not openly crying or acting up. Consequently, no one felt the need to sit with this child and guide him into and through the grief process to reconciliation. I promise you that children who do not grieve their loss at the time of the event will grieve later on — either two years later, ten years later or even 30 years later. This delayed grieving can have devastating consequences in their adult lives.

My close friends Ray and Candice had been married for 15 years and had four children between the ages of 5 and 13 when they finally decided to divorce. From the outset, they were determined to set the standard and do everything they could to make the split amicable — no fighting, name-calling, emotional blackmail or verbal sparring. Both parents explained the situation to the children, but I always worried that they only talked about the details and ignored the emotions of the divorce. Candice, especially, focused on logistics: where their dad would be living, the nitty-gritty of parenting time and even specifics about finances. But neither of them ever talked to the children about the emotional side of the breakup. They hid their own emotions and concerns behind happy faces and never asked how the children felt.

No matter how friendly their parents act during a divorce, in their heart of hearts, the children are distressed. They don't want their mum and dad to dissolve the marriage; they don't want to settle for seeing one parent on a part-time basis. When I raised this issue with Candice and Ray, they brushed aside my concerns. 'Oh, the kids are fine. We are doing this the right way,' they insisted. Later, when both Candice and Ray remarried, there were more mutual expressions of goodwill and cheer, and the children were expected to take the changes in their stride.

Overall, it seemed that they did. Growing up, none of the four children exhibited any signs of distress or maladjustment. From the outside looking in, you could say that Ray and Candice had done well dismantling their nuclear family and moving on with life.

Then their daughter Charlotte got married. She was 28, the only girl in the family and the first of the children to wed. Two years later, Charlotte gave birth to her first child. Although it was a happy occasion for the new mother, this event also brought the issues of her parents' divorce into painful focus for the first time in nearly two decades. Cuddling her tiny infant, Charlotte was overwhelmed with love and, suddenly, equally as furious with her own parents.

When Ray and Candice came to the hospital with their respective spouses to visit their new granddaughter, they were greeted by a very angry adult daughter. 'How could you say you loved us and then get divorced — knowing full well you were inflicting such pain on all of us?' Charlotte shouted at them. Framed in the doorway, their arms filled with flowers and brightly wrapped presents, Candice and Ray froze. The smiles drained from their faces. For the first time, neither parent knew what to say.

On what should have been one of the happiest days of their lives, Charlotte, Candice and Ray were faced with the tough, hard work that had been ignored 18 years earlier — work made much more difficult because now the original wound lay buried under the layers of hurt, confusion and rejection that had been accumulating for years.

Consider Support Programmes and Counselling

Through the years of working with bereaved youngsters, I have been reminded again and again how beneficial support groups are for children in the midst of a significant loss. Their grieving family members simply are not able to assist them at that time. This is precisely why RAINBOWS was founded.

In addition, some bereaved children and adolescents need counselling. This depends on the child, the situation and the family's abilities to communicate. As a compassionate companion, you must decide whether a particular child's grief reactions are normal or whether they're troubled and require professional intervention. If so, it is then up to you to raise the issue with the child's parents or other caregivers. Be aware that they may be overly sensitive and resent your suggestion. Do remind them, though, that effective counselling need not be expensive (depending on what is available in your area, or through specialist support groups) and doesn't necessarily need to be a long-term commitment.

Children need love the most when they deserve it the least.

Often extreme behaviour occurs only after a child has sent subtle distress signals that weren't noticed. In other instances, despite our best efforts, the grieving child simply won't or can't open up. Then it is our obligation to get the child to counselling. If the child refuses to go, insist and take her anyway. Think about it: what would you do if a child said, 'Hey, I don't want to go to school'? Wouldn't you send her anyway? Needing the skills of a counsellor during a difficult time is a much more crucial situation.

Reaching Out

When I started working with bereaved youngsters, I met children who insisted that they were OK — that there was 'no problem' — despite the often obvious emotional turmoil they were in. Quickly, I realized that all of the children I saw were more than willing to share their pain. I only needed to be patient, to reach out a second or third time — and then wait until they were comfortable with me. Grieving children are exceptionally sensitive. They need sincere, genuine attention from caring adults. They are depending on us during a difficult time and need to feel our strength. It's up to us to reach out to them. Our role is to be flexible, enthusiastic and sensitive to the child's needs. Here are some other specific ways to reach out to grieving children.

SHOWING COMPASSION TO A GRIEVING CHILD

Showing compassion to a grieving child is often a spontaneous decision made out of love and a genuine concern for the child's well-being. These feelings will guide you better than any handbook on helping a child grieve a loss. In fact, the 'rules' for being a compassionate companion can be boiled down to the following simple principles.

* Work to build a good rapport with the child, so that you both feel comfortable with each other.

* Be patient, even when the child rejects your help.

* Initiate conversations to help the child talk about his loss.

* Don't give advice.

* Be a loving listener.

* Use healing rituals and activities to help the child understand and process her feelings.

* Allow the bereaved to work through their grief.

* Remember that the grieving child is probably angry with God. Don't quote from the Bible or assure the child that 'God has something great planned for you'. The bereaved just wants the pain to go away!

* Give affirmation and encouragement.

* Set aside special sharing times.

* Stay for the duration.

Create a good rapport with the child. Good rapport ensures that the child feels comfortable with you. To create a positive relationship, it's important to:

• Maintain a calmness about your demeanour when you are with the grieving child. Don't be rushed or superficial.

• Be aware of the child's moods and what is currently happening in her life. Remember that other highly charged events, such as a tragedy at school or a national crisis, can reignite her feelings of loss.

• If the relationship permits, be willing to touch or hug the child. If you are a family friend or member of the community, limit your contact to patting the child's hand or touching his shoulder. Some children openly demand this kind of attention, others ask for it indirectly, while still others will shrink from any physical contact. Always use discretion and common sense.

• Stay in touch. Phone the child often and send cards to let her know you're thinking about her. Mark your calendar to send cards or phone on the anniversary of the loss (1 week, 1 month, 1 year later) and at other significant times, too.

Focus on the child's strengths. A significant loss usually damages a child's self-esteem. When a loved one dies or is absent from daily life, the bereaved child feels incomplete. He senses that a part of his identity has disappeared. He struggles to reclaim the sense of self that is missing.

Reassurance and praise are vital to grieving youngsters. We need to highlight who they are as human beings. Look for occasions to praise them, such as when they do something well or behave generously towards a sibling, classmate or friend. The child needs this reinforcement. If you are with a child who has not opened up yet, you can compliment her cool jeans, great smile, hair colour or her interest in sports or music. This type of reinforcement might just open the door to getting the child to trust and feel comfortable with you.

Be understanding and patient. Bereaved youngsters often act out their feelings and thoughts. They are angry, rebellious, difficult and express their frustration through their actions. Often, we are upset and disappointed because their behaviour seems so negative and spiteful. There are times when we may be tested to the very limits of our patience.

When a grieving child acts out her feelings — and taxes your endurance — stop and ask yourself, 'What is this child trying to say to me?' Taking this perspective can help calm you down and diffuse the situation while providing helpful insight.

Easy to do? No. Responding with understanding and patience requires an inordinate amount of tolerance on your part, but in the end it is worth all the effort, time and aggravation.

Being a compassionate companion does not just happen. Like all other relationships, it takes time and consistency. It is one encounter linked to another. It is remembering what was said the last time you talked. It is showing the child that you truly care.

Sincere tenacity pays off.

Megan was 17 when her mother died. When Megan returned to school after the burial, her history teacher offered to listen and be there for her. Megan politely thanked him but didn't take him up on his offer. Week after week, the teacher sought her out and asked how she was doing. Each time, Megan responded politely and quickly. Seven months later, Megan finally opened up to him. Today, at 49, Megan still talks about this history teacher with great fondness.

Children are not as reticent as adults about establishing relationships, but the bonds won't develop overnight. Eventually, the bereaved child will begin to share his thoughts. When that happens, your obligation is to listen.

The grieving child needs his story — his grief — acknowledged. He needs validation of the painful emotions he is feeling.

The child can then be freed of a great burden. He feels enormous relief. Confusion begins to fade. Fear and anger dissipate, if only for a short while. Hope for the future begins to take root.

Remember that to emotionally survive a death, separation, divorce or family crisis, children need:

• Sufficient time to mourn the profound change that has occurred

• Permission to cry

• Knowledgeable, caring adults who reach out and support them

When, with your help as a compassionate companion, children are able to name and understand their feelings of grief, when they are allowed to express their emotions, then and only then can they begin the healing process that will lead them towards acceptance.

Chapter 7

Four Stepping Stones
to Healing

HEALING THE WOUNDS OF GRIEF is a complex process that involves four fundamental actions — Comprehending, Mourning, Commemorating and Moving Forward. Children and teenagers will reconcile their loss well if they are guided through each of these actions. But grieving children can't complete this journey without support from caring adults. This chapter helps you initiate the healing process and guide the grieving child's steps along the way.

Stepping Stone Number One:
Comprehending

Trent was 10 when his parents divorced. The night his mother told him about the breakup, Trent listened attentively. His final comment: 'Well, Mum, these things happen. Make the best of it and go on.' Trent's mother breathed a sigh of relief. 'Trent's a survivor,' she thought. 'He'll be fine.' And as things turned out, the boy was amazingly stoic throughout the divorce proceedings.

Months later, after Trent's mum had done some reading about the long-term effects divorce has on children, she realized that her son had never mentioned the divorce since the first night. One day, she asked if he'd like to talk about it. Trent didn't skip a beat. 'Mum, talking about the divorce won't change anything!' he barked at her. 'Dad is gone and won't be back!' Afterwards, no matter how many times or ways Trent's mother tried to initiate a discussion about the divorce, the boy refused to talk. Each time, she hugged him and said, 'Talking about it won't change what happened, but it *will* change how you understand it. It will help you make sense out of it.'

Trent was 19 when he finally dismantled his wall of silence and shared with his mother the years of pain he had stored up in his heart. Driving home from college with his mother, after his first term away, Trent mentioned the divorce. His mother was surprised and listened quietly as her son talked about his memories and feelings. From that day on, Trent frequently returned to the topic. It turns out he had many questions and a lot to say.

Years later, Trent's mother asked him what had happened to enable him to finally talk about the divorce. Trent grinned. 'Your persistence and my maturity,' he said.

Children and adolescents must first make sense of their loss in order to grapple with it. Death, divorce and other life-altering events are baffling to youngsters, who cannot emotionally or mentally grasp the concept of what has happened. Young people need someone to gently explain the meaning of the loss.

The easiest way to help a child comprehend what has happened is to ask him to share his story — what happened to him and how it has changed his life. Not once. Not twice. But many times.

How many? *At least 30 times*. When I suggest this in the grief workshops I conduct across the country, it usually elicits a gasp from the participants.

They think I'm kidding, exaggerating to make a point. But I'm serious. Telling her story 30 times means the grieving child finds 30 different people and shares her story once with each one. Or she finds 15 people and shares it twice with each one. Or she finds one really good confidante — a compassionate companion — and shares it over and over again.

> It is the child's telling and retelling of the story that makes it real to her.

Keep in mind that as children mature, their perception of their loss will become more insightful. As they grow up, they may need to retell the story at each new stage of development.

You can gently help a grieving child comprehend the loss that has occurred by using the following strategies.

- Explain to the child what has happened and how it has happened using age-appropriate vocabulary. Do this more than once.

- Take the time to clarify the details of how the child's life and family structure will change since this event has happened.

- Ask children to explain in their words what they believe has happened.

- Provide opportunities for the child to share his feelings and ask questions.

- Have books about loss available for children to read to help normalize their feelings and concerns.

- Purchase a journal for the child and encourage her to write down her feelings and thoughts each day. Writing can help a child express feelings and thoughts she's not yet comfortable saying out loud.

Stepping Stone Number Two: Mourning

When Paige was 11, she got her first babysitting job taking care of Jacob, the newborn son of a couple who lived nearby. Initially, Paige was never left solely in charge of the baby; she merely played with him while his mum did the housework. But by the time she was 13 and Jacob was 2, Paige was his only babysitter. The two of them became inseparable.

Two years later, 4-year-old Jacob was diagnosed with cancer. During the boy's 12 months of gruelling treatments, Paige spent every free moment at the hospital with him. Later, she helped take care of him at home. One day, Jacob didn't wake up. His fight for life had ended. Consumed with grief, Paige wanted desperately to talk about the little boy she had grown to love so dearly. But whenever she mentioned Jacob to his mum and dad, they broke down and cried. At home, Paige followed her own parents around the house, telling them how much she loved and missed Jacob. One day, Paige's father told her she 'needed to snap out of it'. Her mother wasn't any more understanding: 'Why are you so upset?' she asked. 'He wasn't your brother.'

The only sympathetic adult Paige found was her teacher. 'You seem a bit preoccupied,' the teacher said to her one morning. 'Perhaps you can stay after class today and help me change the notice board and we can have a chat.' At the end of the day, Paige had barely started working when she began to talk about Jacob and, for the first time, express her deep feelings of grief out loud. 'Jacob's death must be very difficult for you,' the teacher said. 'I think you're being very brave to talk about him.' Paige felt relieved. Every Friday for several weeks she stayed after class to help with the notice board — and talk.

Mourning is saying out loud what is being felt so intensely inside. It is the expression of the jumbled feelings of grief. For example, a child may say:

'I miss my dad so much.'

'I don't like having only one parent coming to school plays.'

'I don't miss all the fighting, so why am I upset about the divorce?'

'I want to be back home again with all my stuff.'

Our role as compassionate companions is to encourage grieving children to verbalize their feelings of loss. Once these feelings are outside — in the light — the children will be less afraid. Once the conflicting emotions are outside of their hearts, they will have power over the loss event. Then they can begin the work of healing their hurt and moving on.

Often, we want to help the grieving child to talk, but simply don't know how to get started, what to say or how to say it. For most of us, this is a learned skill. In chapter 8, which discusses heartfelt conversations, you'll find practical advice about how to talk with children and teenagers about sensitive issues. For now, though, the following strategies will help you with the basics:

• Ask the child to tell her story — the details of what happened to her (even if you know the details, she needs to tell it from her head and heart).

• Provide special times with the child to ask him how he is feeling about what has happened.

• Act as a role model for the child. Do this by being comfortable with your grief, which will allow you to share your emotions by words or tears.

• Send 'thinking of you' cards or notes throughout the year, especially at birthdays, anniversaries and festive occasions.

• Teach feeling words to the child.

• Acknowledge and affirm the child's feelings; help her work through them.

• Create an atmosphere that encourages the child to ask questions and clarify misunderstandings.

• Have the child join a peer grief support group in the community, such as RAINBOWS.

Stepping Stone Number Three: Commemorating

On a frosty spring morning, fire raced through the two-storey house that belonged to Sue and Todd and their three teenage children. The family was on holiday; they returned to find their home gutted and all their possessions destroyed. 'At least we're safe,' Sue told the others. 'Thank goodness, no one was hurt.' It was a litany they would hear over and over again from relatives, friends and neighbours.

While their house was being rebuilt, the family moved into a rented house and got back to their normal routines of work, school and sports, something in which all three children excelled. Six months later, they were able to return home — to new furniture, new appliances, new clothes. 'Isn't this great?' Sue asked. 'Yeah, super,' her eldest, Bruce, 17, replied sarcastically as the girls — Bonnie, 15, and Tessa, 13 — trudged through the unfamiliar surroundings. Before long the three youngsters gravitated to the living room. Bruce kicked at a footstool, then waved an arm at a blank wall and empty shelves. 'All my football trophies are gone!' he exclaimed. 'It's like everything I've done that's important or means anything to me has been wiped out.' Bonnie and Tess nodded. Years worth of medals, ribbons and certificates for gymnastics and volleyball had disappeared. Team photos, souvenir programmes — the memorabilia of their young lives — had been taken from them for ever. 'I guess all that stuff was more important than I realized,' Bonnie said sadly.

On the Saturday morning of the family's first week back home, the doorbell rang. Sue peeked out of the window, then called her children downstairs. 'Hurry up!' she shouted as she threw open the door. Standing outside was a cluster of the children's teammates bearing gifts — not the traditional housewarming presents, but photocopies of team pictures, boxes of sports memorabilia, a collection of championship ribbons and even several 'extra' trophies that they had gathered for their friends. 'We thought you might like to have these,' one of the boys said as the entourage trooped in. 'This is amazing,' said Bruce. 'It means more than you can imagine.'

By noon, the room had acquired a truly lived-in look and the empty walls and shelves had been filled once again with reminders of past athletic triumphs and struggles. 'Now, this is home,' Tess declared and dropped happily onto the sofa.

Remembering soothes the pain of loss.

Commemorating the past or the person who is absent from the grieving child's life is essential to healing. Most children need to be assured that it's OK for them to cherish their memories. Many will even look for someone to help them remember or, like Bruce, Bonnie and Tess, will ache for tangible reminders of life before the loss event.

Children are imprinted with the good and bad times in their lives. These experiences are part of their identity and determine how they view and experience life. If they are told not to mention happy memories or good times that occurred before the loss, they are being asked to deny who they are and their personal history.

How painful and confusing it must seem to a child not to be able to talk about a loved person who has died or about the days when the family laughed and played before the divorce. Too often, divorced parents destroy wedding photos or cut the ex-spouse out of them. What a tragedy for the children! These pictures document their early family history.

The truth is that commemorating teaches children that life has value. Remembering teaches that love is important, despite the emotional pain that may accompany it. After a life-altering event, such as a death, separation or divorce, children need to establish ways to remember the absent person and the family as it existed before the loss event.

Depending on the specific loss that the child has experienced, there are a number of things you can do to help him remember and honour the past.

AFTER A NATURAL DISASTER OR COMMUNITY CRISIS

Children need to feel connected to the larger community. They can participate in remembering by:

- Helping victims by offering to pick up debris or by providing clothing, food, shelter and child care services.

- Joining with other children and adults for a prayer vigil, candle ceremony or other commemorative service.

- Making cards or presenting symbolic gifts to those who were hardest hit by the crisis.

- Planting a garden, bush or tree to symbolize what has been destroyed or damaged.

AFTER A DIVORCE

The family's roots need to be honoured for the sake of the children. This can be done by:

- Keeping all family photo albums and wedding pictures.

- Saving keepsakes and heirlooms for the children.

- Passing on family jewellery such as the engagement or wedding rings.

- Sharing why you fell in love with your child's other parent.

- Talking about your former spouse's good qualities and traits.

- Reminiscing about the happier times.

AFTER A DEATH

The loved one can be honoured in the following ways:

- Attending a funeral service.

- Having a journal on display for friends and family to write their memories or thoughts of the deceased for the children.

- Compiling a memorial booklet.

- Preparing and delivering a eulogy or tribute; visiting the cemetery.

- Displaying favourite photos.

- Planting a tree or flowers in the deceased person's honour.

- Talking about the deceased loved one, again and again.

- Reminiscing about the ways the deceased influenced a child's life.

- Giving children a journal in which to write their thoughts and feelings for years to come.

When my father died, I saved an inordinate number of things that had belonged to him. These were inconsequential items, such as dance cards from his school days, business cards from his entire working career, copies of his CV, photos, certificates and diplomas, gloves, hats, ties and scarves (all showing signs of wear and certainly tattered). Unable to part with any of the mementoes, I boxed them all up for safekeeping. Well-meaning friends said I was ' overdoing it' and badgered me to dispose of the items, but I refused.

After a few years, I decided to sort through the boxes and 'toss the stuff'. Even then, I couldn't. Instead, I reorganized the collection and put it away again for safekeeping. I'm glad I did because now, every Christmas, I give each of my sons a small box of keepsakes from 'PawPaw'. These relics from my father's life — insignificant though they may seem — have become treasures to these three grown men.

Stepping Stone Number Four: Moving Forward

When Angela was 15, her mother was killed in a car crash. Following the accident, the quiet, reserved teenager grew even more subdued. Although she diligently adhered to her normal routines at home and school, Angela seemed removed from her family and friends. One day she told a favourite aunt that nothing mattered since her mother's death. 'Life will never be the same,' she said. The aunt nodded. 'In many ways, that's true,' she told Angela. 'But life doesn't stop. One day will lead into another, just as it did before your mother died. Life will go on.'

That night, Angela went outside and watched the full moon rise over the horizon. She saw the silvery orb lift into the sky and traced its path through the stars, as she had often done as a small child at her mother's side. Looking at the constellations, Angela thought about how these patterns in the sky had been unchanged for thousands of years, heedless of the many people who had lived and died there. That night, she realized, her aunt was right. Life continued.

Grief is a journey through complex, foreign terrain. The grieving child needs someone to guide him through this unfamiliar territory. Once a child fully understands that a loss event has for ever altered his life, he can, at last, move forward. This realization comes slowly, a little bit at a time. An adult who has taken on the role of a compassionate companion helps the child reach this stage but doesn't try to hurry the process. Grieving is a solitary experience. The child must move forward at his own pace.

Sometimes children seem to get stuck in grief. They appear to not want to proceed with their lives. This holding back often occurs because children cannot visualize what life will be like if they accept what has happened. They equate accepting the loss with liking it. Our role is to explain the difference.

No matter what the loss, we need to keep nudging along the grieving child towards healing.

• When a loved one dies, a child may tenaciously cling to precious memories of that person, fearful that the passage of time will erase these recollections or cause them to fade. You can explain that the deceased will always remain part of the child's personal history and will always remain with her in her heart and reminiscences.

• After a divorce, a child may refuse to accept the reality of her new life. She clings to the past as a way of preserving the nuclear family she had once been part of. You can assure the child that her parents will always love her. Help her recognize that she can have strong, loving, *separate*, *individual* relationships with each of her parents. If one parent has abandoned the child — which is not uncommon after divorce — reassure the child with comments such as, 'This is not about you. It's about your parent's own capabilities. You are not responsible for your mother's (father's) actions.'

• A natural disaster or national crisis may make a child or teenager feel insecure and fearful of the future. In some instances, everything they have known and taken for granted is suddenly threatened. You can comfort him by assuring him that responsible adults are working to resolve the situation and to prevent the problem from recurring. The child should also be told that authorities and responsible adults are doing their best to re-establish daily routines and get life back to as normal as possible.

If a previously planned school or family celebration falls during or immediately after a natural disaster or crisis, it is usually best to go ahead with the event, altering or changing it as seems appropriate or rescheduling it as a memorial to be held later. Celebrations depict life moving forward and can help heal the wounds of a community and even a nation. Such events also focus children's attention on the future and prompt them to look ahead.

No matter what caused the traumatic change in the family or community structure, our role is to guide grieving children towards integrating their loss into their daily lives and moving on. Realizing that a happy life is still possible really does help in the recovery. The darkest night is always followed by a new day. This is what hope is all about.

Chapter 8

Heartfelt Conversations

SIX MONTHS AFTER HER MOTHER DIED FROM BREAST CANCER, 9-year-old Karen spent a weekend with her grandmother. On Friday evening they ate pizza, and on Saturday afternoon they went to the cinema. That evening, Grandma suggested they make chocolate chip cookies, Karen's favourite. Since Karen's arrival, her grandmother had been aware of an unusual reticence about the young girl, but she said nothing. As they worked together in the kitchen, the atmosphere was quiet until she handed the mixing spoon to Karen and asked her granddaughter to stir the ingredients.

Karen stabbed at the dough.

'Karen, you seem upset, what's the matter?' her grandmother asked, with concern.

'Oh, nothing,' the girl replied. The older woman nodded and for a few moments they worked in silence. Then Karen spoke up again. 'I don't have anyone to talk to. Mum is gone! We used to talk all the time — about every-thing – but now, I feel weird just thinking about talking to anyone else. I don't know what to do!'

Grandma looked at the child. 'Yes, we all miss your mum. It must be particularly difficult for you, being the only girl.'

'I'm angry! It just isn't fair.' Karen shoved the bowl away and stared defiantly at her grandmother.

'You're right,' Grandma said quietly. 'It isn't fair. Your mum was so young. And you and your brothers are young. Mums aren't supposed to die. Unfortunately, cancer is a disease that can attack people at any age. And when this happens, families hurt. For you, Karen, it must be really hard because you and your mum talked about everything. I can understand why you are so angry.'

Karen nodded and her grandmother went on. 'Let's play a game. I'll name someone I think you might want to talk to and if you think it's a good fit, you get an extra bite of the cookie dough!'

Bereaved children are psychologically and emotionally bruised and bat-tered. To heal their scarred souls, they need repeated opportunities to talk about their loss, ask questions and rage against the unfairness of the event. Each of us can single-handedly help ease the emotional pain of grieving chil-dren. Healing will occur when children have someone with whom they can talk and who listens to and understands them.

Talking and listening to grieving children are skills that can be learned. This chapter provides simple techniques that RAINBOWS has used success-fully with thousands of grieving children. Here you'll find information on good questions to ask (and which to avoid), how to be an active listener and examples of healing conversations. The chapter also includes playful activi-ties to encourage sharing in children who have difficulty facing their loss and discussing their feelings about it.

Talking with a Grieving Child

At a recent grief workshop, I brought up the importance of meaningful conversations with children. One recently divorced woman complained that she talked to her children 'all the time', but that the kids never seemed to reciprocate. 'I may as well talk to the wall,' she said. Many of the other adults in the room nodded in agreement.

'Do you really talk to the children?' I asked. 'Yes,' the workshop participants insisted. So I asked them to pick a typical day from that week and write down exactly the questions or comments they remembered directing to their children, grandchildren, nieces, nephews or students. A few minutes later, as the adults handed in their lists, I could tell by their contrite expressions that they were not entirely pleased with the results.

Here's what the 'conversations' looked like.

'Hurry up or you'll be late for school.'

'Eat your breakfast.'

'Don't forget to …'

'Why isn't your homework done?'

'How was the game? Did you win?'

'Get ready for bed.'

'It's your turn to empty the dishwasher.'

'Clean up your room.'

'When I was your age …'

The truth is that we don't engage children often enough in meaningful conversations, in the kind of back-and-forth dialogue that leads to insight and understanding. It seems to me that life — our work life, family life and even play life — has been squeezed so tightly that we don't have the time — and rarely do we take the time — to communicate well. Failure to communicate is a misfortune in the best of circumstances. When a momentous event has turned a child's life upside down, the inability to communicate is a tragedy.

Starting a discussion about a painful topic feels awkward, but talking about the loss event is crucial to the four stepping stones of healing I discussed previously: comprehending, mourning, commemorating and moving forward. As children are able to release their pent-up grief emotions and express them out loud, they are finally able to begin sorting through the pieces of their loss. It is only then that they can reassemble their worlds. The process is similar to doing a jigsaw puzzle. Think of the last time you worked on one. You opened the box, emptied out the pieces, turned them all over and sorted through them. Only after you were able to evaluate all the pieces and arrange them in some sort of order were you able to put together the picture.

Grief is the same. Unfortunately, while most children want to talk about the loss, they are afraid to speak of their pain out loud. I think they fear that saying the words — articulating the pain — will only intensify the hurt. I have seen it in their faces. They start; then fear washes over them and they stop. We need to repeatedly, ever so gently, encourage them until they are able to open up. When their pain is finally outside of themselves, their fear will dissipate.

INITIATE CONVERSATIONS ABOUT THE LOSS

Children need to speak out loud about their pain. To recover from grief, the child needs to tell and retell his experience. It is up to you, the compassionate companion, to create opportunities for these stories to come out. *You* must bring up the topic. You can begin these conversations simply and in a non-threatening way:

'Taneesha, how are you today?'

Ask about her friends, school, teachers or an activity she enjoys. Inquire about her favourite music group or sports team. At some point

Heartfelt Conversations

during the conversation, gently ask: 'How are you feeling about (the loss event) today?'

Usually, children respond with 'fine' or 'OK' or some other one-syllable answer. Don't readily accept this reply. Delicately push a bit: 'Are you really OK? You've gone through a difficult time.'

I call this 'knocking on the heart's door.'

Next time, push a little more: 'Last time we talked, you said you were fine. What is the hardest part of (the loss) for you?'

If the child replies, affirm and acknowledge what is being said to you: 'That must have been a difficult time for you.' 'I can hear your anger.' 'You handled that situation well.'

This affirmation is salve for the emotional wound.

It may take many attempts over weeks or even months before the bereaved child or teenager opens up. He'll talk when he is ready, when he feels comfortable with you, and when he knows he can trust you. In the meantime, follow the strategies below.

Revisit the subject often. Sometimes a simple observation opens the door to conversation: 'Apple pie! Do you remember, that was always Grandma's favourite dessert?'

Share your own feelings. By doing so, you set the stage for honest and open communication. If you are sad, admit it; if you are confused or overwhelmed, share this with the child or teenager. But don't monopolize the conversation. Rather, share your feelings as a matter of honesty and setting the stage.

Don't give up. Yes, it's frustrating. You take the grieving child to lunch and, despite your attempts at talking about the loss event, all she wants to discuss are her friends or plans for summer holidays. This will happen. But your efforts are not entirely lost. You have opened the door. You have sent her a strong and powerful message that you care.

Wait for an answer. Too often, a well-meaning adult asks the grieving child, 'How are you?' If the child doesn't respond immediately, the adult

205

quickly fills in the gap with more questions, 'Are you still playing netball? How's school going? What are you doing in the summer holiday?' When we ask a question, we need to sit silently, wait for the child to answer and assimilate what is being said.

Remember that children grieve in spasms. They may talk about the loss event for a few minutes, then stop and change the subject or announce that they want to watch TV. You haven't done anything wrong. The child is simply sending the signal that, for now, he's finished talking about it.

HARMFUL AND HELPFUL QUESTIONING

There are only two reasons to ask questions: for clarification or to encourage further dialogue.

Any questions you ask a grieving child should be simple and easy to understand. They should also encourage the child to share, rather than put him on the defensive. Here are some guidelines to make your questions as useful as possible.

Avoid 'yes-or-no' questions. When you ask yes-or-no questions, they have the potential of ending the sharing. For example: 'Are you sad your mummy died?' If the child says yes, the dialogue is over.

Instead, ask: 'How do you feel about your mummy's death?'

This kind of open-ended question invites the child to share all of the feelings she may have surrounding the death.

Avoid 'why' questions. Why questions put the child on the defensive and may prompt him to close up. For example, if a child says he's sad or angry or depressed and you ask why, you are challenging him to defend or explain his emotions.

Instead, say: 'Could you describe the events that caused you to feel this way?'

Avoid 'what', 'where' or 'how' questions. Interrogating questions are grilling and uncomfortable.

Instead, use clarifying questions: 'That must have been awful for you. Could you tell me more?'

ANSWER ALL QUESTIONS AND CONCERNS

Children and teenagers are rarely told the details about their loss. Instead, they often know only the end result: someone has died; their parents are divorcing. Like anyone, they want to know how this could have happened. Why has their world been turned upside down? We can help by offering to clear up their confusion.

When a child or teenager asks a question, we need to respond as honestly as we can. If we don't know the answer, we can commit to finding out for them — and then follow through. If we're unsuccessful, we need to tell them. At least they'll know that we kept our word and tried, for their sake.

Some questions defy explanation. When faced with a query that cannot be answered, redirect the question to the child. Using this technique invites the child to share what already is on her mind and in her heart and opens the door to further discussion.

For example:

Child: 'Why do you think my real mummy gave me away?'

Adult: 'Jamie, I don't really know. Do you have any ideas?'

FOCUS ON FEELINGS

Joel was 5 years old when his father, a police officer, was shot and killed. Several years later, Joel's mother remarried and life seemed to return to normal. Then, about the time Joel turned 9, he started dressing almost exclusively in dark — usually black — clothing. Joel rarely smiled; his disposition always had an edge to it. His shoulders were slumped, his words mumbled. His brothers would constantly say, 'Joel is in another one of his moods.' But no one really knew what was going on inside the boy. And no one tried to find out.

Grief is about feelings. Putting words around their emotions gives young people the ability to sort through them. People learn while they talk!

HEALING RESPONSES

When you finally get a child to open up to you, the intensity of his feelings might surprise you. When a child makes an honest confession to you about how he's really feeling, it's important to respond without judgement and in a way that gets the child to continue to share. Here are examples of some healing responses as well as some responses that miss the mark.

When the child says:	Do reply:	Don't say:
My life is a mess.	It sounds like you are going through a difficult time. What is happening?	You poor thing. I feel so sorry for you.
I'm scared.	Tell me what you are afraid of.	There is no need to be.
I hate my dad.	What bothers you about him?	You mustn't talk that way.
I don't know what to say to my mum.	Shall we practice some ways for you to approach her?	That's OK. I'll talk to her for you.
I am angry with God.	Are you able to tell me why?	That's a terrible thing to say.
My dad isn't guilty and shouldn't be in prison!	Can you explain what happened?	The legal system is corrupt.
This is the worst thing that's ever happened to me.	Can you tell me more?	Your situation isn't so bad. Let me tell you what happened to my nephew.
Will there be another terrorist attack?	How would you handle it if there were?	No. That will never happen again.
I feel terrible.	Describe what you are feeling.	I know just how you feel.

As a child relates the story of what happened, she usually stays focused on the details. This is certainly fine, but you'll also want to continually ask her how she *feels*, because her grief is contained in her emotions. Part of your role is to assist the child in moving from her head into her heart, where her feelings live. For example:

Adult: 'Shara, what happened in your family?'

Child: 'My mum and dad divorced.'

Adult: 'Would you like to tell me how that has been for you?'

Child: 'Well, my dad lives far away and I only see him in the summer. I have to take an aeroplane by myself to visit him.'

Adult: 'How do you feel about that?'

Child: 'I'm scared of flying. And it is lonely on the plane. I don't know anyone.'

Adult: 'Have you told your mum or dad how you feel about travelling alone?'

Child: 'No.'

Adult: 'Do you think you would want to?'

A child's ability to share his feelings depends on his age and his family's comfort level with this type of honest discussion. Below are general guidelines outlining the increased communication skills linked with each age group. Remember, however, that just because a child reaches a certain age doesn't mean he will suddenly be able to start talking about his feelings. Much depends on coaxing and practice.

Birth to 3 years old. Very young children are unable to verbalize their feelings. They can only express emotion through their behaviour — crying, withdrawal, refusing to eat.

4 to 6 years old. Young children continue to act out their emotions but also begin to use simple words to describe feelings.

6 to 13 years old. Children begin to acknowledge their feelings but attribute them to external sources. For example, they might say, 'You make me angry' rather than 'I am angry.'

14 to 18 years old. Adolescents are able to identify and acknowledge their feelings.

ENCOURAGE, BUT DON'T LECTURE

A simple preposition can make a huge difference in how you approach your conversations with a grieving child. Rather than talking *to* the child, it's important to try to talk *with* him. When we talk *to* a child about a loss, he perceives it as lecturing; when we talk *with* a child, the child gets to share his thoughts, questions, beliefs and feelings with us.

Adult: 'I can see that you are very upset about _____. Do you want to talk?'

Adult: 'You really loved _____, didn't you? What are some of the special things about him that you admired?'

Adult: 'I am feeling really sad about _____. How are you doing?'

If, after a few nudges, the child doesn't seem to want to talk about the loss, let go of the topic. Instead, engage him in conversation about the news, sports, videos — any subject that interests him. A grieving child cannot flip the 'on' switch and discuss a painful loss just because you are ready to talk about the event. Later, on a different occasion, reach out to him again. You may recall, it took me more than a decade to get my son to finally open up about the divorce.

Consider the following conversation.

Adult: 'Frank, you have been so sad since your mum and dad divorced. Do you want to talk about it?'

Teenager: 'No, I'm OK. That's their problem, not mine.'

Adult: 'Well, Frank, I just want to let you know I really care about you and I am here for you. I can't imagine how you must feel.'

Teenager: 'It's awful. I never get to stay home much. I'm always moving back and forth from Mum's house to Dad's house.'

FIVE CONVERSATION HABITS TO AVOID

It's painful to see a child in the midst of grieving. As part of our desire to help, it's understandable that we might want to step in and solve problems for the child or offer advice. For real healing to occur, though, the child needs to come to her own resolutions. The next time you're engaged in a conversation with a child, try to avoid falling into one of the following conversation patterns.

The fact-finder: seeks information, ignores child's feelings
> *Child:* 'My parents are divorcing.'
> *Don't say:* 'No kidding. Are you going to live with your mum or your dad?'
> *Instead, say:* 'How do you feel about that?'

The fix-it: tries to be a problem solver
> *Child:* 'I don't like the man my mum is dating.'
> *Don't say:* 'I'll talk to your mum.'
> *Instead, say:* 'Can you tell your mum how you feel?'

The adviser: tells child what to do
> *Child:* 'I miss my friends when I go to my dad's house on weekends.'
> *Don't say:* 'You must see your dad every other week.'
> *Instead, say:* 'Have you been able to talk this over with your dad?'

The judge: evaluates the child's feelings
> *Child:* 'I hate my mother.'
> *Don't say:* 'You are too angry!'
> *Instead, say:* 'I can hear in your voice how upset you are.'

The questioner: interrogates the child for more details
> *Child:* 'My sister died.'
> *Don't say:* 'How old was she? How did she die? Which hospital was she at?'
> *Instead, say:* 'Could you tell me what happened?'

Adult: 'How is that for you?'

Teenager: 'It's a nightmare. My stuff is always where I'm not. Then I get into trouble at in school because I usually forget homework or gym clothes at someone's house.'

Adult: 'How frustrating that must be for you. Do you think there is some way that it can be organized so you won't get into so much trouble at school?'

Teenager: 'What do you mean, like having two sets of gym clothes?'

Adult: 'Yes, is that possible?'

Teenager: 'I dunno. But I guess I can ask.'

Adult: 'Are there other things about the divorce that you struggle with?'

Listening to a Grieving Child

I was visiting some friends one evening. The family consisted of a mum, dad, grandmother, a daughter who was 6 and a son who was 10. The three adults and I were sitting in the living room talking when Craig, the son, stomped down the stairs and slumped into a chair.

'Craig, what's wrong?' his mother asked.

'I have no friends!' Craig replied.

Across the room, the boy's father looked up. 'It's no wonder, you're too bossy,' he said.

Craig's mother quickly added. 'Don't be ridiculous. The phone is always ringing. And Anthony practically lives here.'

From the chair where she sat knitting, Craig's grandmother added her own comments to the mix: 'Now, now, dear,' she advised, 'you don't need those kind of friends; they aren't polite.' No one had noticed that Craig's younger sister, Melissa, had slipped into the room. When the others had

WHY CHILDREN DON'T TALK TO THEIR FRIENDS ABOUT LOSS

Although children talk to each other about many personal subjects, loss and the emotions of grief are rarely discussed. There are many reasons for this reticence.

The child who has experienced loss hesitates to talk about the event because:

✳ He doesn't know how to bring up the subject.

✳ She's afraid she might cry.

✳ He worries that his friends will treat him differently.

✳ She thinks her friends won't understand her feelings because they haven't had a similar experience.

At the same time, even the most well-meaning friends may stay silent because:

✳ They don't know about the loss.

✳ They don't know if they're supposed to talk about it.

✳ They want to protect their friend and think it's kinder to not bring up the subject.

✳ They feel awkward and don't know how to raise the issue.

✳ They don't know what to say.

finished commenting, Melissa spoke up. 'Craig, why do you feel that way?'

With a look of heartfelt gratitude, Craig turned to his sister and told her about the teasing he'd been subjected to in the school playground that afternoon because he had just started to wear a heavy leg brace. Though she was only six, Melissa had instinctively known how to listen and invited Craig to share, rather than passing judgement on his concerns.

I believe listening, real listening, is the greatest gift we can give one another. Your role as a compassionate companion is to be a good listener: to offer the child an opportunity to share his grief story and to be someone who will acknowledge his feelings. This is the balm he needs for healing his wound of loss. To the grieving child, a good listener says:

> When we truly listen to a grieving child, we use our *eyes* to see the body language, *ears* to hear the words and *heart* to understand the feelings.

You exist. Affirmation boosts self-confidence and helps the child develop coping skills.

You are worthwhile. Being accepted for who she is — not for her grades, athletic ability, or looks — encourages the child to do the work that loss requires.

What you feel, fear and know is important — and important to me. When children begin to move through their grief, the most important message for you to convey is respect for their journey. It is theirs, not yours.

ACTIVE LISTENING

Active listening entails three steps: attending to the surroundings; signalling the child that you are engaged with him and what he is saying; and developing the conversation by asking probing questions.

The following strategies will help you select a location that puts both of you at ease and guide you in using body language that encourages conversation.

• If possible, sit in comfortable surroundings that are well-lit and free of distractions. It's OK to have the television or radio on as background noise, however, since this makes some children more comfortable.

• Do not have a barrier such as a desk or table between you and the child.

• Sit at eye level. Never have a child sit on the floor while you sit on a chair. Even when you meet a child, put yourself at her level when you are introduced. Whenever she is talking, look directly at her, not beyond. Certainly there will be things said that make you uncomfortable, but when this happens, you must continue to have your eyes engaged with hers.

• Use open body language. Keep your arms unfolded; hand gestures should be relaxed and open. Lean forward, since this posture communicates interest. Initially, keep 2 to 3 feet of personal space between you and the child — enough so he doesn't feel crowded but close enough to allow you to reach out and comfort him.

• Keep your voice calm and audible.

• Use phrases that indicate you are paying attention, such as 'Tell me more' or 'I see'. If you remain silent, occasionally nod your head to indicate that you are paying close attention.

To make it clear to the child that you are truly interested in what he's saying, use the techniques below.

Clarify confusing messages. In particular, ask about statements that use the terms 'always' and 'never'. Does the child really mean those words, or is it just a figure of speech?

'Sarah, did I hear you say that your dad is always shouting at you?'

Ask about conflicting verbal and non-verbal messages. These can be conveyed by body language or behaviour.

'You say it doesn't bother you, but you seem tense.'

Allow silence. While most adults are uncomfortable with silent periods during conversations, we must allow them to happen. This is when the internal processing is occurring, when the child or teenager is sorting through the feelings and experiences and trying to put words around them.

Keep your focus on the child. This means that you must set aside your own feelings. You are not there to share them, at least not initially. Your job is to listen and assist the child while she sifts through her story, her experiences and her feelings and responses to them.

When possible, invite the child to problem solve. For example:

'Josh, is there some way for you to talk to your foster family about the extra chores you seem to have?'

Keep your opinions to yourself. The child or teenager is living his own life and struggling through situations totally different from anything you may have experienced. Even if you grew up in a similar situation, don't say: 'I understand what you are going through.' Extenuating circumstances may be radically different.

Don't give advice until asked. Eventually, most children will ask you for insight or a better way of handling a situation. Keep your response concise; otherwise, the child might feel you are lecturing him.

When you don't understand something that has been said to you, reflect back in your own words what you heard and saw. Even if you missed the mark, the message to the child is that you are listening and that you feel it is important to understand exactly what she is saying.

'Jane, did you just say that you have not seen your mum during the last four years?'

Encourage tears. Never hand a tissue or handkerchief to a crying child. Your action may be perceived as a message to stop. Tears are healing and give witness to the hurt the child is feeling. If you also start to cry, it is perfectly OK. It shows the child that you are acknowledging her pain.

Once the child has opened up about the loss, use the following guidelines to further develop the conversation.

Probe by using non-verbal clues. This is a useful strategy if you don't know the child well or if he doesn't seem comfortable enough to talk freely.

'Wes, I see there are tears in your eyes. Are you sure that you aren't upset about what has happened?'

Make comments or pose questions that encourage dialogue. Stay involved in the conversation by asking questions or making comments that keep the child talking.

'You really sounded angry when you talked about that.'

'How did you respond when it happened?'

LISTEN WITH EMPATHY, NOT SYMPATHY

The last thing a struggling child needs is sympathy. Sympathy is the process of feeling sorry for another. Sympathy says, 'I feel …'. When we sympathize with someone, we identify with and take on the feelings of the person sharing. We then tend to give advice or solutions. But in the case of a struggling child, such an approach is a deterrent to grieving. First, this is not what grieving children want or are asking of us when they share their feelings. Second, when we attempt to take away their problems, the message we convey is that they are not capable of resolving the situation themselves.

The opposite of sympathy is empathy — the process of feeling *with* another. With empathy, we:

• Listen without judging.

• Understand without getting involved.

• Ask questions to encourage the dialogue.

An empathetic or compassionate listener doesn't attempt to salve grief, but rather listens, accepts, acknowledges and supports the bereaved child. When used properly, empathy is a key that can open a locked door and invite another to share herself.

> Sympathy fosters pity. Empathy leads to understanding.

217

As an empathetic listener, you will be able to hear feelings the grieving child may not even know exist. When this happens, reflect back to the youngster what you think you heard or are sensing. Then verify with him if this is correct. This process is exactly what good listening is about. It is really a dialogue, except that the child will be doing the sharing and you will be doing the listening and affirming as well as clarifying, whenever necessary.

Consider the following healing conversation, in which the compassionate companion empathizes with the teenager's feelings of loss and helps her to work through her sense of guilt.

Teenager: 'My life will never be good since my twin sister died.'

Adult: 'It must be difficult. I can't imagine how it must be for you.'

Teenager: 'I am miserable every day. If only ...'

Adult: 'If only what?'

Teenager: 'I could have saved her life. It's all my fault.'

Adult: 'How would you have been able to save her life?'

Teenager: 'If I had been in the car with her, I could have told her that truck wasn't stopping for the red light.'

Adult: 'Was your sister a good driver?'

Teenager: 'Yes, very.'

Adult: 'Is it possible she would have seen the truck, too?'

Teenager: 'Probably.'

Adult: 'Is there a chance she thought the truck was going to stop? And maybe he tried and hit the accelerator rather than the brake?'

Teenager: 'Maybe.'

Adult: 'If that's the case, could you or your sister have prevented the accident?'

Teenager: 'I guess not. I never looked at it from that point of view.'

To be an empathetic listener, you need to have a secure sense of your-self. That means 'letting go' of your immediate needs — not looking to be told how generous or kind you are or how much you are helping this child.

In addition, you must be able to stand alongside the grieving child and let her work through her grief. Inner strength and personal growth will come to her as she works through the problem. The highest gift you can give the struggling child is the chance to express herself and reach her own concl-usion about her needs and future.

Playful Ways to Get Children to Share

For several weeks, Martin had tried to talk to his 4-year-old daughter Jenny about his pending divorce from her mother. But every time he asked the child what she thought or how she felt, she'd look at him with her big brown eyes and say, 'I'm OK' and let her voice trail off wistfully. Martin didn't really think Jenny was OK, but he didn't know how to help her articulate her feelings.

Remember, if play is the work of childhood and grief is work, then given the opportunity, a child will grieve through play.

One morning, as they made the hour-long drive to Jenny's grandmother's house, Martin decided he would try once again to talk to his daughter. He reasoned that since they would be alone together on a long drive, he might succeed in getting her to open up. Since the traditional questions never seemed to work, he decided to try a different approach.

Since Jenny was a toddler, she and her dad had had a wonderful ritual of creating bedtime stories together. That morning, Martin decided to create a divorce story and see what happened.

'Hey, let's make up one of our famous stories,' he said to Jenny as he pulled onto the motorway.

The little girl was delighted.

'Once upon a time,' Martin began, 'there was a pretty little girl named Jenny. She had long brown hair and big brown eyes. And she was …?'

Jenny piped up, 'Four!'

Martin went on. 'And Jenny's mum and dad were getting …?'

'Divorced,' Jenny replied.

Martin continued. 'Since Mum and Dad were going to be living in separate houses, Jenny felt …?'

'Sad.' she said.

'Jenny was sad because …?'

'I'm sad because maybe I won't see my dad much and I will really miss him.'

And so the story went on through half the journey. As they talked, Martin didn't comment on or evaluate Jenny's responses. He simply listened.

'You know,' he said when they had finished. 'I love you very much and I will see you often.' Once again, Martin explained the details of the divorce: where he would be living, how far away it actually was and the planned times he would be with her. 'I'll be at every one of your school plays that I possibly can,' he promised. Jenny listened intently.

When they reached Grandma's, Jenny jumped out of the car and threw her arms around her father. 'I feel better now,' she said.

'Good. I do, too,' said Martin.

Talking to children about death, divorce or any other painful transition or crisis can be daunting. However, these crucial conversations can truly be child's play if we use four simple methods and techniques: stories, creative writing, role-playing or drama with props, and art and music.

STORIES

Creating, telling and reading stories appeals to children and teenagers alike. Here are several effective approaches, arranged by age.

Toddlers and pre-school age children: just as Marty did with Jenny, you can ask the child to make up a story with you about what has happened in the family. Or invite him to create his own story, one that begins: 'I wish ...' ; 'If only ...' ; or 'Once upon a time ...'.

Usually, the tale the child weaves reflects the events and emotions he is experiencing.

Pre-school and school-age children. Young children love having someone read to them. The local library and bookshop are good sources for storybooks about various loss events and feelings. Find one that is age- and loss-appropriate and read it to the child.

As you are reading, periodically ask the child if she ever felt or acted like the character in the book. If the child says no, ask if she understands why the character behaved a certain way or felt a particular feeling. You can also ask if she thinks she would do the same thing. If this approach triggers conversation between you and the child, let the discussion flow freely. Don't stop to finish the book and then expect to go back and continue the conversation. It just won't happen. The book is the vehicle to the conversation.

Pre-teens and adolescents. Find a book that deals with the teenager's loss event and buy it as a gift. Read it first to make sure it's appropriate and to garner discussion ideas, then give it to her. 'I was thinking of you when I saw this, and thought you might find it of interest,' you might say.

Because children are afraid of their painful feelings, it may take a while before she even looks at the book. She may even be upset with you for giving it to her. These are typical responses. Don't push. Keep the book out in the open or, if possible, put it in her bedroom. After a couple of weeks, ask if she's read it or make a comment about the content based on your initial review: 'You know, I wonder why the author felt ...' Eventually, the teenager will respond — even if only to say she completely disagrees with everything in the book! Don't be put off — she has just provided the seed for further discussion. 'Oh, and how would you handle the problem?' you might ask. Or, 'What would you tell someone in that situation?'

CONVERSATION GUIDELINES

Make sure the child feels comfortable and safe while the two of you talk. Here are a few strategies to make your conversation as productive as possible.

Make time to talk. Don't wait for opportunities to happen spontaneously. Cars are a great place for conversations with children – the space is confined and you are in control of the distractions. Turn on their favourite radio station, keep the volume low, and slowly move into the topic. Initially ask about other aspects of the child's life – school, friends, music, sports and so on. Translated to the child, your comments say: *Wow, she remembered* or *This person really cares about me.*

Open the dialogue about the loss event with simple, direct questions. They are the most effective. Try to be as specific as possible: 'How are you feeling about Grandpa's death?' The second question could be: 'What are some of the other feelings?'

Listen intently. Paying close attention helps you pick up on clues about unresolved issues and other things the child is thinking, wishing or believing.

Encourage the bereaved child to let you know what she needs. Assure her that it is OK to say: 'I need a hug' or 'I want to talk.'

Assure the child that healing takes a long time. Remind him that grieving is a process – not something to be done to a set timetable.

Nudge him when he gets stuck. Tell him, 'You're doing well.' Remind him to be kind to himself.

Stay in touch with the grieving child. Don't say, 'Call me if you need anything.' Instead, call her regularly.

CREATIVE WRITING

Writing is another non-threatening tool for children to use to express their feelings. There are many avenues available. Try using one or more of these:

Journals. Buy the child a diary or note book and encourage her to write an entry every day. You can offer suggestions on topics to write about, such as her loss, her memories and her hopes or dreams for the future.

Autobiography. Words, photos and pictures cut out from magazines can all be used in creating the child's life story.

Memory book. Provide a scrapbook and list of topics the child might consider in compiling favourite memories of a deceased loved one or life before the divorce or crisis.

Letters. Suggest the child write a letter to the person who has died, moved away, or been injured.

Writing serves several purposes. Keeping a journal helps the grieving child get his feelings out. Once the emotions of grief are expressed, they aren't so frightening. This is essential to *comprehending* and *mourning,* two essential steps to healing. An autobiography, memory book or letter helps in *commemorating* and *moving forward,* the other two crucial healing tasks that children must complete.

ROLE-PLAYING OR DRAMA WITH PROPS

Children are naturally imaginative, and fantasy is a powerful and safe tool for projecting feelings or worries. Props — like a hat, shawl or walking stick — help youngsters portray specific characters. If they don't want to act out a story, they can use puppets or stuffed animals as the main characters.

You can begin the activity by introducing a topic that deals with the loss event. For example, you might say:

'Let's do a play about Grandma.'

'Shall we pretend we are a family that is divorced? Who should be the mum and who should be the dad?'

'Let's do a radio interview about the flood. Do you want to be the reporter or the mayor?'

Let the child guide you. You can offer the suggestion and start, but it is up to her to respond. She may agree with the idea or propose an alternative topic.

ART AND MUSIC

At a grief workshop for teenagers, I handed out modelling clay and asked the youngsters to create images of their losses. The results were varied and incredibly poignant. One boy fashioned a heart with a hole through the middle. A 16-year-old girl carefully sculpted a heart and then ripped it into two pieces. Several of the young people made hearts with pieces missing. One boy took the piece of clay I'd given him, squished it into a ball and pounded the lump against the table. His 'heart' had no shape, but it surely represented his most intense internal feelings.

If only we ask them, grieving children will draw pictures of what they are thinking and feeling — dragons, swirling clouds, raging storms. They'll use colours to express emotions and fears. Red is anger! Blue is sadness!

Similarly, children can express their emotions through music. They don't need lessons, just props: drums for banging out anger; bells to toll sadness; cymbals to clang out their shock. The instruments can be used alone or in combination with stories to emphasize different parts of the tale being told or read.

Art and music can be used repeatedly as the child moves through the grieving process. Each time he allows some of his internal emotion to flow outward through creative expression, he is freed of a portion of his grief.

Each activity is simply a means to an end, a way to encourage a child to express his innermost feelings and fears. Thus, while engaging children in these playful routines, it's essential to ask what they are thinking, believing, feeling and needing.

Once their emotions and concerns are acknowledged, the children can begin to do the work that grief requires.

Chapter 9

Activities and Rituals for Healing

ONE WARM SPRING AFTERNOON, I sat with a group of children who'd each recently lost a parent to divorce or death. The children ranged in age from 9 to 11 and were participating in the RAINBOWS group at their school. Since the previous autumn, we'd met nearly every week to talk about their losses. During that time, we'd dealt with many difficult issues and our sessions had often prompted tears and elicited sad memories. The children were wonderful youngsters, bubbly and full of imagination. When we gathered, they invariably greeted me with brave smiles. Yet I saw the sorrow that lingered in their eyes. Each one of these boys and girls was still wrapped tightly in the mantle of grief, fearful of letting go, hanging on to the strange, melancholy comfort that sadness so artfully weaves around us.

'Today, we're going to have some fun and maybe do some magic,' I announced when they had put down their things and settled around the table where I was waiting. The children's faces brightened immediately. One little girl clapped her hands in delight. 'I love magic,' she said.

While the children looked on, I set out my props: a clear glass bowl, a jug of water and some bottles of food colouring.

'Ready?' They all nodded. As the children watched, I slowly poured the water into the bowl. When the container was half full, I stopped.

'We're going to pretend the water represents a happy heart,' I said. 'Can anyone tell me what types of feelings make our hearts happy?'

One hand after another shot up as the children chimed in with names of positive feelings: joy, laughter, love, pride.

'Now, how about examples of when you laughed or felt joyful or loved or were proud of something,' I continued. Again, they responded with a chorus of answers: a funny joke, a good school report, a birthday party, a new puppy, a visit from a friend.

When the children finally finished, I asked them for examples of things that cause us to be unhappy. Their faces grew solemn. We'd spent months talking about feelings, and much of the discussion had focused on sad events and memories. Anger was one important feeling they'd all shared. The children of divorce were angry with their parents because they had failed to stay together. One boy, whose father had died, was angry with his dad for deserting him.

He raised his hand and was the first to name something that could cause unhappiness. 'Being angry,' he said.

I nodded and invited him to choose a bottle of food colouring to represent how he was feeling. He picked the colour blue to represent his anger. Next, I asked him to put one drop of the dye into the bowl of clear water. As he did so, a ribbon of bright blue swirled into the bowl. Then the other children followed suit. Their list of sad feelings was very comprehensive: loneliness, fear, hate, jealousy. With each emotion named, the children shared an event that precipitated their feeling this way and dribbled food colouring into the bowl. As the dyes were added, the individual colours began to run into each other. By the time all of the children were finished, the clear water had grown dark and murky.

Several of the children made faces. 'That's yucky,' one girl said.

'Yes, it isn't very nice,' I agreed. 'But that shows how sad feelings can affect the 'colour' of our hearts.' The children nodded, and I knew that because of their own experiences they understood what I meant.

'But things can change,' I assured them. When we feel angry or sad or experience any unhappy emotion, we all have options about what to do with those feelings, I explained. 'We don't have to keep those feelings. We can forgive people for hurting or disappointing us. Then we can release these sad feelings and make them go away.'

To illustrate, I slowly poured two cups of 'forgiveness' (bleach) into the water. Like magic, the liquid began to lighten and brighten. The children watched quietly, never taking their eyes off the bowl. I continued adding the bleach until the bowl was full. Then I stirred the contents. Soon, the water was completely clear.

'When you have sad feelings inside, you have a choice,' I told the children. 'You can keep carrying them in your heart or you can let them go.' I gestured towards the bowl. 'Forgiving helps you to be happy inside again. When the sad feelings disappear, the good feelings inside you come back, just like the clear water here, and once again you have a happy heart.'

Ritual is a part of our lives, and healing activities, like the ceremony with the bleach and the bowl of discoloured water, have always been an integral part of RAINBOWS. We use rituals, games and activities in our group meetings because we see repeatedly how they help both children and teenagers process their grief and move on to full recovery.

To successfully work through their grief, children need to acknowledge and talk about the many painful emotions and experiences that loss entails. Although that may sound easy, it's not. Grieving youngsters are nervous, wary. They have already been hurt once by the loss event and don't want to endure more pain. Because of this, they will do anything to deny or avoid the hurtful feelings and memories roiling about inside their hearts and heads. Besides that problem, many children are ill-equipped to talk about feelings. Some don't know what words to use; others have been raised in an atmosphere that discourages or even forbids talking about personal emotions.

That's where ritual plays an essential role. Children heal by *doing*. Games and activities provide a familiar form and structure that help the grieving child feel comfortable about approaching even the most intimidating subjects. When children play games, they feel secure and safe. They're on familiar ground. Games and activities come with rules and directions; they establish parameters that make emotional chaos manageable.

Games and activities can teach children and teenagers to identify feelings and sort out the complex emotions that result from loss. Healing rituals are a vehicle for children to grieve.

The healing activities in this chapter address the different emotional issues that arise as children and adolescents move through the 10 phases of grief outlined in chapter 2. If you're unsure of the stage the child is currently working through, turn back to that chapter to reacquaint yourself with the telltale signs of each.

The games and rituals are tools designed to help you, as a compassionate companion, reach into the hearts and minds of grieving children who range in age from pre-school to adolescence. Some are drawn from the RAINBOWS programme and have been adapted for your use in one-on-one situations, and others have been created especially for this book so you can more easily assist grieving youngsters.

There's no correct order and no limit to how many times each can be played. However, it's important to set the right tone. Avoid using a sombre, now-we're-going-to-talk-about-grief approach. Instead, invite the child to join you in trying a new game you've discovered, or an interesting activity you've found.

Initially, the grieving child may resist participating or may respond at a superficial level. That's OK. It simply means she's not ready yet to talk about

THE HEALING BOX

You might find it helpful to gather up some or all of the materials used in the activities in this chapter and place them in a 'healing box'. That way, you'll have the materials ready when an opportunity presents itself. Plus, the presence of the box makes a visual statement to the child that you are always ready to listen to him whenever he is ready to talk about his feelings. This makes those moments less intimidating and more like play, which is what the child does best.

Here's a list of the items needed for the activities in this chapter. (Bear in mind that each child will naturally gravitate towards certain games and rituals rather than others, so you don't necessarily need each and every one of the items listed here.)

Bleach	Index cards	Pencils
Coins	Lollipop sticks	Pens
Crayons	Lunch bags	Scissors
Empty boxes	Markers	Scrap book
Felt squares	Modelling clay	Sequins
Food colouring	Old magazines	String
Glass bowl	Old socks	Tape
Glue	Paint	Toy phone
Graph paper	Paper	Wool

the hurtful issues and to face the pain inside. Please don't be discouraged. When the child is ready, when she feels comfortable, she will embrace the opportunity you are providing that allows her to confront her pain and move beyond it to the stage where she feels good about life and about herself. You'll see the transformation happening before your eyes.

The activities use many props and materials that can be gathered ahead of time and kept in a 'healing box'. Children and young teenagers enjoy working with props and arts-and-crafts materials. But older adolescents may consider these items juvenile and boring and may simply fumble with the pieces. If a child or teenager seems uninterested, put the game pieces aside and try simply to talk. After all, the trappings of the game aren't what matters. They are merely a means to helping the child confront and resolve the underlying grief issues and, ultimately, process his grief and heal the emotional pain of his loss.

Remember, too, that children associate games with winning or getting prizes. Giving a child a small reward (such as stickers, a small toy, a pack of chewing gum) when he has finished one of the activities is a good idea. By doing so, you acknowledge his efforts and also pave the way for the next time.

RED ALERT

Grief is individual. Every child, even members of the same family, will feel, think and respond differently to the same loss. Our role as compassionate companions is to be present for the child we are with. This means that we need to listen carefully to the child, paying close attention to his words, actions and body language. Even his writings and drawings can provide clues as to how the child is feeling inside.

It's especially important that you are aware of 'red flags' that are signs that the child needs additional help. Some of them are:

* Phrases like: 'I wish I had never been born.'

* Suicidal statements: 'I don't want to live any more.'

* Any comments about risky behaviour, such as drug-taking, alcohol or sex.

* Prolonged denial that the loss has occurred.

* The inability to heal from the loss (The child may exclaim, 'I'll never get over this!').

* Anger that frightens you.

When any of these red flags are raised, or you are simply not feeling comfortable with what a child is sharing, you must talk with her parent or caregiver or recommend therapy. It is always best to err on the side of the child's safety.

Healing Activities for Denial

At the first volleyball game of the autumn season, Ashley, aged 9, raced up to her coach. 'My dad's on a business trip. He can't be here today,' she said breathlessly.

In fact, Ashley's father had died earlier that month. And even though the young girl had attended both the wake and the funeral, she still could not accept the reality of what had happened. For several months, Ashley insisted that her dad was merely out of town 'on business' and would be home soon.

Underlying concern: denial allows the child to avoid the painful emotions that accompany loss. The grieving child often wants to stay in denial because the phase is non-threatening and comforting. To move past denial, the grieving child has to absorb the reality of the loss event and acknowledge that her life has changed because of it.

Objective: to help the grieving child face the truth. To do this, we must:

• Provide her with an age-appropriate vocabulary of words she can use to express both joy-filled and pain-filled feelings.

• Show her how to link feelings to events or incidents.

• Help him to relate his loss event to specific feelings.

• Create rituals that openly address the loss.

 LOLLIPOP PUPPETS

Ages: up to 7

Materials: four lollipop sticks, paper, markers or crayons

Directions: on the sheet of paper, print four pairs of contrasting feeling words, such as: happy/sad; love/hate; glad/angry; good/bad. Ask the child to draw a symbol or face to represent the feeling words. Cut out each and glue them to the lollipop sticks. For instance, on one side of stick one would be a smiley face and the word *happy*; on the other side of the stick would be a sad face below the word *sad*. Explain to the child that sometimes we feel one way and sometimes we feel the other, depending on what's happened.

How to play: describe a series of different incidents (some positive and some negative) and ask the child to use one of the puppet faces to show how she might feel if that happened to her. Eventually, include the child's specific loss event (your mummy and daddy divorced, or whatever loss recently occurred).

Examples:

'You dropped your ice cream cone. How did you feel?'

'You got your bicycle fixed. How did you feel?'

'You broke your doll. How did you feel?'

'You went to a birthday party. How did you feel?'

'You found a coin on the pavement. How did you feel?'

'It rained all day. How did you feel?'

'The day that your mummy died, how did you feel?'

When the grieving child has gone as far as she can with this ritual, she may tune out and stop talking. She may even get up, walk away and start another activity. That's OK; it simply means she's had enough for now. Remember, children cannot sustain the intense feelings of grief for very long.

FEELINGS FLASHCARDS

Ages: all ages

Materials: blank index cards, marker or pen, discarded magazines, glue or tape

Directions: create a set of flashcards that depict both joy-filled and pain-filled feelings.

• For younger children, use pictures cut from magazines.

* For older children and teenagers, write one age-appropriate 'feeling' word on each card. 'Vocabulary of Feelings' overleaf suggests 140 words and phrases from which to choose.

How to play: shuffle the cards. Show the cards to the child one at a time. Ask him to read the feeling word out loud or describe the feeling being shown in the picture and recall a time when he experienced that emotion.

THE STATUE OF FEELING

Ages: all ages

Materials: modelling clay or plasticine

How to play: give the child a lump of modelling clay and ask him to shape it into a symbol of a feeling, event or place that represents the change in his family structure.

If the child is having trouble getting started, you can ask him questions, such as:

'What kinds of negative changes have happened because of the loss?'

'Are there any positive changes for you?'

'How did you feel about the loss when it happened?'

'How do you feel about it today?'

When the child is finished, ask him to explain what the statue means.

SAYING GOODBYE

A child who does not attend the funeral of a loved one can easily deny the reality of what has happened. Each of the following rituals and activities allow the child to say farewell, gently bringing him face-to-face with the loss event. Let the child choose which she would prefer doing.

VOCABULARY OF FEELINGS

Joy-filled words

able	enthusiastic	outstanding
accepted	esteemed	patient
active	excited	pleased
admired	fond	popular
alert	friendly	positive
alive	glad	rejoicing
appreciated	good	remarkable
attractive	grateful	relieved
better	great	respected
brave	happy	satisfied
bright	hopeful	secure
capable	important	self-sufficient
cared for	included	sensitive
cheerful	independent	strong
comfortable	intelligent	tender
confident	interested	terrific
courage	joyful	vital
curious	knowing	wanted
delighted	liked	warm
determined	lively	welcomed
eager	loved	worthy
elated	notable	
empathy	optimistic	
enjoy	outgoing	

- Go together to the cemetery, and let the child bring something to leave behind: flowers to plant, a small flag, a token gift or hand-drawn picture, a letter she's written to the deceased, or a small, symbolic memento from home. Remind the child that the token item will be carried away or eroded by the wind or weather.

- Have the child write a note to or draw a picture for the deceased, conveying his thoughts, feelings and words of goodbye. Tie the note or

Pain-filled words

abandoned	fed up	shocked
accused	frustrated	shy
afraid	furious	stupid
alarmed	gloomy	suspicious
angry	guilty	tempted
anxious	hate	tense
apprehensive	helpless	terrified
ashamed	hopeless	tired
bad	humiliated	torn up
bashful	impatient	trapped
bitter	inadequate	troubled
bored	left out	uncomfortable
confused	like giving up	unhappy
depressed	listless	unloved
despised	lonely	unpopular
difficult	miserable	upset
disappointed	mixed up	useless
discouraged	pain	vengeful
disgusted	put down	weak
doubtful	reluctant	worn-out
dreadful	resentful	worried
embarrassed	sad	worthless
envious	scared	
exhausted	self-conscious	

picture to a helium balloon and release it either at the cemetery or a special place the child chooses for the occasion.

- Invite the child to create a personal memorial service; this can be held at home, in the garden, a park or the cemetery — wherever the child chooses. Ask the child to write an epitaph for the gravestone.

- Ask the child to write the life story of the deceased and then tell what has happened to the family since the person's death. The story can include poignant or funny memories and relate what's missed most about the deceased. Afterwards, you can have a special ceremony at the graveside, beach, or any other special place. This story can be buried, burned, tied to a balloon and released to the sky, or taken back home and saved.

Healing Activities for Bargaining

Two weeks after his father moved out in what his parents called a 'trial separation', 10-year-old Daniel wrote his dad a letter. In a mix of childish joined-up writing and printing, he begged his father to come home: 'I'll be good,' Daniel wrote. 'I'll clean my room and do the washing up. I'll never talk back again.'

Later, Daniel took a bus to his father's workplace and left the letter with his dad's secretary. He did this, he said, to make sure the letter didn't get lost in the post.

Underlying concern: a child thinks that by striking the right deal with his parents, God or whomever, he can stop his mum and dad from divorcing or separating or he can protect a terminally ill family member or friend from death.

Objective: to teach the child that he has no influence over adult matters or certain kinds of natural events.

 'IF I WERE A SUPERHERO ...'

Ages: 5 to 10

Materials: paper, pen or pencil, an envelope or bag

Directions: on separate sheets of paper, write out the names of events that could occur in a child's life over which he would have no control, such as natural disasters, community crises, a parent losing his job, a death, a divorce or an aeroplane crash. Try to include some events that have happened in the past year or two that the child can remember, and be sure to include the loss the child has personally experienced. Place the sheets of paper in an envelope or paper bag.

How to play: ask the child to describe his favourite superhero. Encourage him to tell you what qualities he admires in this person. Next, ask the child what powers he would like to possess.

Finally, have the child pull a slip of paper from the envelope or bag. Tell him he is the superhero who must use the powers about which he fantasized earlier to 'fix' the problem or situation. The goal is to guide the child into the realization that even a superhero can't fix everything. And certainly neither can a child.

'THAT'S LIFE' CARD GAME

Ages: all ages

Materials: eight blank index cards, marker or pen

Directions: ask the child to name eight important life events. The situations should include both happy and sad events, such as marriage, death, divorce, war, earthquake, leaving school, passing the driving test, moving to a new house, first date. Write one event on each card.

How to play: the dealer shuffles the cards and gives four to each player. The adult chooses a card from the child's hand, reads the card out loud, and lays it right side up on the table. Then the adult asks a series of questions about the event, encouraging the child to talk about the event: what he thinks about it, how he would feel if it happened to him and coping strategies to survive such events. The activity should lead to back-and-forth dialogue about the life event that is being discussed. Then the child takes a card from the adult's hand and asks the adult questions about the event.

Suggested questions:

'What causes _____?'

'How could we stop _____ from happening?'

'If not us, who could change or alter it in any way?'

'Is there any way we can prevent _____?'

'If you did have the influence, what could you do?'

'What could be positive results of _____?'

Healing Activities for Guilt

Douglas was 5 years old when his father was paralysed in a car crash. Several months after the accident, I talked to Doug about what had happened.

'If I'd only gone with my dad, he wouldn't have been hurt,' the boy insisted, his voice brimming with urgency. 'If I'd been in the car, I could have stopped the accident. I just know it.'

'Do you know how to drive a car?' I asked Douglas quietly.

The freckle-faced youngster shook his head and clenched his hands into tight fists.

'Could your feet have reached the pedals and pushed the brakes?'

'No,' he whispered and slouched lower into the chair.

Slowly I leaned towards the silent child and folded my hands over his. 'Doug, sometimes things just happen and there's nothing we can do.'

Underlying concern: because of the stage he's at developmentally, a child inhabits a small, self-centred world. In his universe, he wields ultimate control. Unfortunately, when loss occurs, he feels that he was somehow responsible for the tragedy.

Objective: to help children to acknowledge what happened, to understand the reasons for it happening, and to realize they didn't have the power to change the course of events.

 ## SOCK PUPPETS

> *Ages*: pre-school to 10 or 11 years
>
> *Materials*: two clean, discarded socks; markers
>
> *Directions*: ask the child to draw a face on each sock.

How to play: each player chooses a sock puppet. Then the puppet held by the adult questions the other puppet about the child's loss.

Suggested questions:

'I know that (name the loss event). How is it for you?'

'Can you tell me what happened?'

'Why do you think this happened?'

'What is the hardest part of ____?'

'What would make it easier for you?'

'What do you need?'

NOUGHTS AND CROSSES YES OR NO

Ages: all ages

Materials: paper, pencil or pen, coin

Directions: draw a noughts and crosses board with squares large enough to accommodate the coin you are using. Explain to the child that this is a different kind of noughts and crosses in which no one wins or loses. It is a game in which we get to talk about blame.

How to play: have the child choose X or O and toss the coin on to the game board. After the coin lands successfully on an open square, select one of the scenarios below to read to the child (or make up others that are appropriate for the child) and ask if she believes she is to blame for what happened in that situation. If she says 'yes' she marks the square after she answers.

You promise to walk the dog, but forget to.

Your mum becomes ill.

Your mum shouts at your dad.

Your sister cries when you tease her.

Your room is a mess.

Your dad moves out.

You lose a favourite toy.

Your grandmother seems sad.

After each question, ask her about her answers. For example: 'What could you do that would cause your grandmother to be sad?' 'If your sister cries when you tease her, what do you think you should do?' Listen deeply to what she has to say, without trying to correct her. If a question arises that she cannot seem to answer, take the time to talk it through, even if you never talk about any other scenarios. *Never force a child to talk.* If she simply does not want to discuss a particular scenario, make a mental note of the topic to revisit it at another time and proceed with your turn. If the child does not feel to blame, talk about who is responsible.

When it is your turn, toss the coin on a block and have the child read you a scenario. Your participation will keep the conversation more open and give her the chance to see what you think about things in your life. It may take a few tosses of the coin each turn to find a blank spot and the two of you may not achieve a full line. The game is over when either a winning line or a full game board is achieved.

 THE PHONE CALL

Ages: all ages

Materials: play phones or handpieces from real phones, if available

How to play: adult and child have a pretend telephone conversation about a problem or situation. The child plays himself and the adult plays the role of the real-life person the child wants to talk to about the problem.

If a play or real telephone isn't available, simply pretend with your hands that you're holding a phone and 'call' the child. Young children especially enjoy the motions and words that go with a phone conversation:

'Ring. Ring. Hello. Who is it? May I talk to _____ please ? This is _____ and I'm calling because I heard you're worried about _____. Why don't you tell me about it?'

Encourage the child as he starts talking. Remember, the goal is to let the child 'practice' or 'run through' what's on his mind. The activity boosts the child's self-confidence and gives him courage to have a real conversation about whatever's bothering him with the person he said he wanted to talk to. In the case of a death, the child can pretend he's talking to the deceased person. Be especially aware of any feelings of guilt the child might express.

Healing Activities for Fear

After her grandfather died, 8-year-old Carla was extremely sensitive to any mention of illness in the family. When her mother caught the flu, the child immediately collared her dad: 'Is that something you can die from?' she asked anxiously. Later, Carla's aunt underwent routine surgery for carpal tunnel syndrome. 'Why did she have to go the hospital?' Carla wanted to know. 'She won't die, will she?'

Underlying concern: for children, loss generates fear on many levels.

• Fear of the unknown. Life has changed; the future becomes uncertain.

• Fear that 'it' will happen again. Dad moved out; will Mum go too? Last spring, a fire destroyed the school; will there be another fire?

• Fear that there's no responsible adult left to take care of them. Children are afraid that the key people they have depended on in the past can't or won't help them any more.

Objective: To help grieving children and teenagers distinguish between imagined fears (situations that can't hurt them) and real fears (situations that are of real concern).

WHAT'S REAL?

Ages: all ages

Materials: one paper bag, one piece of wool or string (45 to 60 cm/ 18 to 24 inches long), small note cards or pieces of paper, pens or pencils

Directions: both adult and child write down their fears and worries on the pieces of paper (one concern per piece) and then drop the papers into the paper bag. (Children find it comforting to know that adults have fears, too. So in this activity, your honesty is really helpful to them.)

How to play: lay the string or wool on the floor or table in front of the players to form a dividing line between real and imaginary fears.

Shake up the bag with the slips of paper. Players take turns pulling out the pieces of paper one by one. Each time a fear is revealed, the players decide on which side of the dividing line to put it.

When the bag is empty, ask the child to stuff the imaginary fears back in the bag and to toss the bag in the bin. 'Throwing away' the unreal fears means the child doesn't have to worry about them any more.

What are left are the 'real' fears. Although some may be easy to resolve, others might prove quite formidable. Help the child to carefully think through each concern and to identify the resources he can use to successfully cope with each situation. For example:

'Who can help tutor you so you won't fail maths?'

'Who can you call when Dad comes home drunk?'

'What should you eat if Mum forgot to make dinner?'

When you've finished, put the slips of paper with 'real fears' in a special bag or box and assure the child that you'll review the problems together at a later date, 'to see if we've handled them correctly'.

What if you're completely stumped by a problem or situation? Suggest that you both take time to think about a solution.

'Where can we get the help we need on this?'

'We may not have the answer, but someone else does; we need to figure out who that person is.'

Make a date to get together soon to discuss your ideas.

'THE WISEST LINK'

Ages: all ages (this game usually works best with two or more children, but can be played with only one)

Materials: strips of paper, pens or pencils, a paper bag or small box

Directions: give the children several strips of paper and ask them to write out any questions they may have about the personal crisis or loss they are experiencing. When they've finished, they put the questions in the box or bag and then shake it up.

How to play: starting with the youngest, have the children take turns pulling out a question and reading it out loud. If someone knows the answer, he or she can jump up and tell the others. Reward each correct answer with a small prize (sweets, coins or one less chore that week). If none of the children know the answer, then the adult responds.

If there is no 'correct' or one answer to a question (for example: 'What is heaven?'), each person gets a chance to respond.

Healing Activities for Anger

Since he started school, Bradley had been friends with boys from many different ethnic and racial groups at his large and diverse urban school. Bradley, who is Afro-Caribbean and the son of a police officer, was in the first year of secondary school when his father was stabbed and critically wounded when a demonstration got out of hand at the local mosque.

For several days, Bradley didn't go to school and shuttled back and forth to the hospital with his mother. Seeing his father lying helpless and linked to half a dozen tubes was a frightening experience for the boy. 'Dad's going to be fine,' his mum said, but Bradley heard the worry in her voice.

Finally, Bradley went back to school. All morning, he was rude to his Muslim friends and refused to eat lunch at the same table. When one of them called him at home that evening, he wouldn't come to the phone. Two days later, he got into a fight with the boy who had called.

'This is about your father, isn't it?' Bradley's mother asked after she was called to school to pick up her son.

Bradley shrugged.

'You think you have to be angry with your friends because of the guy who knifed your dad?'

'They're not my friends!' Bradley yelled at his mum. 'They just pretended they liked me. I hate them, all of them! I want to go a different school. I don't want to ever see any of them again.'

Underlying concern: the reality of the loss or crisis has settled in. The divorce, death, fire or move is a truth that can't be denied. The realization that he can't change what has happened fuels the child's anger over the loss event and the changes that have occurred in his life because of it.

Objective: these activities have a multiple objective.

1. To help the child identify (name) the cause of his anger and to affirm that he has the right to be angry. Anger is a normal response to loss; it's a sign that we are upset about what has happened.

2. To discover how the grieving child handles his anger. (Many children act out their rage with destructive, threatening behaviour. Younger children might hit a sibling or friend, kick the dog, break a toy or tear a page from a book. Pre-adolescents and teenagers might shoplift, smoke, start drinking alcohol or play truant.)

3. To teach the child appropriate ways of coping with anger, which might include punching a pillow, riding a bike, kicking a football, running or other physical activity, using a punchbag, writing a letter to the person who upset them, throwing water-filled balloons at a tree or other harmless object that represents the anger, or filling a water gun with food colouring and squirting it at a tree or other chosen object.

🎲 ANGER TOWER

Ages: up to 8

Materials: 5 to 10 boxes of various sizes, such as jewellery boxes, shoe boxes, and large cardboard boxes from the supermarket

How to play: ask the child or children one at a time to say out loud what they are angry, upset, or feel hurt about. As each child speaks, she chooses the box that is the right size to contain her anger. When she's finished, she puts the box down. If they wish, the other children can comment about her situation and offer suggestions on how she can handle her feelings of distress. Otherwise, the play moves on to the next child. When he's finished, he puts his box on top of the first and so on as the game moves around the circle.

When all the boxes are piled into a tower, invite the children to knock it down — they can kick the boxes or push over the tower. It's a wonderful activity for getting children to articulate their anger and then providing them with a safe way of lashing out and expressing their feelings.

🎲 ANGER CHAIN

Ages: pre-school to 10 or 11 years

Materials: markers, glue, craft paper in a variety of colours

How to play: ask the child to think about people or circumstances that upset him or hurt his feelings. If he wants, he can assign a specific colour to each person or circumstance. For example:

brothers = red	parents = blue
sisters = yellow	friends = purple
chores = green	school = brown

After choosing the colours that fit his reasons for being hurt or angry (or any others not mentioned above), ask the child to cut the coloured paper into strips. Then make him glue the strips together end-to-end, or first glue each strip into a circle and attach each circle to the next to make a chain. Each piece of paper represents a person, thing, or event that upsets him. The child can write or draw the event on the paper or just keep the symbolism confidential.

As the child is assembling the chain, encourage him to talk about the object he is making. Link by link, ask him what caused him to be upset and how he handled the distress the last time. Reinforce good coping mechanisms and suggest alternative, constructive activities that he could try in place of any negative or destructive behaviour.

 Graffiti Wall

Ages: pre-teen to adolescence

Materials: large sheet of paper (e.g. wallpaper), pen, markers

How to play: the youngster creates his own graffiti wall of anger on the paper. On the top half of the page, he writes, scribbles or draws the people and things that make him angry.

On the bottom half, he writes out positive ways he can deal with each anger situation he's put on the wall.

Healing Activities for Isolation

When Jared's father died, life seemed to end for the 9-year-old boy. His mother stopped cooking and cleaning; some days she didn't even get out of bed in the morning. Jared's teenage brother began to hang out late into the night with his friends, drinking beer. Neither of them ever mentioned Jared's father.

Christmas came one month after the funeral. This had always been a special time for the family. But that year, there was no tree and no gifts. In the morning, Jared went to church by himself. Later, at noon, he made a peanut butter sandwich and ate a lonely lunch in the deserted kitchen. Although Jared waited all day for his aunts, uncles and cousins to visit, no one came to the house. That evening, Jared went down to the cellar, where his father's model train collection was stored. One by one, he pulled out the engines and carriages, hugged them to his chest and began to talk about his dad, his voice echoing softly in the empty room.

Underlying concern: for many reasons, including cultural traditions and family dynamics, a grieving child may be denied the opportunity to talk about his loss.

Objective: to find out whom grieving children can talk to about different aspects of their lives.

TRUST BUS

Ages: pre-school to 8 years

Materials: 'Trust Bus' picture, paper, crayons, markers

How to play:

1. Trace or copy the Trust Bus picture.

2. Have the child fill in the faces and write in the names of the people he trusts.

3. Ask him to name the things he can talk about with each person on his bus.

WORD SEARCH

Ages: pre-teen to adolescence

Materials: Word Search Puzzle (opposite), pencil

How to play: the child reads each question on the puzzle page. Then she underlines the name of the person or thing that answers it and circles the words in the puzzle.

THE JOURNAL

Ages: all ages

Materials: blank manuscript books or journals, pen or pencil

Here's how: immediately after a loss event (or before, if you can antici-pate the loss) give the child the journal and writing or drawing materials. Explain that it's for her thoughts, memories, fears, dreams and hopes for the future — to be expressed any way she wishes (prose, poetry or pictures). This is an extremely powerful gift.

Healing Activities for Pining

Four-year-old Grace rarely saw her parents. Her father frequently travelled on business, and her mother's time was taken up with to a busy schedule of lunches, charity dinners, concerts and gallery openings around town.

WORD SEARCH PUZZLE

Ask yourself the following questions. Then underline the answer from the list below. Finally, search for the words in the puzzle and circle them.

Questions:

Who do I talk to when I'm happy?
Where do I go when I'm sad?
Who listens to me?
Who do I talk to about the change in my family?
Who understands my feelings?
Who do I want to talk to?
Who makes me laugh?
Who makes me feel good about myself?

Answers:

aunt	mother	school	friend	neighbour
uncle	father	church	park	temple
sister	teacher	library	grandma	
brother	coach	room	grandpa	

X	F	I	D	X	L	S	R	P	E	T	H
R	R	H	E	C	I	O	A	W	N	J	U
E	I	C	G	B	B	F	G	U	H	J	J
H	E	W	H	H	R	R	A	P	C	X	I
T	N	T	G	U	A	P	D	N	A	R	G
O	D	I	E	N	R	R	E	R	O	R	U
M	E	Y	D	A	Y	C	E	L	C	S	K
N	T	M	Y	D	C	H	H	T	C	G	B
P	A	B	R	O	T	H	E	R	S	N	U
R	O	O	M	A	S	Q	E	H	W	I	U
P	B	B	F	N	P	J	S	R	G	R	S
S	C	H	O	O	L	E	L	P	M	E	T

Although Grace wasn't physically abandoned, she certainly was emotionally deserted and felt she was unloved and unwanted. One day, sitting at her mother's dressing table, Grace found a tissue her mother had used to blot her lipstick. The white sheet bore a perfect red imprint of her mother's mouth. Grace picked up the tissue and touched the lip print to her cheek, imagining her mother by her side. It was a reassuring feeling. Grace hid the tissue in a drawer and kept it for a very long time. Often, when her mother was gone for long periods, Grace held the paper handkerchief to her cheek, comforted by the memories of her mother that it evoked for her.

Underlying concern: the grieving child who pines for the person who is missing from her life craves a comforting, tangible reminder of the individual she has lost.

Objective: to help the grieving child create a tangible memorial of the loved one who is absent from her life.

MEMORY BOX OR MEMORY BOOK

Ages: all ages

Materials: small box with a lid, scrapbook or blank manuscript book

Here's how: the grieving child uses the book or box to organize and save pictures or written reminiscences, photos and souvenirs that remind her of the person she longs for.

Here are some suggested items to include.

A small item of favourite clothing

Ticket stubs from a concert, film or event they attended together

Photographs

A list of the person's favourite foods or songs

Stories about the person who is gone

A page of special memories

A written description of or story about the person being remembered (including both positive and negative characteristics)

A drawing of the person

A letter from the child to the person who is gone

Sympathy cards, a copy of the death announcement or other items from the funeral that the child wants to keep

The Memory Book or Box is a dynamic creation. It may change over time as the child matures.

PORTRAIT OF A LOVED ONE

Ages: all ages

Materials: paper or canvas, markers, crayons, paints

Here's how: the grieving child draws a picture of the deceased and chooses a special frame. The framed picture is hung in any room the child chooses. (This can also be done with a favourite photo.)

LOVING REMEMBRANCES

Children and teenagers can participate in creating special ways to remember the loved one who has died. Here are some suggestions:

• For festivities and special occasions, ask the children to pick out a candle for the deceased to be lit at home in memory of the deceased.

• Plan an outing or memorial service to mark the loved one's birthday, anniversary of their death, or other special occasion. Take the children out of school for the day; talk about the deceased.

• Invite the child or teenager to choose one or two items that belonged to the deceased that they want to keep as a 'for ever treasure'.

Healing Activities for Belonging

For the four years following her parents' divorce, 15-year-old Ali shuttled back and forth between her mother's house and her father's flat. At first she'd been the focus of attention in each household. But slowly things changed. Her mum remarried and spent more time with her new husband than with Ali. Her dad had a steady girlfriend and was rarely at home any more.

Most weekends and evenings, Ali drifted between the shopping centre and friends' houses. She began to have sex with older boys in the neighbourhood. At 16, Ali was pregnant — and thrilled. 'I want a baby,' the teenager told one of her teachers. When asked why, she said simply: 'Because then I'll have someone I belong to, someone to love and someone who loves me back.'

Underlying concern: so much has changed that the grieving child barely recognizes her life. Often, she feels like an outsider — especially if there are new people involved in her parents' lives.

Objective: to show the grieving child that even though her life and some of the people in it have changed, she still belongs.

BELONGING BINGO

Ages: pre-school to 10 or 11

Materials: paper, marker or pen, small coins, small prizes (optional)

Directions: trace the prototype 'Belonging Bingo' card on a sheet of paper (or make copies from the book).

How to play: Have the child fill in each blank with the name of a place he goes to (school, scouts, park, gym and so on) or the name of an activity he participates in (football, maths club, hockey and so forth).

When the card is ready, ask the child questions that he can answer using the words in the squares.

B	I	N	G	O
		FREE		

Suggested questions:

'Where do you feel you're accepted?'

'Where is it you're comfortable?'

'Where do you feel safe?'

'Where do you feel listened to?'

'Where do you feel uncomfortable?'

'Where do you feel liked?'

'Where do you feel loved?'

'Where do you feel happy?'

'Where do you feel relaxed?'

'Where do you feel welcome?'

'Where do you feel appreciated?'

Each time the child answers a question, he covers the appropriate square with a coin. When the child has five coins in a row or on a diagonal, the child yells 'Bingo!' and either gets to keep the coins or is rewarded with a small prize, such as a pack of chewing gum or stickers.

ROAD MAP DETOURS

Ages: pre-teen to adolescence

Materials: Road Map of Life, pencil or pen

Directions: trace the map or make copies of the page.

How to play: this activity helps the teenager create a chronological time line of changes in her life through the metaphor of a map. Starting with Event 1, get the teenager to fill in each blank rectangle with a significant family change she's experienced.

Then, underneath each change, have the teenager write down the adjustments she's made that help her deal with the situation.

LOVING LEGACIES

After a loss, children often feel adrift. We can take steps to help them feel anchored and centred.

• Letters and stories are powerful tools for forging a bond with children. By writing a letter to a beloved child, a critically ill family member or friend can create an invaluable treasure for the child to cherish for years to come. Parents can do the same before, during, or after a divorce.

ROAD MAP OF LIFE

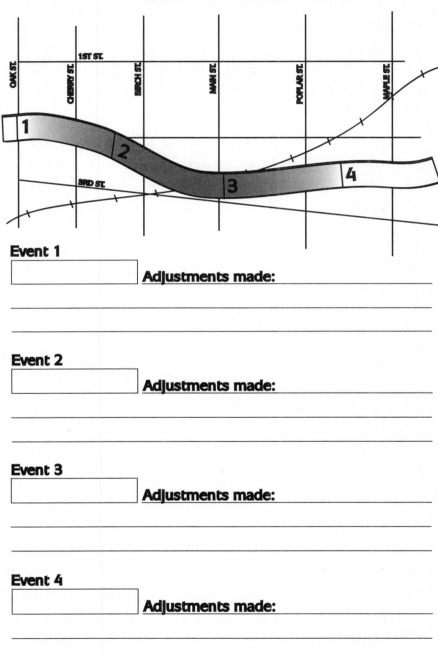

Event 1

| | Adjustments made: |

Event 2

| | Adjustments made: |

Event 3

| | Adjustments made: |

Event 4

| | Adjustments made: |

- Ask friends of the deceased to write letters to the children so they will have remembrances of their absent loved one.

- Tape record or video tape family members as they recall important, funny or poignant moments of the family's history. Adults who are not comfortable being taped can write their stories to be passed on.

Healing Activities for Depression and Sadness

Jordan was 7 when she started playing volleyball. The tiny, athletic girl was passionate about the sport and by the age of 12 was on a team that practiced and played all year round. At the age of 15, Jordan was captain of her school team. The next year she joined the regional team, and her teacher began talking about a potential sports scholarship. Then, Jordan's left knee began to give way. After every practice and game she was confined to the sofa with an ice pack on her sore knee. Three operations in less than 18 months did not help to correct the situation. The cartilage was worn away, the doctor said. Jordan's volleyball career was over. 'But volleyball is my life,' the teenager wailed.

At home, the friendly, outgoing adolescent became sullen and withdrawn. She spent hours in her room listening to music. She stopped calling her close friends, all of whom were on the team, and had little to say when they came to visit. When questioned by her parents, Jordan insisted she was fine. 'I don't care about volleyball — it doesn't matter,' she said. Once driven and focused, Jordan was listless and lost.

Underlying concern: the grieving child feels overwhelmed by the conflicting emotions and lifestyle changes associated with the loss event. Life feels out of control.

Objective: to help the grieving child to process her pain, let go of negative feelings and feel empowered and whole again.

 PAPER PROFILE

>   *Ages*: all ages
>
>   *Materials*: sheet of paper, scissors
>
>   *How to play*: hold up the sheet of paper and explain that it represents the child before the loss event.
>
>   Ask the child to fold the paper into as many squares as possible.
>
>   Ask her to name a thing or event that has hurt or upset her. When she does, have her make a cut into or snip off a corner of the folded paper.
>
>   Repeat until the child has identified all the things that have been bothering her.
>
>   Carefully unfold the paper. Let the child see that even though the sheet of paper has been altered by the snipping and cutting, it is still the same piece of paper. Similarly, even though she has been affected by the changes in her life, she remains the same unique and wonderful person she was before the loss event. Loss has affected her life, but not changed who she is.

LOVE BOX

Keep all of the support cards and letters that are received immediately after the death of a loved one; add others that are sent later. Store them in a box — a 'love box' — to reread on days when your children and you are down in the dumps about the death of the loved one. The many cards and notes comprise a wonderful testament to the deceased's life and will really pull you up and out of your sadness!

Healing Activities for Accepting Loss

T.J. was 10 when his parents divorced. The youngest of three boys, he was the most distressed by the event. For years, T.J. fantasized that his mum and dad would remarry. Every time money was tight or his mother seemed particularly worn out by the challenges of being a single parent, T.J. reminded her that if she hadn't got divorced, life would be easier. For years, he demanded answers to hard questions: 'Why did you divorce Dad?' 'How can two people stop loving each other?' 'Didn't you ever think about how this would affect your children?'

When T.J. was 16, his General Studies course included researching and writing an essay on 'The Morality of Divorce'. The boy spent hours in the library reading and digging up statistics and analysed the subject from both a religious and societal perspective. When he finished writing, T.J. asked his mother to type his essay. She expected to read a diatribe against divorce, a veiled condemnation of her for having left T.J.'s dad. Instead, she found that her son had written a well-considered and balanced analysis of a complex issue. His last sentence was especially telling and revealed how far he had come in accepting the bitter reality of his parents' situation and decision. 'Divorce,' T.J. wrote, 'is a painful solution to an otherwise unsolvable problem.'

Underlying concern: although the grieving child doesn't like the changes that have occurred in his life, he is able to acknowledge them.

Objective: to help the child learn to live with the changes in his life.

CREATE A FAMILY COAT OF ARMS

Ages: pre-school to 12 or 13

Materials: felt, markers, crayons, sequins, scissors, glue

Here's how: explain to the child that long ago, many aristocratic families had coats of arms to proclaim the family motto and portray the family's unique characteristics.

Because the loss event has changed her family structure, she needs to think of her family unit in a new way.

What motto best describes her new family unit? What are the characteristics that make her new family structure unique or special? Use these to create a family coat of arms.

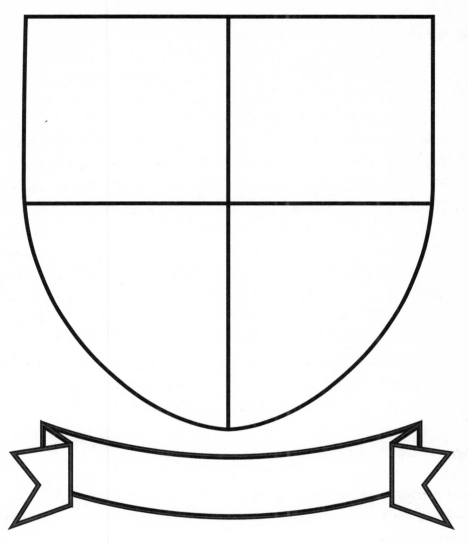

1. Trace the coat of arms pattern onto the felt and cut out the shapes.

2. With as little help from you as possible, let the child decorate the shield so it represents her concept of her new family unit.

 SMART CHOICES 'VIDEO' GAME

Ages: pre-teen to adolescence

Materials: paper, pen or pencil

Directions: the grieving teenager uses the template opposite to create a non-violent 'video' game that focuses on smart choices and positive steps. The object of the game is to help the robot move through three obstacles of his choice. In the boxes marked 1, 2 and 3, the teenager draws creatures that represent his feelings about three obstacles in his life. The first level represents an 'annoying' obstacle, the second a 'serious' obstacle and the third a 'monstrous' obstacle.

How to play: ask the teenager to think about positive ways he would handle each obstacle. Starting with Level 1, have him write down at least one positive thing that will help him overcome this obstacle. Then do the same for Levels 2 and 3. Ask him to show how his suggestions can help the robot overcome the obstacles.

LET'S MAKE LEMONADE

Ages: all ages

Materials: glass of water, lemon (cut in half), sugar, teaspoon

How to play: pretend the glass of water represents the child. Ask her to think about and say out loud the names of the people, things and events that have made her sad. Each time she names someone or something, have her squeeze a few drops of lemon juice into the water. When she's finished, let her taste the mixture she's created. She'll probably make a face because the mixture is sour. Now, ask the child to consider what would happen if she let go of those unhappy feelings.

Pretend the sugar represents acceptance. Add a teaspoon or more of sugar to the water, stir, and let her taste it again. Ask her how the sugar changed the taste of the lemon water and how she thinks acceptance might make her feel.

SMART CHOICES

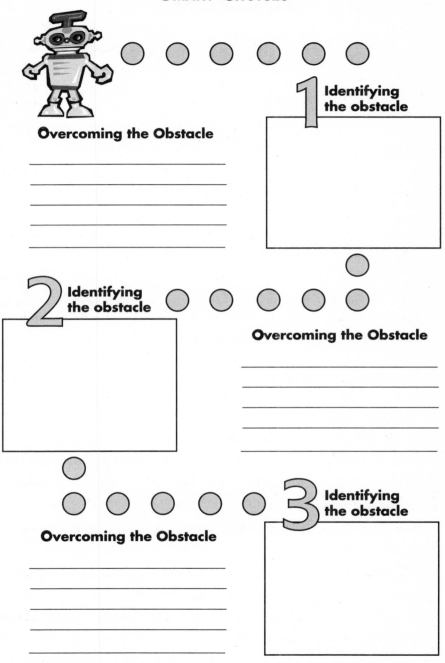

Overcoming the Obstacle

_____
_____
_____
_____
_____

1 Identifying
the obstacle

2 Identifying
the obstacle

Overcoming the Obstacle

_____
_____
_____
_____
_____

Overcoming the Obstacle

_____
_____
_____
_____
_____

3 Identifying
the obstacle

Sunny Day/Rainy Day Activities

We can take advantage of quiet afternoons and lulls in our busy schedules to touch base with the children and get a pulse on their feelings. Here are helpful 'spur-of-the-moment' activities for children, regardless of what stage of grieving they're currently working through.

For children up to the age of eight:

• Buy or make bubbles with washing-up liquid to blow in the garden or at the park. Suggest that each bubble contains a dream or hope for the future.

• Hand out pieces of thick coloured chalk and invite your child or children to become a pavement artist for the day. The challenge: to decorate the driveway or pavement with BIG pictures of feelings, family and so on.

• Spend an hour playing 'dolls' house' with your young child or children. Introduce loss-related topics like visiting rights (after a divorce) or a funeral (after a death) to help children sort out their feelings and work through their confusion.

All ages:

• Whenever you pass a fountain or wishing well, give the children coins to toss in and use to make a wish. Invite them to share their dreams with you.

• Invite everyone to draw a 'family portrait'. Let each child decide who's included and who is not.

• Invite the children to use pictures cut from magazines and newspapers to create a collage representing their family, their loss and their dreams of the future. Use the finished product as a conversation starter. You can make a collage, too, and compare.

♡♡ HEALING CELEBRATIONS AND RITUALS

Celebrations are a special part of life, and they can be a valuable way to remember a person who is gone from our lives as well as a unique healing tool to create new, positive memories.

To celebrate the family, start new rituals: have pizza every Friday, make Saturday breakfast croissant time, prepare Sunday brunch together — even the youngest can help. After a death, these times can be used to specifically talk about — or not talk about — the deceased. After a divorce, they can be used to talk about future plans.

To celebrate a deceased loved one, try one of these rituals.

* On the deceased's special days — birthdays, anniversary of their death — have a party in that person's honour. Prepare the person's favourite foods; set a place for him or her at the table. A young child might want to put a favourite stuffed animal or doll there. Use the time for remembering and telling stories about the loved one.

* If the deceased was a collector, continue to add items to the collection. The children will enjoy spotting an item in the shop or park to bring home and contribute. They'll feel the deceased is still part of their lives, only in a different way.

* At weddings, raise a toast for the deceased.

* Play the deceased loved one's favourite music for the family. The familiar songs will help everyone feel the loved one's presence.

♡♡ FAMILY MEETINGS

Select one night a week or month for a family meeting. Every family member attends and contributes to the agenda. Each person's thoughts, ideas and complaints are presented; problems are resolved together. The meeting gives children a real voice in the family. It is amazing how children respond when they feel they are integral to the family's existence and success.

Chapter 10

Troubleshooting

CARLOS WAS 16 WHEN HE STARTED GETTING INTO TROUBLE. First, his school reports got worse, then he became involved in minor fights. Soon after getting his driving licence, he had a car accident, which he attributed to the other driver's 'road rage'. The incident was followed by minor scrapes with the police. Carlos's father dismissed the problems as 'normal' teenage mischief.

Finally, Carlos was arrested for shoplifting. As the young man waited at the police station for his dad to arrange bail, one of the policemen decided to talk with him. Carlos wasn't at all communicative, but the constable, who was good with teenagers, kept pushing him about his actions. 'You live in a nice area and go to a good school,' the policeman reasoned. 'This doesn't make sense.'

As one hour went into another, Carlos finally started talking. 'My parents divorced when I was 7, and from then until I was 15 there was really nobody around for me. I lived with my dad, who works night shifts. Every day when I left for school, he was just going to bed. He doesn't like cooking, so I got my own frozen dinner or got money for fast food.

'I am really good at basketball,' Carlos went on to say, 'but my dad never comes to any of my games or my school activities.'

'Has your dad ever hit you?' the policeman asked.

Carlos shook his head. 'No, he doesn't even know I exist.'

Last year, the boy's father remarried. Carlos told the policeman that he doesn't have any feelings about his stepmother, one way or the other. According to Carlos, she just seems to shout at him all the time, and she grounds him almost every week. When his dad comes home, he listens to Carlos complain about his stepmum and then, sure enough, he reinforces the punishment without asking Carlos for his side of the story.

'No matter what I do, it's never good enough,' Carlos confided. 'Even when I clean the house or get good marks, he never says anything.' The boy hesitated, then went on sadly. 'I'm not sure my dad likes me.'

When Carlos's father arrived at the station, the policeman pulled him aside to talk. The father's perspective was straightforward and blunt: he worked hard to support his wife and son, but things weren't easy financially. He thought Carlos understood why he wasn't at his matches or other events. 'What else can I do? We go out to dinner sometimes, the three of us, or to see a film. At the weekend, we watch TV together.'

The policeman asked Carlos's dad to come into the room where the boy was waiting. With father and son face-to-face, the policeman began to relate the exchange he had had with the boy's dad. Carlos smiled woefully. 'It's one thing to watch TV together and another to have conversation across the dinner table,' he said. This comment opened the way for Carlos's dad to explain how pressured he was feeling and how hard he was trying. For a short while, the policeman sat there watching some honest communication occur between the father and his son — probably for the first time. As the two continued talking, the constable quietly left them alone.

A child's or teenager's troubled behaviour is a serious issue that, if not resolved, can derail his academic success or haunt him into adulthood, diminishing his potential and quality of life. In some cases, negative behaviour is even a cry for help from a young person contemplating suicide. Consider Carlos — a young man heading in the wrong direction, with no one trying to stop him. He was feeling lonely — ignored by his dad, whom he loved, and displaced by his stepmother, whom he believed didn't like him. When Carlos tried to get his dad's attention or praise, his actions were overlooked. Fortunately, the police constable understood that children act out their emotions and took it upon himself to probe. Once the boy's problem was identified, the real feelings and needs of both son and father could be shared. Only then could they begin to rebuild their relationship.

Like the policeman, we, as caring adults, can reach out and help troubled children and teenagers. This chapter provides both valuable insight into the factors that contribute to a grieving child's troubled behaviour and practical coping strategies that help young people resolve issues and embrace positive behaviour.

Troubled Symptoms and Behaviour

Each child has a unique story and relationship to loss. We can't assume that we understand a child's pain or that all young people will respond similarly to a crisis. Some children become fiercely independent. They think their parents aren't capable of protecting them, so they decide they have to look after themselves. Others become paralysed with fear and indecision. The key to identifying the source of the troubled behaviour and developing coping strategies lies in the heart of the individual grieving child. To help, we must stay focused on the child and customize our approach accordingly.

Here are some of the more common troubled behaviour patterns youngsters may display, as well as some symptoms of emotional turmoil.

Troubled Behaviour

• Drug and alcohol abuse.

• Gang activity or other trouble with the law.

• Truants or is expelled.

• Sexual activity.

• Talk of suicide.

• Physical aggression, violence.

• Exaggerated clinging.

• Eating disorders.

Troubled Symptoms

• Isolation, withdrawal.

• Depression, apathy.

• Anxiety.

• Preoccupation with further loss.

• Persistent fears of catastrophe.

• Resists forming new attachments.

• Total denial of loss event.

Unlike healthy responses to loss, which are moderate and short-lived, a child's troubled behaviour or symptoms are extreme and persistent. Troubled behaviour in bereaved youngsters usually stems from denial, anger or fear related to a loss event. But problematic behaviour may also be linked to a burst of hormones or energy, a statement of independence, or ordinary teenage angst. When a child or teenager acts up, we must work to get to the source of the troubled behaviour. Since children are not adept at articulating their feelings or needs, they act them out, 'talking' to us – as it were – through their actions. If we don't react immediately, they increase the 'volume' by escalating the misbehaviour — until someone hears their pleas and responds. Our challenge is to identify the catalyst for the troubled symptom or behaviour and to teach the youngster how to develop coping strategies.

Admittedly, discovering what is at the root of misbehaviour can be a difficult task. And sometimes the answer is far from obvious. Consider the case of Rachael.

When 11-year-old Rachael was marched into the head's office, her teacher had a list of complaints to lodge against her: Rachael had been late almost every day for two weeks; during that same period, she had not handed in any homework, had fallen asleep during class and had been involved in several disputes in the playground. 'Today was the last straw,' the teacher said. 'I don't want Rachael in my class any more.'

Mr McCarthy, the head, motioned Rachael into a chair. 'What's going on?' he asked, looking her squarely in the eye.

'Nothing.'

'Rachael, you've been in this school for 5 years. You know the rules and yet you're not doing what's expected. Is something wrong?'

The girl was silent.

Mr McCarthy tried a different approach. 'OK, let's talk about today, then. Nothing else, OK?' Rachael nodded and the head continued. 'Why were you late for class today?'

Without hesitating, Rachael responded. First, she had to wake up her little sister, who didn't want to get out of bed. Then she had to make breakfast for both of them. Then she had to walk her sister to her classroom. 'I just couldn't get to my class by the bell!' she exclaimed.

'There was no one at home to help?'

Rachael shook her head. 'Mum's on a cruise.'

Mum, it turned out, had recently remarried and gone off on holiday with her new husband, leaving a freezer full of meals for the microwave and her 11-year-old daughter in charge of the household. As soon as the head understood the nature of the problem, he was able to step in and get help. Notice how he approached the situation.

- Rather than focusing on Rachael's troubled behaviour, he probed for the reasons behind her actions.

- He began with general questions: 'What's going on?' and 'Is something wrong?'

- When the girl failed to respond to these, he narrowed the focus: 'Why were you late for class today?' The question was specific and made it easy for Rachael to give concrete answers.

When you're faced with a child or teenager who is acting up, you can have the most positive impact when you take the time and invest the patience to search for the cause and help develop the solution. I believe strongly there are no bad children — only children who have had difficult things happen to them and who are searching for a voice to talk about events and someone with whom to share their experiences!

Denial-based Behaviour

Fifteen-year-old Morgan was in her study group room, waiting for the change-of-class bell, when she was paged over the school intercom and asked to report immediately to the head's office. 'What's up?' her closest friend asked. Morgan shrugged. 'Oooo, somebody's in trouble,' another student teased. Morgan laughed, grabbed her books and nonchalantly headed towards the door. But walking through the corridors and down three flights of stairs, she worried: What had she done? Had something happened at home? Why did the head need to see her?

The scene in the administrative office reinforced the teenager's concern. Sitting at his desk, the head was sombre and unable to meet her eyes. Stationed along the wall stood her form tutor, his happy-go-lucky appearance replaced by a mask of sadness.

The head teacher cleared his throat and asked Morgan to sit down. Her Uncle John, he explained, was on his way to pick her up. 'Why?' Morgan asked.

Both men fidgeted uncomfortably. The young girl looked sharply from one to the other. 'What's happened?' she demanded.

'Your mother died this morning,' her form tutor said abruptly.

Morgan froze, thinking, 'That's *impossible*. Mum's not sick. She's hardly ever ill.'

'What did you say?' the teenager asked quietly.

'Your mother died this morning.'

'I'm so sorry,' the head murmured.

But Morgan didn't hear him. She sat quietly, waiting. When her uncle arrived, she stood up and without a word to anyone walked out of the door with him.

Once in the car, Morgan turned in fury to her uncle. 'What happened? How can Mum be dead?' And that was when she learned the awful truth: her mother had committed suicide.

From that moment on, Morgan asked no more questions. Everyone said she went through the funeral service and burial 'like a trooper', her emotions in check. Her grief invisible. Her shame buried deep inside.

For two years, Morgan maintained the status quo of good student and cooperative, obedient child. Then, at 17, she changed. Her appearance, once modest and casual, became studied and provocative. She dropped her old friends and began hanging out with a different crowd. 'Teenagers! What can you expect?' her father said and shrugged off her behaviour.

Soon Morgan began dating more and more frequently. The boyfriends came and went. These were not the clean-cut boyfriends she had once spent time with, but guys who were older and had bad reputations around town. Morgan's dad grew concerned and threatened to throw her out if she didn't 'sort herself out'. She laughed in his face. Finally, Uncle John intervened. He began meeting Morgan once a week for dinner. Initially, they sat in silence.

Finally, after several such encounters, John brought up the suicide. Morgan's eyes filled with tears and she bit her lip to keep from crying.

When her uncle suggested they go to the cemetery together the next week to visit her mother's grave, Morgan exploded. 'Why should I go to see her when she never cared about me?'

'Do you really believe that?' Uncle John asked.

'Yes.' Morgan turned towards her reflection in the restaurant window. 'She never even said goodbye,' she mumbled bitterly. 'Now I don't care about her any more, either.'

For the first time since her mother's death, Morgan allowed her emotions to bubble to the surface. Though she didn't realize it, she had just taken the first step towards recovery on her journey through grief.

As they drove home, Uncle John offered again to take his niece to the cemetery. 'Morgan, are you sure you wouldn't want to go to your mum's grave? I'll go with you and stay right there.'

'If I go, so what?' Morgan replied. 'She's dead. What would I do there?'

Uncle John was quiet for a while, then he said: 'This may sound strange, but you could write a letter to your mum, ask her all of the questions that are still unanswered and share with her your personal feelings and thoughts.'

Morgan told Uncle John she would think about his suggestion. And she did all week. On Saturday morning, the teenager woke to the sound of rain hitting the bedroom window. She slipped out of bed and got a pad of paper and a pencil. Then she crawled back under the covers and started writing. Before long, she had filled ten pages with her thoughts. When she was finished, Morgan phoned her uncle. 'Can we go today?' she asked.

Uncle John came over straight away. For nearly an hour, as the rain faded into mist, the two drove in silence. At the cemetery, they both got out of the car and walked towards the grave. A short way from the gravestone, Uncle John stopped and let Morgan go on alone. When the teenager reached her mother's grave, she hesitated a moment, then sat down on the wet grass. As Uncle John watched from a safe distance, Morgan pulled the neatly folded letter from her pocket and began to read it out loud. Tears streamed down her cheeks. Then the tears turned to sobs.

Finally, Morgan got up and walked back to Uncle John. He hugged her, and then put his arm around her shoulders and walked her back to the car. Overhead, the clouds broke and a band of blue sky shone through. Morgan looked up and said, 'Goodbye, Mummy. I love you.'

Gradually, Morgan began acting like her former self. Although she seemed older and wiser, she also was at peace with herself and her mum.

What Happened Here ...

For two years, Morgan denied and was unable to face the painful truth of her mother's suicide. The girl's change in personality and provocative clothing were outward signals of her emotional distress. While Morgan's dad was unable to hear his daughter's cries for help, Uncle John recognized the problem and reached out to his niece as a compassionate companion. He demonstrated his concern and patience by repeatedly inviting Morgan to dinner. Cautiously, he opened the door for conversations about her loss. Eventually, Morgan responded by yelling at him about her mum. Rather than judging the girl's statements or being hurt by her tone, Uncle John listened and offered suggestions to guide the troubled adolescent through her grief, all the while reminding Morgan that she was not alone.

What You Can Do to Help

• Continually provide opportunities to be alone with the child. He will never confront his loss in a crowd, no matter how well he knows the other people. You can go for ice cream or fast food, take a walk in the park, or have a picnic. Allow at least 60 minutes of uninterrupted time together at each meeting.

• The first few times together, don't bring up the loss. These are simply opportunities for establishing rapport and trust, building the foundation for future conversations.

• When you mention the loss, do it gently and watch the child's response. If you see him 'shut down', back away from the topic. But do try again another time on another outing. And again. And again.

• If the child seems reluctant to talk about the loss face-to-face, you can suggest having conversations through e-mails, letters or phone calls. You can ask the child for suggestions. Work with him to be creative.

• Remind him that he is not alone during this time. It really does help.

• Be patient.

Anger-based Behaviour

One Friday after school, 11-year-old Karl got into a shouting match with his younger brother. The disagreement was starting to get physical when the boys' mother walked in on them. She sent the younger boy into the garden and suggested Karl go for a bike ride, which he did. Thirty minutes later, Karl stalked back into the house. He slammed the door, walked past his mum and said, 'And I'm not talking about it!' Before she could reply, he stormed up the stairs and slammed his bedroom door.

After a while, Karl's mum followed.

'Can I come in?' she asked from the hall outside his room.

'No,' he said. Then: 'OK, I don't care.'

Karl lay face down on the bed. His mother sat beside him. 'What's wrong?' she asked.

'Nothing,' he snapped.

TROUBLESHOOTING PARENTS' BEHAVIOUR

After a loss, parents often depend on their children for emotional support. The situation is understandable, because grieving parents are in deep pain, but it's unfortunate, because this creates unwarranted dependency stress on the children.

As a parent, ask yourself the following questions.

* Is your child your confidante – the person you talk to about adult issues?

* Does your child know too many specifics about the person you are dating or trying to date or about any intimate sexual activity in which you are involved?

* Does your child know the facts about your financial situation?

* Do you talk with your child about the pitfalls of life, marriage or any other struggle you might be challenged with at this time?

* Do you expect your teenager to run the household or handle major tasks like laundry or meal preparation?

* Is your child solely responsible for the care of her siblings?

* Is your child your regular companion to social events, films and other outside activities?

'Are you sure?' she asked again, softly.

'I already told you — I'm not talking about it!'

Karl's mum started rubbing his back. She expected him to pull away, but he didn't. After a few minutes, she asked again why he was so upset.

Karl was silent for a moment, and then said bitterly that he hated his brother.

'What happened?' his mum asked.

'He should never have been born.'

A 'yes' response to even one of the above questions indicates that you might be putting too much pressure on your child or teenager. You are expecting her to deal with adult-sized responsibilities before she has the skills to cope with them properly. While children and teenagers should be expected to do housework and be entrusted with certain family-related responsibilities, they should not have to assume the largest share of the job. Also, while it is perfectly OK to tell your children you are dating, you need to avoid giving them the details. Generally, children are uncomfortable with a parent going out on dates. Talk with them in generalities about your relationships. And yes, you can certainly tell your child that you cannot afford something or that it is too expensive, but avoid making him feel that the family's financial situation is his responsibility. In particular, refrain from saying things like, 'If your dad gave us more money ...'.

Simply put, children and teenagers lack the emotional maturity to assume an adult role in the family. Pressure to do so can contribute to troubled behaviour.

When she asked a second time what the other boy had done to upset Karl, he repeated his comment.

Still rubbing the boy's back, the mother probed further. 'How's school?' she queried.

'I hate it.'

'Anything happen you want to tell me about?'

'Nope.'

Neither one moved. Finally, Karl picked up his head and said, 'I hate Fridays!'

His mother was really surprised. 'I thought children loved Fridays — no homework, and then it's the weekend. Something has really upset you. Do you know what it is?'

Karl fired back, 'Yeah, tomorrow is Saturday.'

The boy's mother sighed. Her son's responses were disjointed and made no sense. Still, she persevered — all the while rubbing his back. 'Can you tell me about Saturday ...?'

Karl turned over on the bed and faced her. With tears welling up, he said, 'Every Saturday, Dad says he'll be here at 10 and he never turns up. I really miss him, but I know he won't come.'

At long last, Karl acknowledged the source of his anger — not his brother's birth, nor Fridays — but his father's absence.

WHAT HAPPENED HERE ...

Karl's misbehaviour grew from his anger with his father. Rather than simply discipline the boy for fighting with his brother, Karl's mum took the time to search for the root of the problem. First, she sent the boy for a bike ride because she knew he needed to exhaust himself before he could really understand why he was angry. And she was wise enough and patient enough to continue to gently push him to search for his answer. When Karl's responses to her questions didn't make sense, she kept searching with him. Finally, she understood the wonder of touch. To a child — especially one who feels hurt, worried, or sad — physical contact is both soothing and comforting. When children and teenagers are upset, they should not be left alone for any length of time. If necessary, take a break and come back to them. They need you now more than ever!

THE ROOTS OF ANGER

Anger is a strong feeling of disapproval or irritation that results from a real or felt wrong. Despite society's implication that anger is an inappropriate emotion, it really is a healthy response to a hurtful action, event, or verbal statement. I certainly can understand why children of loss are angry with everyone and everything around them: life has been unfair, and someone or something they love and cherish has been taken away from them through no fault of their own. In the long term, however, anger is emotionally draining and counterproductive. That's why grieving children need our help in working through their hurt or rage to a healthy resolution.

A loss event usually involves both primary and secondary losses. Primary loss occurs when a loved one dies, a parent abandons the family or leaves after a divorce, or a close friend relocates to a new city. In these instances, anger could be directed at:

• The parent who left or died.

• The parent who, in the eyes of the child, failed as a spouse and thus 'forced' the other parent out of the house and family.

• Parents who 'allowed' a sibling to die.

• God — for punishing the child with this loss or for not stopping it.

• Friends or classmates — for having a 'normal family'.

• Adults in general — because children think adults caused the loss through specific actions, decisions or negligence.

• The parent with whom the child lives, because he feels safe with this person; he assumes the person won't abandon him, so he can take out his emotions on him more freely.

At the same time as the child experiences turmoil because of the primary loss, she also must deal with secondary or hidden losses. These can be many and varied. Here are only a few.

• Change of self-identity or a loss in self-confidence. These are factors that can be altered with divorce or separation, parent remarriage, the death of a close family member or the arrival of step-siblings. For example, children and teenagers may feel disconnected from their mother if she takes back her maiden name or assumes her new husband's name. A young child who was identified as 'Daddy's little girl' or 'a chip off the old block' may feel displaced if Dad suddenly is gone. For other children, the arrival of step- or half-siblings may alter their birth order or sense of seniority in the family. Finally, a child who becomes part of the foster-care programme endures a complete break with family ties and traditions.

• Change in security. A shift from a two-parent to a one-parent family threatens the child's emotional, physical and financial well-being. The child worries, 'What will happen now? Can one parent take care of everything seeing as it took two before?' Some children become fiercely independent, because they think their parent is not capable of protecting them and that they must do it for themselves.

• Change in family structure. 'Who is my family now? What is my role?' the child wonders. What does a child do on Mother's Day after Mum dies or deserts the family? Now that Dad is no longer around, who will take the child to football matches at the weekend? Think about the enormous responsibility that is implied when a well-meaning adult tells the child, 'You are the father of the house now' or 'You must take over your mum's role with your brothers and sisters.' Then there are the more subtle signals that a child's family isn't 'normal', such as when there's only one name on a school form that asks for the signatures of both parents.

• Change in life goals. Perhaps the child dreamed of becoming a police officer, like Dad. If Dad dies at a young age on duty, what happens to the child's career plans? Or maybe when Dad and Mum were married, the child's university education was assured; now it is not financially feasible.

What You Can Do to Help

Teach the child appropriate ways to express anger. After loss, children and teenagers often respond with destructive anger. They let the world know they're upset, but in doing so, they can either hurt themselves or others or destroy property. We need to teach them ways to express anger constructively. Constructive anger acknowledges a child's feelings without threatening or hurting anyone or anything.

Here are some effective strategies you can introduce to the child to help her manage her anger constructively.

Redirect. Rather than kicking the dog, hitting her sister or throwing rocks at the garage window, the child should be encouraged to find a positive outlet for her feelings. Suggest hitting a punchbag, pillow or an old beanbag; drawing or painting pictures or writing a letter to the person with whom they are upset. The very act of writing about or drawing what is troubling them inside pulls the emotions out and is a great first step to resolving the anger. Afterwards, the letter or picture can be given to the person or ripped up. These 'safe' acts of destruction are cleansing, too.

Be physical. Research confirms that rigorous physical activity, such as running, bike riding, or rollerblading helps diminish the force of the anger and allows the child to more easily identify its root causes.

Don't be afraid to cry. Teaching children that crying is healthy encourages the uninhibited flow of tears. After tears are shed, the child feels calmer and is able to look inward at the source of the anger.

Use the 'I' message. This approach is a tool of honesty that helps the child talk through the source of his anger and the reasons behind it. To use it, coach the child to clearly state the issue and then express his feelings or beliefs, thereby acknowledging them. When a child reframes his conversation in terms of his own honest feelings rather than what he feels someone else did or *should* do or be doing, the person he is confronting is less likely to become defensive, and the channels of communication remain open between the two. Here's an example to get you started: 'When you _____, I feel _____ because _____.'

Identify the source. The following questions can help the child — and the adult — discover the source of anger. These are questions you present to the child for her to ask herself.

* 'With whom am I angry?'

- 'What happened to cause my anger?'
- 'Is the anger covering another feeling — hurt, frustration, fear?'

Help the child resolve the underlying conflict. The best gifts we can give children are the skills to manage their emotions appropriately. Children and teenagers need to know that conflict can and should be resolved. Otherwise, it will continue to escalate. Here are seven steps for coming to a peaceful resolution that children can use any time they are angry.

1. Identify a trustworthy adult with whom you can talk about what is bothering you.

2. Recognize the type of anger — constructive versus destructive. If you're expressing anger only to get even or get revenge (to hurt or harm), rather than to resolve the matter, this expression of anger is not positive. Think about the reasons you have for not wanting to work through the situation.

3. When you are able to confront the person with whom you are angry, say what you are feeling. Be sure to express your thoughts in terms of 'I feel' rather than 'you should' or 'you did'.

4. Be honest without being verbally abusive.

5. State what you want and need.

6. Listen to the other person's perspective.

7. Negotiate an agreement that works for everyone. Feel free to offer your suggestions and ideas, but also be open to compromise.

Fear-based Behaviour

Maddy was 6 when her parents divorced and 8 when her dad remarried. At 12, she and her two brothers began living with her father and stepmother and her stepmum's three sons. Suddenly, life really changed for Maddy! Now she had five brothers to contend with and three parents to love and obey.

Maddy tried to make the best of things. Though she missed her mum, she also liked her stepmother a lot. As the two spent more time together — cooking, going shopping, doing homework — Maddy grew increasingly confused about the relationships that had emerged following her parents' divorce. Did she really have *two* mothers, or was this other woman just her 'dad's wife'? More important, how should she act when both her mother and her stepmother were present at the same time — like at her volleyball games or school events? Whom should she go up to first? How should she introduce them to her teachers and friends? And on Mother's Day — should she give a card to each of them? There was a school dance coming up — should she go dress shopping with her mum or with her stepmum? Both seemed to be looking forward to the outing!

Maddy had many questions but was afraid to ask for help. She feared that raising the issues would hurt one or the other 'mum's' feelings, or even make her dad feel caught in the middle. 'Why can't I have a normal family?' she complained to her friends. 'Life would be so much easier.'

Eventually, Maddy decided the only way out of the dilemma was to ignore everyone. By the age of 16, she was withdrawn and sometimes edgy. Maddy's parents — all three of them — noticed the change, and each asked her what was wrong. 'I'm fine,' she always replied.

At first, the parents attributed the problem to 'teenage angst' and reassured themselves that 'it was just a phase'. 'Happens to them all,' they assured each other. But every day, Maddy grew more distant, more difficult, and more depressed. Finally, the adults met for coffee to discuss the situation. Certainly, no one could figure out what was at the bottom of Maddy's personality change.

After a lengthy discussion, the adults decided that Maddy needed professional help. Together, the three of them told her that she was going to go to see a counsellor. Maddy wasn't happy about the decision, but she didn't protest either, as her parents had feared she might.

Eventually, Maddy confided her fears and anxieties to the counsellor. Afterwards, the therapist arranged for a series of family meetings where Maddy was able to share her dilemma with all three of her parents. Maddy's mum responded by publicly giving her daughter permission to care about her stepmum. Even then, change came slowly. It took Maddy a few more years of maturing before she felt completely comfortable loving both her mums.

WHAT HAPPENED HERE ...

Initially, Maddy seemed to adjust well to the many changes in her family. It wasn't until adolescence when one issue — how to deal with two mothers — really caused Maddy difficulty. For a teenage girl struggling with normal adolescent identity issues, the ongoing conflict she faced was certainly understandable. Once Maddy's parents focused on her behaviour changes and recognized the underlying causes, they were able to guide her through her fear.

WHAT YOU CAN DO TO HELP

Be there for him. Continually provide opportunities to be alone with the child.

Stick to specifics. When you feel it's time to address the behaviour that has you concerned, bring it up by using concrete examples. For instance, with Maddy: 'Maddy, most girls your age are always out having fun with their friends, but hardly anyone calls you, and you seldom see anyone. Do you know why that is?'

When you bring up issues, do it gently and be sensitive to the response. If the child shuts down, back away from the topic. Return to these conversations again — another time on another outing. And again. And again.

Offer suggestions for ways to communicate his feelings, such as letters and phone calls. The child can offer suggestions, too. Be creative.

Remind the troubled child that she is not alone during this time.
Your support really does make a difference.

Pursue counselling. If you are concerned that the child is slipping further from you emotionally or getting into serious trouble, you must insist that she go to counselling.

Identifying What Motivates the Misbehaviour of Young Children

Besides responding to emotion-driven forces, grieving children misbehave for other reasons as well. Noted psychiatrist Alfred Adler believed that all behaviour is goal-directed and has a purpose. He identified four forces that serve as motivators for misbehaviour: attention, power, retaliation and inadequacy.

A significant crisis in a child's life heightens these forces and is often seen as misbehaviour. Let's look at how they influence a child's actions and what we can do in each instance to modify the child's negative behaviour.

ATTENTION

Rick was 7 years old when his parents divorced and his father moved out. Afterwards, his parents worked hard to maintain a cordial relationship and to ensure that the children had ready access to their father. As often happens, Rick's dad was more lenient with the children after the divorce than he had been during the marriage. Sensing that he was loving his children against the clock, he tried to be the perfect parent: he organized outings, learned to cook, and planned his schedule around the kids' activities. No matter what Rick's father did, however, the boy got into trouble. Often, Rick was deliberately disobedient. Sometimes he fought with his siblings, demanded his own way and refused to put away his toys. Still, Rick's father

MAGICAL THINKING

Magical Thinking helps children respond to many of life's situations. We all engaged in it when we were growing up. It's a child's way of fantasizing about how he'd like the world to be or providing explanations for things he doesn't understand. Under ordinary circumstances, Magical Thinking is harmless and adds to the wonder of childhood, with its tales of imaginary friends or familiar stories of the Tooth Fairy, Easter Bunny, Bogey Man or Santa Claus.

When trauma occurs, however, children often revert to Magical Thinking as a means of coping with or understanding complex events, especially if no one has talked to them about what has taken place. When this happens, Magical Thinking blurs reality and can fuel self-blame, exaggerating children's vulnerability and guilt. Remember, children believe that the world revolves around them. They think: 'I caused this, so I can sort it out.' For example, listen to what 6-year-old Tim told his dad after his parents divorced: 'It is my fault you and Mum divorced, because you were happy before I was born.'

Sometimes Magical Thinking stems from things adults say to children. On a visit to a local nursery school where I had been invited to talk to the children about death, I asked the class if they knew anyone who had died. Almost every child raised a hand. Then I asked the children to go around the room and tell me who died. For most of them, it was a grandparent, followed by a variety of beloved pets. I followed that question with another: 'Do any of you think you caused the death?' In the front row, Paul's

never raised his voice or punished the boy. Then one day, Rick went at it again. He ignored his chores, talked back to his dad and even hit his little sister. Finally, Rick's dad had had enough. He confronted the boy, reprimanded him severely, and sent him to his room. 'I have had enough,' the dad said. 'You, young man, had better change your ways — now!' Rick, who'd been protesting loudly, suddenly fell silent. A calm came over his face, and he said quietly, 'My dad's back.'

hand shot up immediately. With the fervour of a 5-year-old, he said that his grandmother's death was his fault. I asked him if he would tell us what happened and what caused him to feel responsible. Without hesitating, Paul explained, 'Grandma always said, 'Paul, you will be the death of me!' So when Grandma died, I knew I did it.'

When children are not told the specifics about a loss or traumatic event, they come up with their own explanations. Magical Thinking allows children to put their child-size arms around a frightening incident. They use it to draw their own conclusions, make order out of confusion, or assign blame.

The child's thoughts may have no bearing on reality, but they do provide insight into what he understands about the loss and how far he has progressed through the grieving process. Magical Thinking usually is limited to children aged 4 to 8, but teenagers may use it as well. In teenagers, it may have even more disastrous effects, since they are more likely to develop an eating disorder, abuse drugs or even commit suicide as a result of their misguided beliefs.

To uncover the Magical Thinking a child or teenager is using to deal with a traumatic event, try asking specific questions about how she feels and interprets the loss. For example, you might ask, 'How are you feeling about _____?' or 'Do you think someone caused this?'

Children thrive on attention, but after a loss event, they are often ignored. Adult family members may be immersed in their own grief or too preoccupied with new responsibilities and concerns to pay heed to the children. Or, as in Rick's case, parents will do everything they can to make their limited time with the children happy, instead of realizing that the children just want it to be the way it was. In other instances, children who are feeling lonely or isolated will test limits and family rules in an effort to have someone pay attention to them. Others misbehave because they mistakenly think their actions could reunite their divorced parents.

To modify attention-seeking misbehaviour:

- Find ways to give the child positive attention and recognition while ignoring (as much as possible) the negative behaviour.
- Praise the child or teenager's accomplishments.
- Schedule alone time with the child so he can have your undivided attention.

POWER

After a workshop, a woman came up to me and asked if I could help her understand her son's behaviour. Nine months earlier, she explained, her husband had died of cancer. The time between diagnosis and death had been bittersweet, especially for their 16-year-old son Neil, who had become especially close to his dad during that period. They spent hours together and, for 18 months, it seemed as if the father was the boy's whole world.

'How's Neil doing now?' I asked.

That was the problem, it seemed. Neil had always been a good, well-behaved child. Since his father's death, he had changed completely, his mother said. 'He yells at me all the time and tries to run my life — telling me who I should see and talk to, what time I should come home at night, even how to manage my money. He doesn't listen to me at all. Last night we got into a terrible argument and he tried to push me!' She looked away and whispered. 'I'm almost afraid of him. My own son!'

'Could someone at the funeral have told Neil that he was now the man of the family?' I inquired.

'Yes, and I know exactly who. The last words Neil's dad said to him were, 'Be strong and take care of your mum.'

'That's what your son is trying to do,' I said gently. 'He's proving he's strong enough to fulfil his father's final wishes.'

When a child struggles for power, he wants to be in control and demonstrate his strength. Like Neil, children may be motivated by a deathbed wish or the misguided advice of a family member or friend ('Be strong for your father now. He needs you.'). After a divorce, children may play one parent against the other as a way to gain power over a situation or to get something they know ordinarily wouldn't be given to them. The mistake is to try to force your will on them. It only adds fuel to the fire.

To modify power-motivated behaviour:

* Remove yourself from the power struggle. Do not push the child into a corner.

* Provide options, not ultimatums. Instead of saying, 'You're grounded!' say, 'If you continue this behaviour, you will be grounded.'

* Be firm as well as kind. Rather than saying, 'You're a bad boy! Stop hitting your brother,' say, 'I love you, but your behaviour is not acceptable.'

RETALIATION

Cassandra and her kitten Jasmine had been inseparable since the tiny tortoiseshell had been found sleeping in the garage two years earlier. But after Cassandra's 16-month-old baby brother died, the little girl turned vicious towards the cat. Instead of caring for the animal as she had before, she tortured it mercilessly — pulling Jasmine's fur, lifting her up by the tail, and even throwing her across the living room. Cassie's parents reprimanded her daily for her conduct and even threatened to find a new home for Jasmine. Beyond that, they were so bereft by the death of their infant son, they paid little attention to their daughter and never had the energy to sit and talk with her about her behaviour.

One night, Cassandra's mum and dad went out and her grandfather came over to babysit. Within minutes of his arrival, Cassandra threw Jasmine across the room. Grandpa immediately sat down with the little girl, put his arm around her and asked what was going on. 'I've never seen you be cruel to this little cat before,' he said. Cassie burst into tears and buried her face in her grandfather's shoulder. He said nothing but held her while she sobbed.

'Do you want to tell old Pops about it?' he asked gently after the tears had subsided. Cassie sniffled and shook her head. Grandpa waited quietly. Then, without another word from him, the little girl unleashed a torrent of distress: she felt lonely; she was angry at her parents; she believed it was their job to have taken care of her little brother and if they'd done it right, he wouldn't have died. Finally, Cassandra admitted she was afraid that maybe her parents wouldn't take good care of her and that she would die, too.

'I love Jasmine,' she said softly. 'I don't know why I'm so horrid to her.' But Grandpa understood.

The desire for revenge works hand-in-hand with sustained anger and the need for power. Grieving children who try to retaliate for their loss are angry over what has happened and desperate to gain some semblance of control over life. They want to 'get even' with those whom they believe have hurt them or with the world because it has allowed their pain. Often, these children act cruelly and become bullies. Typically, they direct their reprisals at their classmates, the resident parent, a relative or, like Cassandra, at a family pet.

> Adversity used wisely strengthens self-confidence and instils courage.

To modify revenge-based behaviour:

• Give the child extra care and attention.

• Concentrate on the child's positive behaviour and praise it extensively.

• Teach the child how to release anger in appropriate ways that don't involve hurting people, animals or things.

• If the behaviour persists, consider counselling.

INADEQUACY

Michaela, 13, had moved six times in 10 years, relocating from one foster family to another, from one house to another, from one school to another. It was little wonder, then, that she felt she didn't belong anywhere and had no one who really cared about her. Despite the kind overtures from her current foster family, Michaela was withdrawn and sullen. She slept an inordinate amount, did poorly in class and would not interact with the other children in the family or at her new school. Whenever Michaela was asked a question or invited to join in an activity, the teenager lowered her eyes and her voice and said either: 'I don't know,' or 'I don't want to.'

Children who seem determined to display personal inadequacy often feel helpless in the face of events and circumstances. They have probably endured many disappointments in life and lack faith in their own capacity or power. They don't make friends readily and do poorly in school. They

---

DECIPHERING A TROUBLED CHILD'S MOTIVES

How do you know what a troubled child needs when she misbehaves? You can usually pinpoint the subconscious goal behind children's actions by identifying the response the behaviour elicits in you. If you feel:

* ANNOYED, the child or teenager wants your ATTENTION.

* CHALLENGED, the child or teenager feels a need for POWER.

* HURT by what the child or teenager has done or said, the child's purpose is REVENGE.

* DESPAIR and want to give up, the child or teenager is feeling INADEQUATE.

truly cannot cope and try to advertise this fact to the world. Their protestations of their lack of self-worth are designed to ward off demands or expectations from adults and peers alike. Like Michaela, these children may suffer from depression that, if not tended to, may become chronic.

To modify this type of behaviour:

• Avoid criticism.

• Focus on the child's strengths.

• Provide loving attention.

• Recognize the possible need for professional counselling.

Preventing Youth Suicide

There are at least two suicides every day by young people under the age of 25 in the UK and Republic of Ireland. Experts believe that the majority of youth suicides result from depression, which is treatable. This means most youth suicides could be prevented if those close to the youngsters understood what makes adolescents vulnerable to suicide and heeded the warning signs — or if the teenagers had one adult who believed in them and whom they felt they could trust.

THE CAUSES

Depression often results from unresolved grief. Breakdown of the family unit can be a factor. Geographic mobility also can contribute. A move when an adolescent is already insecure can leave the teenager fearful, lonely and bereft. Personal loss — the breakup of a teenage romance or close friendship, or failure to win a coveted award — can be part of the scenario as well. It isn't one loss or failure that pushes a child to suicidal thoughts, but rather an accumulation of losses for which the child has been unable to grieve.

THE WARNING SIGNS

Youth suicide rarely occurs spontaneously without warnings. The majority of youngsters signal their intentions beforehand. We need to be alert to:

Suicide Threats

• 'I want to die.'

• 'I hate life.'

• 'I don't want to live any more — it hurts too much.'

• 'I wish I'd never been born.'

• 'You're going to be sorry when I'm gone.'

• 'I want to go to sleep and never wake up.'

• 'I am going to kill myself.'

Personality Changes

• Unusual withdrawal, aggression or moodiness.

• Severe depression or feelings of hopelessness.

• Statements that express intense loneliness or boredom.

• Trouble at school or with the police.

• Tendency to take life-threatening risks.

• Changes in appetite or sleep patterns.

• Dramatic drop in school performance.

• Loss of friends.

• Themes of suicide, death or depression in essays or art.

• Making final arrangements, such as giving away prized possessions or writing a will.

• Previous suicide attempts.

WHAT TO DO

Adults are sometimes too frightened to believe that the warning signs a troubled child is displaying could really mean he is contemplating suicide. Friends may be aware of the teenager's suicidal intent, but don't disclose the information because they have been sworn to secrecy or don't believe the person will go through with it. Often, if a teenager makes an unsuccessful attempt, others assume the threat is now past; in fact, the crisis is still very real.

If you suspect a child is considering suicide, don't hesitate to take the following steps.

Act on your concerns. If suicide clues are evident, respond immediately — don't wait.

Ask questions. Asking questions might save a life. Your actions will not put ideas into a child's or teenager's mind that aren't already there.

'Is life really that difficult?'

'Do you wonder sometimes if life is worthwhile?'

'Do you think you really don't want to live any more?'

'Do you realize that death is a permanent solution to a temporary problem?'

'Is there anyone who can help you with this problem?'

'Do you have a plan on how to end your life?' (The existence of a specified plan indicates imminent danger and the need for immediate professional help.)

Be supportive. Listen intelligently and empathetically; let the child/teenager know you would like to help.

Stay calm. If you are alarmed, say: 'This is difficult stuff to deal with, but I will do my best.'

Give the child or teenager realistic feedback. Don't offer advice or share your opinions. Reflect back what has been said to you.

Ask to remove pills or weapons from the youngster. Say: 'I want to help you, but am uncomfortable that you have ____ in your possession.'

Never promise that you will not tell anyone. Say: 'I must take whatever steps I feel are necessary to help you.'

Urge the child or teenager to seek professional help. Offer to make the referral and accompany him on the first visit.

Get immediate help. Accompany the child or teenager home to their parent or caregiver, to the hospital, doctor or counsellor.

What Not to Do

When it comes to helping a child you fear might be considering suicide, nearly *anything* you do to express your concern is better than ignoring the problem or hoping to 'wait it out'. Still, here are a few pointers for approaching this difficult and complex situation.

Don't assume the child or teenager is 'not the type' to commit suicide. The pain that leads a child to contemplate suicide knows no economic, social or physical boundaries.

Don't leave a young person alone if you believe the risk of suicide is imminent.

Don't be afraid to be the first to mention suicide. Generally, the child or teenager is relieved that you are willing to discuss the subject.

Don't react. When you get the child to open up about her feelings, don't act shocked at what she tells you.

Don't debate whether suicide is morally right or wrong. Your opinions may make the child or teenager feel guiltier and more depressed.

Don't feel that you need an answer to every question or issue raised. If the child asks, 'What is the meaning of life?' it's OK to say you don't know and that scholars have spent years studying the same question. Perhaps you can search for the answers together. Make it clear that you are present to help solve problems.

Don't deny or downplay the youngster's feelings or intentions. Acknowledge the child's feelings without judging or reinforcing the negative. Say: 'I believe that you are feeling miserable right now. Let's talk about it.'

Don't abandon the child or teenager because the problems are too overwhelming. Follow through in getting help. Don't be another loss or rejection the teenager must face.

Don't assume the child or teenager 'will get over it'. Reach out and talk to the youngster immediately.

Don't take sole responsibility for 'saving' the child or teenager. Get help. No one person can handle this situation alone.

Recovery Tools

Children and adolescents who are causing distress in the family, classroom or community can frustrate and discourage us. Yet if we continue reaching out to them, we can lead them through the troubled times and into acceptance of the loss event that lies at the heart of their distress. We can help them change their reaction to the loss and ultimately become stronger because of it. Two specific tools help alleviate troubled behaviour: discipline and forgiveness.

Discipline

After a loss, parents and caregivers tend either to be overly solicitous and lenient towards bereaved children or to assume that they are much more mature than their age would indicate. There are many reasons for these changes: adults may not have the energy to sustain consistent disciplinary practice, or they may feel guilty about the loss; many single parents are exhausted and feel they deserve 'time off' almost at any cost; a newly single parent may be uncertain what rules and parameters to establish with the child; family and friends may feel uncomfortable 'burdening' the child with expectations or worry that they will somehow alienate the child.

In fact, after a major loss, children need more structure than ever. They need to know that someone is in charge — and that it's not them! If we excuse the misdeeds of grieving children and allow them to consistently flout normal rules of conduct, we are sending them a message that they are for ever damaged by the loss and will never be able to measure up to the usual standards. On the other hand, when we insist on good behaviour, we not only assure children that they are cared for and protected, but we also convey our abiding faith in their ability to grow beyond the pain of the loss.

DEALING WITH TANTRUMS

Young children have temper tantrums for a number of reasons:

✳ They need or want something that is not being communicated.

✳ They are testing the adult's resolve.

✳ They are tired or frustrated.

✳ They feel powerless.

A tantrum is a young child's way of being heard. We need to put aside our frustrations and feelings of embarrassment and focus on working out what the child is trying to communicate. Some ways to do this are:

✳ Get at eye level with the child and calm him as much as possible

✳ Hold, touch or rock the child so he feels cared for.

✳ Try to understand what she is asking or saying.

✳ Acknowledge his anger and frustration.

✳ Explain that her behaviour will not resolve the problem.

✳ Try to negotiate a workable solution that fills the child's need.

✳ Do not give in to unreasonable demands. Instead, walk away and ignore the child's behaviour, if possible.

When a youngster's behaviour requires you to discipline and enforce limits, remember the following important steps.

- Remain calm and use eye contact and relaxed body language (arms unfolded, hands still, sitting comfortably) in order to open communication.

- Put yourself at eye level with the child and notice his body language, particularly slumped shoulders, sad eyes or an angry stance.

- Listen intently to what the child says.

- Repeat the child's statements and comments, using her own words: 'What I am hearing you say is …'

- Be honest with your thoughts and feelings, but limit the expression of them during the conversation.

- Allow silences — this is when the internal work is happening.

- Don't lecture. Be kind and firm.

- Don't solve the problem. Instead, guide the child in arriving at a solution.

FORGIVENESS

Several years after my divorce, I had arranged for a panel of five teenagers to participate in a workshop on grief. Each of the children lived in a single-parent home and was willing to answer questions from the audience about their feelings and experiences regarding their new family structure. My 16-year-old son Michael was one of the participants. To this day, I can't remember the question that prompted this response from him: 'I will never forgive my parents for the divorce!'

Listening to him, feeling the intensity in his voice, was like having someone plunge a knife into my heart. I sat there confused and thinking, 'But we have a good relationship. How can he be saying that?' Later, while driving home, I asked Michael about the comment. 'Well, Mum,' he said matter-of-factly, 'one day you were married, and the next day you and Dad were divorced. No one ever thought about us.'

I was stunned. But as he went on, the reality was clear: despite our best intentions, we had not prepared the boys ahead of time; we had not assured the children that *they* were our primary concern; we hadn't asked them for any input about the custody or parenting arrangements. We had simply followed traditional practices.

That night, unable to sleep, I sat at the kitchen counter and wrote a letter to Michael and his brothers (see 'Asking for Forgiveness' on page 298). My heartfelt words didn't discuss the reasons for the divorce or try to blame anyone; I simply asked their forgiveness for what had happened in our family. The next day, I placed a copy of the letter on each son's pillow. Michael was the first to come to me with tears in his eyes. He threw his arms around me and said: 'Mum, I *do* forgive you.' And for the first time since the divorce, he cried.

Forgiveness isn't something we do for or to someone who has wronged us. It is a gift we give ourselves. Forgiveness brings personal peace. I saw the transformation in my sons, saw them relax and blossom after they forgave the injury the divorce had imposed on the family. Forgiveness is healthy. A California study confirms that people who forgive endure fewer incidents of anger and physical symptoms of stress than those who don't.

To help a child who has suffered a loss work towards forgiveness, guide him through the following process.

1. Take the first step. Begin by identifying the person you feel has hurt you — it may be a parent or friend who died, a drunk driver who caused a fatal accident, a relative who abandoned the family. Don't wait for this person to apologize first — he may not be able to or may be unaware of the pain he has caused. Simply forgive him.

2. Realize that the person who wronged you may have acted out of her own pain or ignorance. An old adage says: *Behind every unkind deed, there is a sad story.* Try to see things from the other person's perspective.

ASKING FOR FORGIVENESS: SUZY'S LETTER TO HER SONS

Dear Michael, Tom and Tim,

From the time I was 5 years old, all I ever dreamed of was being a mother ...

Sixteen years ago, I carried my first child close to my heart. Through the entire 9 months, fear and excitement walked with me. The day you were born, Michael, love welled inside me until I thought I would burst. The first time I held you, I whispered: 'I love you, and I will never allow anything or anyone to ever hurt you.'

As time grew close for the birth of my second child, I realized that fear and excitement had only been infrequent visitors to me. The love I already had for you, Tom, kept them away. When you were placed in my arms, my first words were: 'I love you' and that solemn vow: 'I will never allow anything or anyone to ever hurt you.'

The joy of the news of my third pregnancy was clouded with the diagnosis of a difficult birth. When Tim's first cry bellowed, I thanked our Lord through streams of tears for this healthy son. Once again, as I held your tiny fingers in my hand, I said: 'I love you,' and I promised to never let anything or anyone ever hurt you.

As you boys grew, I was able to comfort a hurt feeling, bandage a cut finger or kiss a skinned knee. I was keeping my promise. As time passed, all of you got bigger and stronger, but my marriage was crumbling around me. No matter what I said, what I did or what I changed, I couldn't save it. Choosing the divorce was the most difficult decision of my life, because it meant my sons would be hurt. I was the one to break that first promise!

In the years that have passed, I have struggled to make our life special. In doing that, many things were not as I wanted them to be. Because I had to work extra jobs, I was gone from you so much. Each time I started the car to pull away, I would cry because I wanted to stay at home with you. The days, so many of them, when I was exhausted and moody, I snapped at you — the three people who didn't deserve it.

There are scars you will carry always because of the divorce of the two people you love most in this world. Because of this, I must ask your forgiveness ...

I am sorry for not being the perfect parent I wanted to be.

I am sorry for not loving your father any more.

I am sorry for being too strict at times and too lenient at others.

I am sorry for not being as wise as I thought a parent needed to be.

Yet you taught me about being a real parent with your unconditional love for me.

Boys, now that you are almost grown, I realize more than ever that you will be leaving home in just a few years. The yesterdays cannot be recalled, only the tomorrows better lived. I am continually humbled by your gentle hearts.

I love you with all of mine.

Mum

THE MEASURE OF SUCCESS

I believe a young person's success in navigating through the grieving process can be measured by the following criteria.

* As children – and later as adults – can they make and sustain commitments?

* Do they have working relationships with friends, family and colleagues?

* Is their self-esteem strong?

* Can they handle defeat or disappointment?

* As adults, do they parent their own children well?

* Are they successful in the job or profession they have chosen?

* Are they well-adjusted and content in life?

3. Remember how bad you felt when you hurt someone — either deliberately or unintentionally — and then how good you felt when you were forgiven. This memory will help you to begin to let go of the hurt.

To simplify the concept of forgiveness for younger children, you might want to work through the 'Let's Make Lemonade' activity on page 260.

One of the hardest things a child of loss will ever be asked to do is to forgive the person or event that has hurt her so deeply. To do so, she will need to sort through her troubling behaviour to identify what is at the root of it, what needs she feels are going unfulfilled, and what emotions she has harboured within her heart. Only then will she be able to bring her true feelings out into the light of day, acknowledge them and work towards forgiveness. For it is with forgiveness that she will finally be able to move forward to a new and brighter tomorrow.

Part Three
The Hope

Harbingers of Hope

Dear God,
As I reaffirm my commitment
To reach out to the children and adolescents around me,
Please give me the words to help them
Sort through their feelings,
Let them know how really special they are,
How good life really is,
And to be that Harbinger of Hope for their tomorrows.
I ask you to help me
Be the role model children require.
May my voice speak the words they need to hear.
And be able to offer the support that provides them consolation.
For these are the gifts that instill hope.
God, I shall try to be Your arms for hugging,
Your ears for listening,
And Your heart for loving.
Through these times of terror and unprecedented fear
Strengthen my resolve
So that I may be strong and able
To give the children all they need.

Chapter 11
Still a Family

AT A DIVORCE WORKSHOP I WAS CONDUCTING, Claudia stood up during the Q & A session and began to rage against her daughter's father. From the time Colette was an infant, he'd ignored her. After the divorce, he'd pick her up for weekends and leave her with his parents while he went off fishing or golfing.

Recently, however, her former husband had acquired a steady girlfriend and developed an intense interest in the child. Suddenly, he is being 'super-Dad' to Colette — begging for extra time with her, taking her to the adventure playground and treating her to cinema trips and ice shows. 'I am so furious,' Claudia said. 'I don't have enough money to do things like that.'

Gently, I asked Claudia why she was upset about the hands-on parenting time her ex-husband was finally showering on Colette.

'He wasn't there before, what's he trying to prove now?' she said. 'That other woman probably just wants to take my place.'

So many emotions and resentments were crowding in on Claudia! Is it possible, I wondered, that Colette's father hadn't really known how to parent before, that he'd had no reasonable role model himself, and that he had felt uncomfortable and inept about being alone with Colette after the divorce?

'Look at the situation from Colette's perspective,' I urged. 'You and your former husband are still her parents, even though you live in separate homes. At long last, Colette's father is giving her lots of attention and love. She can only benefit.'

One Child, Two Families

After a divorce, it's natural to feel hurt, to be angry, and to mourn unfulfilled dreams and expectations. And, as in Claudia's case, it's easy to fall into the trap of questioning your former partner's motives and to feel that you're in competition with him for your children's affections. You may even feel that by minimizing your former partner's influence, you're protecting your children. In reality, though, the opposite is true. For while you have severed your marriage bond with your partner, the bond between child and parent — both mother *and* father — needs to remain strong and unquestioned.

One of the most difficult things to come to terms with after a divorce is the fact that your child's family is now different from your own — and it is crucial that he is able to interact freely in both your family and your former partner's. To exclude members of the child's 'other' family is to exclude a part of the child's very identity and can only end up hurting the child.

Similarly, if your partner dies, you may rage against the unfairness of the situation and may find it too heartwrenching to speak about your deceased mate or visit his side of the family. As the years pass, you may find yourself growing apart from your former in-laws. But it's imperative that you allow and encourage your children to keep in contact with their deceased parent's family. By maintaining this link to the past, they are better able to get a complete picture of their personal histories and carve out their own identities.

Re-creating Your Family

Loss affects both the nuclear and extended families and your children's place in each. You can't pretend you are the same family unit as before, just with one person missing. But you can rebuild the structures and sustain the interpersonal relationships that ground your children and nourish their links to everyone involved. The following six resolutions will help you re-create the strong sense of family that your children need to thrive.

Resolution 1: I will keep my children connected with extended relatives. Despite a separation, divorce or death, the grandparents, aunts, uncles and cousins are still family members. By including these family members in your activities, you help your children maintain their sense of identity and 'connectedness'. Invite extended relatives to parties, celebrations and special school events. Send them current photographs of the children. Encourage the children to send seasonal greetings and birthday cards to the relatives. There are many creative ways children can stay closely linked with relatives of a former or deceased spouse.

Resolution 2: together with my children, I will create new family traditions. Families have certain ways of doing things together. Family traditions intensify this sense of oneness. When a family changes, you may not want to or even be able to maintain past traditions. It's OK — and even healthy — to do things differently. This year, as birthdays, festivities and special events come up, talk with your children about new ways to observe these occasions.

After my divorce, I was unable to buy my children the kinds of presents and treats they were accustomed to, so I improvised. When the first birthday came, I wrote 'Happy Birthday' in soap on the bathroom mirror so my son would see it when he got up. For dinner, I made his favourite meal and drew a special placemat. When their birthdays came around, I did the same for the other two boys. In my stepfamily, we incorporated these now well-used 'traditions' into their birthday celebrations. And to that tradition we added a red plate that says 'Your special day' around the rim. The birthday celebrant chooses the dinner and type of birthday cake. Now my grandchildren are looking forward to enjoying these traditions, too!

New traditions don't have to be expensive or elaborate. What matters is that they are ritualistic, inclusive and special to your family. An activity as simple as walking the dog together every Sunday evening can be a new family tradition.

Resolution 3: if divorced or separated, I will not speak negatively of my ex-parter in front of our children. If widowed, I will not place my deceased partner on a pedestal. You know how it goes: the divorced partner is portrayed as someone who can't do anything right. The deceased partner is depicted as a saint. Either situation creates an unrealistic picture for the children.

Whether your partner is gone because of a divorce or death, your children still need to look to him or her as a role model. For their sake — to help them retain a sense of family connection to the absent parent — resolve to eliminate the verbal put-downs and negative comments that seem to come so easily after divorce. If you are widowed, help your children to remember their absent parent as a real person with both personal strengths and human weaknesses.

Resolution 4: I will spend time alone daily with each of my children. By doing this now, you create a close relationship with your children that paves the way to future discussions about important feelings and events. Set aside at least 10 minutes every day for each child. Right after school or at bedtime usually works well. Ask specific questions, such as: 'How was school?' 'Was one class really good or bad today?' and 'Who did you sit with at lunch?' Usually, you'll get routine reports on their activities, but occasionally these talks lead to deeper conversations. When a crisis occurs, your children know you are available for them to talk to about it.

Resolution 5: we will share family meals as often as possible. Eating together sends a strong message of cohesiveness to your children. When you sit down to share a meal with one another, you make a statement: *we are family.* It doesn't matter if the meal is homemade, a freezer-to-microwave or ready meal or a fast food takeaway. Sharing at least one meal a day is an ideal goal. If this is unrealistic for your family, work to share at least four or five meals every week, even if you need to adjust the mealtime to fit individual schedules.

Resolution 6: I will take time for myself. Holidays and long weekends away from home are fantasies for most single parents. But regularly scheduled breaks are do-able. A change in routine re-energizes physically and calms mentally. Set aside at least 30 minutes every few days to do something you personally enjoy, such as walking, reading, exercising, or watching television. If possible, treat yourself to an hour off. Taking time for yourself may sound self-serving, but ultimately, you gain patience and perspective — two tools you need for the daunting but rewarding challenge of re-creating family.

Making the Transition

Carving out a new identity for your family after a loss can be a complex process, but it needs to be done in order for both you and your children to move on with your lives. There are special factors to keep in mind depending on whether the loss was a divorce or a death. In the rest of this chapter, I'll discuss the unique concerns of each situation and give you practical strategies for moving through this difficult but necessary transition period.

THE NEXT STEP FOR PARENTS WHO ARE DIVORCED

A complete divorce involves three elements: legal, physical and emotional. Until all three are accomplished, you are not fully divorced. While the legal and physical aspects happen on a set timeline and are usually dictated by the courts, the emotional part of divorce can take years to achieve and can only be accomplished by you. Yet divorcing yourself emotionally from your partner and rebuilding a separate, positive, nurturing life is the most essential of these tasks — and the most crucial one for allowing your children to heal and rebuild their own lives.

To complete the emotional phase of the divorce and provide the best possible environment for your children, you'll need to work on the following two fundamental tasks.

Become an emotionally stable parent for your children. To do this, you'll need to grieve the loss; wrestle with your feelings — the good, the bad, and the ugly; forgive your former partner; and rebuild your self-esteem. For help in working towards these goals, consider joining a support group, reading books and articles that offer advice on the subject and seeking counselling if you feel it would be helpful.

Many newly divorced men and women jump into dating, taking up new hobbies, moving to a new town or travelling. While these can add to the richness of your life, they should not be substitutes for the grief work. One divorced father called his support group his 'class' because the group taught him positive ways to uncouple from his former wife.

Even if the marriage failed, the divorce can be successful!

Develop a positive post-divorce relationship with your ex. Your goal is to create a relationship that is kind, supportive and works on behalf of the children.

Recently, I was at a conference where I regularly present workshops. Just before the session began, a woman from the audience came up to me. 'I've heard you speak four times,' she said. 'The first time, I left the room furious with what you'd said about developing a post-divorce relationship. I hated my ex-husband and wanted nothing whatsoever to do with him. I could see no reason for it.' But, she added, there were always the children — three of them. 'Their birthdays, school activities and sports kept bringing us together.' Eventually, the woman said, she saw how the animosity was hurting the children, so she worked hard to process her feelings. 'You were right,' she told me that morning. 'And I just want to say *thanks*.'

Life goes on and brings an endless sequence of events — school activities, weddings and eventually the births of grandchildren — that involve the children and the divorced parents. If you continue to harbour bitterness or resentment towards your ex, your anger will eat away at the inherent joy of these events for everyone involved. In the end, the people you'll end up hurting the most will be your children. If a child or teenager suffers through joyful events because he's worried that his divorced parents will make everyone uncomfortable, imagine the additional misery he experiences when a tragic event such as a serious illness or death in the family forces his parents together. Marcel was 12 and the oldest of four siblings when his parents divorced in the early 1960s. It was an ugly affair that trailed bitterness and rancour in its wake. The judge split the children between the parents, sending Marcel and the next oldest to live with their father. The boys were never allowed to mention their mother in his presence.

Years later, when Marcel shipped off to Vietnam for military service, he listed his mother as the emergency contact, should anything happen to him. Why? Because he knew she would have the decency to inform his dad, while his father, sadly, would never call or communicate with her — even if Marcel were killed or injured. As it turned out, Marcel was seriously hurt in battle. His mother got the call late one evening. When she telephoned her former husband to tell him the unfortunate news, he hung up on her. Distraught and in tears, she phoned her former brother-in-law and asked him to convey the message to Marcel's dad.

WHAT IF ONE PARENT IS DECLARED UNFIT?

Under certain circumstances – usually in cases of abuse or neglect – a court may declare a family member unfit to act in the normal role of parent or relative and forbid that adult to have any contact with the child. When this happens, another loving adult needs to talk with the children to explain the court's decision and the reasons behind it, so the children don't blame themselves. The explanation can be presented in a matter-of-fact way, withholding judgemental statements. As we know, even if a parent has abused a child, in most cases the child still loves the parent.

Sometimes a child's mother or father may simply not be a good role model or a responsible parent for a child. If this is the case, it's better to help the child establish a relationship with that individual rather than cut off all contact. The relationship might not meet our standards of a healthy bond between parent and child, but it can still be a good 'working relationship'. In extreme situations, this relationship could be shaped through supervised

Children of divorce deserve better from their parents. Fifteen years after my divorce, my youngest son, Tim, was gravely injured while serving in the Peace Corps. The doctors weren't certain he would survive. After hearing the news, I was on the next flight out with my former husband, Jim, as well as with Tim's brothers and stepfather. Mercifully, Jim and I had resolved all of our divorce issues years before. There was no lingering tension, no underlying animosities. Standing on each side of Tim's bed, we held his hands and prayed together for his recovery.

Can you imagine how Tim would have felt lying there if we were still filled with disdain for each other?

Can you imagine how Marcel — another child of divorce — would have felt if his parents had ever both visited him at the same time during his lengthy convalescence — and focused all their attention on *him*?

parenting time or through communications such as e-mail, letters or phone calls. In other circumstances – when a parent is depressed, never really does much with the children when they have them, never takes the children to their home or keeps their home in conditions not up to one parent's standards – it is still important that the child develop a bond.

I have seen children be content with and loving towards a clinically depressed parent who gave them only marginal attention. I have also seen children accept alcohol or drug dependency as a disease and move past that to love the parent simply as a person and respond to her with great compassion. Often these children mature into wonderfully compassionate adults. On the other hand, children who are denied the opportunity to have a relationship with a parent – for whatever reason – can spend their entire adulthoods 'looking' for this lost parent connection in unhealthy relationships – either emotionally, professionally or personally.

As parents, we owe it to our children to recognize the destructive nature of our hostility and bitterness. Despite what happened in the past, each child is entitled to two parents who are mature, responsible, and concerned enough to shelve their anger and work towards creating an environment where their children can interact comfortably with *all* members of their family.

Residential Parenting

If the custody agreement means your children spend most of their time with you, then you are probably extra weary. Under the best of circumstances, parenting benefits from having two people to master the details. As a single parent, it's easy to fall into the victim trap. You've probably caught yourself thinking, 'There's so much to do and too little time' or 'My former partner has more money and spoils the kids; I'm just the disciplinarian.' I've heard any number of negative comments from custodial parents, perhaps some of them true. What is more important is the amazing and wonderful responsibility that the custodial parent assumes.

The custodial/residential parent has the opportunity to nurture a child's recovery from divorce and the transition from a two-parent home to two

DATING AFTER FAMILY LOSS

After a family loss, the parents – whether divorced or widowed – have an unspoken obligation to choose their dates carefully and to ensure that the adults they introduce into their children's lives are good, upstanding individuals. I don't recommend starting to date until the family has a firm footing in the rebuilding process, but once you do, be aware that dating can add a new dimension of people, children, lifestyles and traditions. This period can be filled with great experiences, treasured memories, awkward moments, broken hearts and, possibly, a new stepfamily.

If you are a single parent and new again to the dating scene, here are a few questions to ask yourself about the people you are considering dating.

* Do they like children in general?

* Do they want to meet your children?

* Do they avoid disciplining your children? Setting rules and boundaries is not appropriate for them at this stage.

* Are they jealous of the time and energy you spend with your children, or are they flexible and understanding of the chaotic schedule that life with children sometimes entails?

* Do they help your children with homework or any other task with which the kids need adult assistance or guidance?

* Are they respectful towards your children?

* Do they want to develop a relationship with your children? Would they be willing to attend any of the children's school functions or invite them along when the two of you go out?

homes. Initially, I tried to be Mum and Dad — and failed miserably. Then I made a conscious decision to have a healthy, functioning family and refocused on being the best parent possible. I enrolled in classes and read insightful books on parenting. As the custodial parent, I got involved in events, projects and sports that I had always urged my sons' father to do with

* Are they courteous to your children rather than being negative, sarcastic, or putting them down?

* Do they respect your relationship with your child's other family?

* Are they patient with your children's insecurities about their relationship with you?

* How do they handle your children's inappropriate behaviour towards them?

* Do they understand the inherent difficulties of being a single parent?

* Do they respect and honour your parental role and responsibilities?

* Are they respectful to you, and do they treat you well?

* Are they willing to participate in family traditions and rituals that were established long before they entered the picture?

* Are they at all abusive – emotionally or physically?

* Do they abuse drugs or alcohol?

* Are they interested in working with you to strengthen your family unit?

* Do they have children and, if so, what is their relationship with them?

* Are they able to apologize or forgive when the need arises?

them alone. I helped Mike make his pinewood car for Cub Scouts; became acquainted with the rules of basketball, football and baseball so I could be a knowledgeable fan to cheer Tom when he played each of them; and encouraged Tim's involvement in school politics and a local drama group. At the same time, I worked hard to foster the relationship that the boys had with their dad.

As custodial parent, there are many ways to nurture your children through the divorce and build a healthy, productive family life. Here are some suggestions.

- Keep your former partner aware of activities and events in your children's lives. It means the world to the children to have both parents involved in their activities.

- Divide the children's school papers and awards between the two households.

- Encourage your child to have daily contact with the other parent.

- Be accommodating and willing to adjust schedules when special circumstances or events come up.

- Be kind to the child's 'other' family. Refrain from making negative comments about the other parent, former in-laws and other relatives.

- Do not undercut the other parent's discipline.

- Do not ask children to be message carriers to the other family members.

- Discipline when necessary. Your child is still looking for and needs a parent, not a playmate. 'No' is a love word. But do offer more compliments and praise than corrective comments.

- Don't overindulge or spoil your children to compensate for their loss or other family shortcomings. Buying apologies is not effective or worthwhile and teaches children to take advantage of you and the situation.

Non-residential Parenting

Being a parent in a married household by its nature means that you are with your child on a daily basis. Yes, you may take holidays without them or be away on business trips, but overall, from birth throughout the next 18 years, you are involved with your child each and every day.

Now that you are divorced, you need to establish a new type of relationship with your beloved child. Being the non-custodial or non-residential parent is extremely difficult. You miss your child constantly and may feel that you don't have significant input into your child's life and upbringing. You may feel left out and anxious.

Still, in spite of not being physically present every day, you can have a very positive and strong relationship with your sons and daughters. The process takes patience and perseverance and will be painful at times, but don't give up!

Here are some ideas that work.

• Keep the channels of communication open at all times. If possible, talk to your children daily. Parents often are astounded at this suggestion. Yet, if you talked to your children every day while you were married, why would you not do it just because you live elsewhere? Your former partner and family members alike should encourage this close connection. Of course, there will be times when the child will be too busy or not available, but it's important that you try again the next day.

• Mail or e-mail your children cards, articles from the newspaper, cartoons and jokes. This provides a link and also lets your children know you are thinking of them. Children really believe that when you aren't with them physically, you don't think of them or miss them.

• When you see a little trinket that your child might enjoy, buy it. This could be her favourite sweet or magazine, a CD or a voucher for a fast-food restaurant. This small gift lets your child know that you were thinking about her.

- Introduce yourself to your child's teacher and the other staff at the school. Ask for copies of all communications that go home — offering to pay the postage, if necessary. Attend as many school functions as possible.

- With your child's help, start a scrapbook or memory box commemorating things you have done together. Include written memories, photographs, ticket stubs and other mementos.

- Be dependable. Your reliability gives your child much-needed stability. Part of being dependable means being on time, keeping your word and following through on your promises. For example, if you say you're going to be at one of your child's school activities or open days, be there. If something unforeseen happens and you're not able to make it after all, apologize for breaking your promise. And possibly most important, only make promises you can keep.

- Be kind to the child's family. Refrain from making negative comments about the other parent, former in-laws and other relatives. Remember that while they may be your 'ex-family' they are still your child's current family. Also, recognize that plans really do change. Be flexible: give in on parenting time for special circumstances.

- Do not undercut the other parent's discipline.

- Do not ask children to be message carriers to the other family members.

- Spend time alone with each child when just the two of you talk, read, take a walk together or engage in some other activity both of you enjoy. You don't need to have the TV or CD player on all of the time for background noise. In addition to these regular one-on-one times, create special outings for the two of you where you do something you know the child particularly enjoys.

- Go to the library and learn more about the subjects that interest your child. While you're there, borrow books that talk about divorce. Read them together.

- When your children are with you, do not include your current 'friend' except on rare occasions. The children need you, not a group visit.

- Remember your child's birthday and other key dates. Find ways to make these special occasions memorable by creating new traditions while keeping some of the old. A 2 o'clock birthday party at a local restaurant with your table wrapped in crêpe paper and decorated with balloons is just as memorable as a fancy event at the family home.

- Handle the teenage years gracefully. Your child will become more distant and want to spend more time with friends. This is normal. Maintain a steady, constant presence and the child will eventually return to you.

- Discipline when necessary. Your child is still looking for and needs a parent, not a playmate. 'No' is a love word. Do offer more compliments and praise than corrective comments, however.

- Don't overindulge or spoil your children to compensate for your absence or other shortcomings. Instead, take time to talk through your feelings with your children. Buying apologies is not effective or worthwhile and teaches children to take advantage of you and the situation.

Easing the Move between Two Families

Even when a child is comfortable in both of her divorced parents' homes, the physical move from one to the other can leave her feeling out of sorts. This is yet another time for you and your former spouse to come together and put your child's needs above your own. Consider the case of Charlene.

Charlene was 2 when her parents divorced. By the time she was 6, they had each remarried, giving the little girl four 'parents'. Charlene sees her daddy and step-mum every other weekend and every Tuesday night for dinner. Now that her dad and step-mum have a new baby, Charlene misses them even more when they are apart. For about a month, every time she had to separate from them and come back to her mum and step-dad, Charlene acted out her emotions. As soon as she'd walk in the door, Charlene would throw her overnight bag on the floor, stalk past her mum and start petting the dog. When her mum and step-dad approached her for a hug, she turned away from them. Obviously, her mum and step-dad felt embarrassed in front of the 'other side'. But Charlene's actions made the child's dad and step-mum feel awkward as well. When they began to leave, Charlene would run to her dad, sobbing uncontrollably and beg him not to leave. By this point, all four parents felt terrible and helpless.

Finally, the adults talked and worked out a plan. Now, on Sunday evenings, they all sit down together for a few minutes at the kitchen table. Charlene's dad pulls her up onto his lap and, after a few minutes of cuddling, starts talking about the next time they will be together. He then walks her to the refrigerator where her mum has a calendar with heart stickers marking every day Charlene is going to be with Daddy. When they're finished, her dad transfers Charlene into her mum's arms. 'Bath time. Tomorrow's a school day!' he cheerfully reminds her. Then he and the step-mum kiss Charlene goodbye and leave — smiling and blowing kisses as the little girl goes upstairs.

Like Charlene's parents, you can help make your children's transition from one home to the other easier and less awkward for everyone involved. Here are some tips to follow.

- Have the children packed, calm and ready on time to be picked up.

- Return the children clean, happy and calm. Talk about your time together and when you will see each other again.

WHOSE HOUSE IS IT, ANYWAY?

After a divorce, most children move between the two separate residences occupied by their divorced parents. Although the houses or apartments belong to the children as well as to the adults, children's parents, relatives and friends often use the terms *your mum's house* or *your dad's house* to distinguish between the two. These terms deny the children any sense of ownership. It's better to say: *your home with your mum* or *your home with your dad*.

- Send the children off to have a good time; be cheerful and encourag-ing. Never lament about how lonely you are when they are away from you. This is also true when you are returning them.

- Before the children leave, remind them to love their other parent and enjoy their time with him or her.

- Never discuss issues or problems in front of the children, even though it may seem convenient to bring up conflicts while the kids are being picked up or dropped off. All parent-to-parent disagreements should occur in private.

- Resolve conflicts in a way that doesn't involve the child. Never threaten to withhold parenting time as a means of solving a problem such as late or missing support payments.

- If children don't want to spend time with the other parent, you need to discover why. There are many possibilities: maybe they miss their friends; they feel disloyal to the custodial parent; they worry about the parent being alone while they are away; or the image of their other parent has been negatively tainted by you or another relative.

- Establish goodbye and welcome-home traditions to ease the transitions from one residence to another. For instance, sit and read a story, share a favourite food treat or play a favourite board or card game.

The Next Step for Bereaved Parents

When a beloved spouse or child dies, we are in shock. We can barely make it through each day, much less gather the energy to parent our bereaved children. Too often, we layer our grief with guilt or we push ourselves into super-parent mode, casting aside our needs and grief emotions to 'be there and be up' for our children. Neither approach is helpful in the long run. If you are a bereaved parent, first and foremost, listen to yourself and your needs. Work towards balancing your need to heal and your responsibility to help your children through their trauma as well as their ordinary days. To achieve this:

Don't hesitate to take people up on their offers to help. Tell them what you need and how they can help the children and you. Maybe Uncle Joe can teach your son how to bat, or your neighbour can drive your daughter to dance class.

Make stability a goal. Try not to move homes, change the children's schools or do anything drastic for at least a year. The children need consistency.

Be cautious about bringing new people into the family. Although you're undoubtedly lonely, consider waiting at least 6 to 12 months before you start dating. Even though the children probably won't say anything, they feel threatened because they think your new 'friend' is replacing their deceased parent or is taking away from their time with you. It is always best to have the family heal its loss before adding people into the new family unit.

Plan ahead for upcoming events. Don't leave a special day — especially seasonal festivities and significant events like birthdays or the anniversary of the death — to chance. Always ask the children what they want to do. Keep some of the old family traditions and create new ones as well. After the death of a loved one, you may be overwhelmed at the thought of preparing Christmas dinner, for example; perhaps this is the year to spend the holiday with friends or to travel to be with relatives for the weekend.

If your child has died, keep in mind that you still have living children. They need your love and attention now more than ever. You will need to put forth extra energy to overcome any survivor guilt they may have or feelings that they should have died, not their sibling. The surviving children deserve to live in a happy home. This should be the impetus to move yourself through the grief process and restore happiness.

Extend the children's support network. Whenever possible, encourage your children to keep in contact with their deceased parent's family. Your partner's parents, siblings and extended family members can and should still play an important role in your children's lives. And by staying in touch with them, your children get a more complete picture of their identity and family history, as well as another link to their deceased parent.

Chapter 12

Caring Communities: Shaping a Brighter Future

TWIN BROTHERS JAMES AND SEAN endured near indescribable misery in their childhoods. From the boys' infancy through to early adolescence, the three adults — mother, father and, later, stepmother — who were the most important authority figures in their lives subjected the two children to a gamut of physical and psychological abuse. By the time they were teenagers, James and Sean had severed all contact with their birth mother, moved in and out of a series of foster homes and were living with their father and his fourth wife. They struggled in their new family, argued constantly with their stepmum and did poorly in school. These two were angry and really sad children who seemed headed for trouble.

James was 15 when he told his good friend Dean that he wanted to run away but was worried he couldn't manage on his own. Dean confided the situation to his parents, who agreed to talk to James about his options.

After many conversations that included James, the school counsellor and his social worker — and with reluctant permission from the boy's father — Dean's parents invited the teenager to live with them. Within months, Sean joined his brother. Incredibly, the two lived with Dean's family throughout their remaining school years.

Today, despite the scars they carry from their abusive childhoods, James and Sean are productive, well-adjusted adults. Both are at university and headed towards rewarding professions. Had these young men not been lovingly guided by Dean's parents and other community members who assumed the responsibility of being their compassionate companions, there is a strong chance that they would have ended up as school dropouts or even on the street.

When it comes to helping troubled children, it is heartwarming to see what one person can do. It is astounding to see what a group of focused, like-minded people can achieve. Though few of us have the resources or ability to open our homes as Dean's parents did, there is still much we can accomplish. Whether as a member of the immediate or extended family or part of the larger community — the school system, faith community, neighbourhood or nation — we can link our talents and energies together to create a safety net for the children and teenagers among us.

Children and teenagers have fundamental needs. Among those who have experienced life-altering loss, the requisites are even more intense:

• To feel unconditionally loved.

• To be safe — physically, emotionally and mentally.

• To feel valued.

• To have adults whom they can look up to and from whom they can learn.

• To enjoy positive peer relationships.

• To be empowered to use their strengths.

• To have a family unit that serves as their anchor and base.

In chapter 2, I talked about the ten phases of grief experienced by children of loss. There is yet one more phase, and it is the most important. The 11th phase is hope. Hope is what lights the path to reconciling loss. It is a voice that continually says: *I will get better. Life will be better. The pain will eventually go away.* We need to offer hope as the incentive for navigating all of the difficult phases of mourning. Hope makes grieving possible.

Whether we are the grieving child's parent, step-parent, grandparent, aunt, uncle, teacher, coach, neighbour or family friend, we — the adults — are that child's hope. By acting as compassionate companions, we give bereaved youngsters the only reassurance they have that their fundamental needs will be met.

The School Community

Every day, many children come to school not ready to learn. They may be hungry, depressed, physically exhausted, frightened or torn by emotional turmoil. How is a teacher to teach a child who has a broken heart or a battered body or whose family has been decimated by loss?

I have a son and a daughter-in-law who are teachers. In recent years, both have gained postgraduate degrees in Education. But neither was ever taught how to address the emotional issues they see children struggling with every day. They were trained how to discipline but not how to nurture. When our teachers are not themselves taught how to address the emotional issues many of their pupils are facing, it becomes nearly impossible to make the school a productive place for all students. While teachers are not therapists, they do need to be armed with the resources to deal with the complex problems presented by a diverse student population.

Except for the unfortunate students who have already dropped out, the great majority of our grieving, abused, struggling young people are in a school building every day. School is the place where we can reach the most children at any given time. It is where students should find staff who are caring, patient, understanding and in control. School is where the unspoken lessons of life must be taught.

There are many ways local education authorities can improve the school's ability to better prepare teachers and to serve the many needs of today's student body. Here are just a few of them:

- Schedule workshops on grief and crisis management for teachers and other school personnel.

- Offer a variety of student support groups at break-time and lunch or after school.

- Provide before- and after-school care.

- Develop a nurturing atmosphere for both students and family members. By this, I mean establish policies and outreach programmes that take into account the many stresses and changes that families and students face today. In addition, encourage teachers and staff to get to know the students personally and ensure that faculty and administration are friendly and approachable.

- Increase the school budget to include more social services.

While the strategies above will improve a school's ability to serve troubled children on a general scale, there are also specific things teachers and staff can do to help individual students, depending on whether they're struggling with divorce, death or some other personal crisis.

RESPONDING TO DIVORCE

During a divorce, school may represent one of the few constants and the classroom teacher one of the few secure elements in a child's life. Here are some of the ways the teacher can help the child:

- Be understanding while still setting expectations. You could say: 'I know this is a difficult time for you. Do you think you can work hard at focusing on _____ for now?'

- Ensure that your curriculum and suggested readings portray many family styles.

- Encourage parents to keep you informed of important events in the divorce process, such as the day the parent moves out, pending court dates and so on.

- Avoid any discussions about the estranged partner.

- Keep in mind that Mondays and Fridays are stressful or sad transition days for children of divorced parents because they're leaving one home and going to another.

- If possible, connect the child to other students who have navigated the divorce process successfully.

- Encourage the child to join a school or community support group.

- Remain compassionate and stable for the child.

RESPONDING TO DEATH

The death of a parent, student, teacher or staff member may occur at any time. Schools can take positive steps to help students cope with these kinds of serious losses.

When a student's parent dies:

- The child's teachers should prepare their students on how to react to their classmate when he returns to school after the funeral services.

- As a school or class, prepare a joint expression of condolence to share with the student whose parent has died.

When a student dies:

• Inform the other students of the death; be honest about the cause.

• Set aside special time to talk about the death process.

• Ask the class what they want to do with the deceased child's desk and chair.

• Give the children a chance to say goodbye. They can write individual letters or cards, which can then be given to the bereaved family or buried with the deceased. Another option is to have the students write messages and attach them to balloons that are released outside.

• Ask the children how they want to memorialize the student, and then help them do it. Perhaps they could make a plaque or plant a tree.

• Talk about the student during the rest of the school year.

When a teacher or other staff member dies:

• Do all of the above, plus

• Hold an all-school memorial service.

• Keep the teacher's picture displayed throughout the rest of the year.

If the student's, teacher's or staff member's death has been a suicide:

• Do all of the above, plus

• Set aside time to discuss suicide, its causes, and its prevention. (See page 290.)

• In remembering the person, focus on his or her life, not death.

• Be consciously proactive and aware of other students who are particularly vulnerable at this time.

• Ask a clinical professional to speak to the students about suicide.

RESPONDING TO CRISIS

We live in uncertain times; many cities, communities and schools have experienced traumatic events. The future may bring more tragedies, more calamitous natural disasters, more large-scale episodes of violence. It is always best to be prepared. Here are some guidelines for both teachers and school administrators.

Before a Crisis Occurs

- Staff should work together to create strategies on how to inform students and parents of what has happened and how the school will respond. Each school needs to know its culture and what will work best for the staff and children.

- Prepare teachers to work directly with their students.

- In each area, create a Crisis Response Team of concerned citizens trained for immediate response to assist teachers and students.

During a Crisis Situation

- Generally, it's best to keep the children in the classroom, since the setting is intimate and familiar. However, not all teachers are comfortable handling these types of situations. It may be necessary to move the students into the gym or assembly hall, where a general announcement can be made. The PA system is really a last resort; it is a formal, distant means of communication.

- Tell the truth, so rumours will be diminished.

- Classroom teachers should share with the students how they are feeling.

- Maintain classroom and school routines as much as possible to help children and teenagers remain calm and focused.

• Be available for children to talk when they are ready. Every student will respond differently. There is no right or wrong way.

After a Crisis

• Inform the students' parents or caregivers of what has been done and what is planned for the future. Honour their wishes about their children.

• Depending on the circumstances, suspend school for a day or two so families have time to be together.

• Ask teachers to set aside weekly 'sharing times' in each classroom to discuss how the children are doing. Then stretch these sessions farther apart throughout the year. Remember, it takes many months for children to process these types of events.

20 School Do's and Don'ts

Schoolchildren live in a variety of family shapes and lifestyles. Recently, I asked a friend about the students in her 11-year-old daughter's classroom. The class has 29 children; of these, 10 live in single-parent homes. Six are children of divorce, two are children of never-married single mothers, one is the adopted child of a single mother, and the other lives with her widowed father and older sister. One of the children has two mummies, and four more live in stepfamilies. The school community needs to be sensitive to and supportive of all these circumstances. The following list details what teachers and other school personnel can do to help children from all types of families feel comfortable and secure in the classroom.

1. Identify children who have had a life-altering crisis in their family. It is important for legal and emotional reasons that the school is aware of each student's family unit.

   • Update emergency records annually, requesting current information — name, address and phone numbers — for mother, father, step-parent or legal guardian.

- Review students' files to learn of any family changes or problems that may have occurred — whether recently or in the past, even while the student attended another school.

- When a new student is enrolled, ask the previous school for a family history.

2. Be aware of your own attitude and feelings. Children are acutely perceptive and sensitive, especially at times of loss. Be sensitive with classroom projects, such as an assignment on mother's or father's occupation.

3. Teach feeling words in the classroom. Being able to link words with emotions helps children describe their own feelings and is beneficial to everyone.

4. Initiate class discussions about death, serious illness, marriage and family (talk about the various meanings of family: newlyweds, empty-nesters, nuclear families, single-parent families and stepfamilies). Such discussions allow the students to understand how their classmates feel about death or divorce in the family. It also helps children learn compassion.

5. Be aware of gift-giving and gift-making. The child should be allowed to decide for whom a gift is intended; you could say that the gift is for an important adult in her life. For example, avoid Mother's Day gifts for mothers only.

6. Be sensitive to school events. Avoid mother/son dances and father/daughter outings. The child who does not have a relationship with that particular parent feels the loss acutely at this time. It is easy enough to have parent/child events.

7. Stay out of custody battles. Unless you have a point to make that involves the child in your class, it is not your place to become involved. There is no need to be intimidated by the parent or the legal system.

8. When there has been a divorce in a family or a new family registers, request the documentation that stipulates who has legal custody for decision-making and picking up the children at school.

9. Schedule parent/teacher conferences before, during and after regular school hours to give working parents the opportunity to attend. Be careful not to remind children to 'be sure to bring *both* parents' to the meeting. If one parent is not currently available or the parents are hostile to each other, the child will remain silent about the conference altogether. On the other hand, be aware that while there might be only one parent there for a child, the chances are also good that three or four 'parents' could show up for one child. Sometimes the adults may request separate meetings. If they are together, the tension may be palpable. The role of the teacher is to keep the discussion focused on the child.

10. Provide both the classroom and library with books about grief and loss events, such as death, divorce and serious illness.

11. Be supportive of the parents' situations. Encouragement, understanding and affirmation are needed most at this time. If possible, work with the school social worker to make books available for the parents to read. Or get a list of local social service agencies.

12. Be sensitive in the communications and letters going home. Avoid writing: 'Dear Parents'. Instead write: 'Dear Parent/Guardian'. And don't assume that family members have the same last name.

13. Understand that there may be financial difficulties. Work with the family if fees are not paid. A mutually agreeable payment schedule should be worked out.

14. Cooperate with parents in sending duplicate report cards, notices of parent/teacher conferences and school activities to two addresses.

15. Keep communication open between you and the parent(s).
   - Keep a record of changes in the child's behaviour or academic performance.
   - Send progress reports when necessary, along with notes of praise.
   - Use the child's progress as a vehicle to open dialogue.

16. Provide opportunities to talk privately with struggling children. These children desperately need an adult who plays a significant role in their lives to listen to them.

17. Don't dismiss or make light of the child's situation. Avoid statements such as, 'it isn't that bad,' or 'time heals all wounds'. The child is living in the present and needs to know how to cope today! Validate his feelings and family struggles.

18. Don't pry or intrude into private family matters. There is a difference between asking the child how he is doing and asking what is going on in the family, or with particular members of that family.

19. When the child is present, don't bring up sensitive issues in front of peers or adults.

20. Respect the child's confidentiality. Disclose details of the situation to proper authorities only if you are aware of abuse or suspect the child may harm himself or others.

The Neighbourhood Community

Lynn's mother had been sick for several days. 'It's just the flu,' her father assured the girl. Then, one night, Lynn was awakened by the siren and flashing lights of an ambulance pulling into the driveway. Lying in bed, she heard doors slam and loud voices — her father's heavy baritone among them. Alarmed, the 15-year-old hurried down the hall and hid behind the kitchen door. Peeking out, she watched as the paramedics rushed through the front door and her dad directed them into the master bedroom. There was a flurry of talk and activity, then one of the ambulance crew hurried out for a stretcher. A few minutes later, Lynn stood helplessly by, weeping, as her mother was wheeled out into the waiting ambulance. Her dad was right behind. Turning to snatch his car keys off the hall table, he spotted Lynn.

'I'm following them to the hospital. Mum will be fine,' he shouted over his shoulder. Then he ran out of the door.

Lynn's mother died that night.

In many areas, the police as well as paramedics would have responded to an emergency call like the one Lynn's father made that night. Imagine the difference for Lynn if others on the response team had noticed her and asked to talk with her. They could have explained the procedures the paramedics were following and possibly have intervened to allow Lynn the opportunity to give her mother a goodbye kiss or hug. Certainly, they could have asked Lynn or her distraught father for the name of a family member or friend to call to come and sit with her. In this instance, there was no one to intercede on Lynn's behalf. Not even the neighbours. Although they were awakened by the ambulance, none of them came round or phoned — perhaps because they assumed everything was taken care of and they didn't want to 'interfere'. Lynn was left alone.

Unfortunately, millions of children and teenagers experience crises and loss events in their young lives, and far too many of them go through the difficult events relatively alone. While it is understandable that the child's immediate family members might be so overcome with grief that they're unable to attend to the child's needs, it is inexcusable that the child be left alone with her grief when she is a member of a community. All branches of the community — residents, social service agencies, faith communities, police and fire departments, medical facilities, libraries — can play vital roles in responding to the needs of children of loss. As communities serving the best interests of our young people, we need to pool our resources and create networks of safety for the youngsters in our midst.

How do we go about doing this? Here are some suggestions.

Create a task force. Invite members from all areas of the community to serve on this committee. The main goal of the group should be to assess the community's resources and needs.

Identify potential crises and develop response scenarios for each. Be sure to include community-wide disasters (flood, fire, flu epidemic), terrorist attacks, episodes of school violence and family loss events. The response scenarios should focus on both the immediate and ongoing needs of the community's children and teenagers.

Educate the community about loss. Host community-wide workshops and sensitivity training sessions on grief and loss issues. These can inform caring adults about the epidemic of grief among our young people, symptoms of normal versus abnormal grieving and specific issues that affect children of loss.

Create a 'Community Resource' booklet. The publication should be distributed free to families through schools, libraries, faith communities, police and fire departments, and social service agencies. The booklet could contain:

- Hotline numbers to reach immediate assistance.

- Information about social service agencies that offer a variety of support services.

- The names and phone numbers of youth officers, community-based counsellors, religious leaders and representatives of support groups and other outreach services — these people can offer assistance and a friendly face to families even before a crisis occurs.

- A listing of community resources established to meet specific needs families might have, such as health care organizations, emergency food and clothes shops or support groups

Make information easily available. Government agencies as well as large not-for-profit organizations produce brochures and leaflets on a variety of crisis and loss topics, including natural disasters, death, divorce, suicide, drug and alcohol abuse and prevention, and crisis response. Obtain these resources and make them readily available in the community.

(continued on page 336)

MAKING A POSITIVE DIFFERENCE

Each of us has a responsibility to have a positive influence on the children we know. Each of us has the power to add to their lives in a way that helps them develop into the best adults possible. Here are some ways we can achieve that lofty goal.

* Be a child's coach into adulthood – motivate, monitor and mentor.

* Set rules, establish routines, offer support and be dependable.

* Make sure that verbal interactions are positive, never sarcastic or cutting.

* Laugh often and try to keep things in perspective.

* Set the standards for children by living them yourself.

* Let children and teenagers know the consequences of their behaviour (and the punishments that will be meted out) ahead of time, so they are responsible for their decisions and actions.

* Help children and teenagers set achievable goals in all aspects of their lives – academic, sports, friendships, and in the family.

* Talk about being responsible and what that means as a child, teenager or adult.

* Help the child to feel that he belongs and is loved.

* Model appreciation of community – local, national and world-wide.

* Teach children to respect themselves and others.

* Encourage a passion for learning and achieving.

* Instil a wonder of life.

* Promote stewardship: a sense of gratitude for what they have and the obligation to give back.

* Talk about the future – their dreams and aspirations – throughout their lives, not just at important milestones.

The remaining strategies are just for parents and caregivers:

※ Make your family a happy place where children feel emotionally and physically safe.

※ Spell out the rules loud and clear. Ask children for their input, but do not waver because you want to be liked or seem cool.

※ Every day, spend quiet time alone with each child. Ask about their day or their friends. You listen; they talk. Don't criticize; instead, affirm what you are hearing. Let them *feel* your care.

※ Ask them questions. Be nosy, even annoying. Let them know you ask because you care about them and want them to ask about your daily life, too.

※ Check up on them. Call the house they say they are visiting. 'Bump' into them at the shopping centre to which they say they are going.

※ Get to know their friends and their friends' families. Ignore their pleas that you not chaperone or act as a coach, scout leader or classroom parent. Offer to drive them where they need to go. (It is enlightening to hear your kids chat with their friends about what is happening in all of their lives.)

※ Become interested in what they enjoy. You don't have to *like* the musical group they are fans of, but go to the concert anyway. Listen to the topics they express interest in and clip pertinent newspaper articles for them. Buy them a magazine that features an article about their favourite team or athlete.

※ Take time to play as a family.

※ Encourage down-time each day to relax without a pre-planned activity or task. I like to think of this as 'hammock time'.

※ Learn to communicate effectively. This means being ready at all times for your children to indicate that they want to talk. Respond immediately. Children don't usually ask a second time.

Offer crisis response programmes and grief support groups for adults and young people. Locally sponsored programmes and groups provide children with:

• An opportunity to understand they are not alone in the difficulties they face.

• A positive social setting where children can learn to trust their peers as well as adults.

• A hands-on experience with proactive problem solving.

Many different kinds of programmes are available. The following are examples of both crisis response and grief support programmes offered by RAINBOWS.

CRISIS RESPONSE: SILVER LININGS

In 1992, a series of torrential storms caused severe flooding in the American Midwest. Parts of Indiana were especially hard hit. In several communities, businesses and schools were forced to close, and hundreds of families were evacuated to emergency shelters. Even after the waters receded, hazardous conditions prompted health officials to keep schools shut and to prohibit families from returning to their homes. For days and weeks, people lived with no sense of normality. Children were especially affected by the disaster and abrupt change in routine. At RAINBOWS headquarters outside Chicago, a call came in from one of the organization's Registered Directors in the affected State. 'What can we do for the children?' she asked.

Prior to this time, children would come to our programmes whose parents weren't divorced or widowed, but who still needed somebody to talk to about a family or community crisis. We would welcome them to the programme rather than turn them away. We found that all of these children were experiencing similar feelings:

- Disbelief over what had happened.
- Loss of emotional stability.
- An unbalanced sense of life.
- Loss of possessions or of personal identity.

Responding to the Indiana emergency, RAINBOWS created the initial version of Silver Linings, a hands-on, group-based crisis response programme for children and teenagers. Silver Linings was first used by adult volunteers working with children in the communities devastated by the Indiana floods. One year later, in 1993, Silver Linings was used to help children affected by the civil unrest that resulted from riots in Los Angeles. Since then, the programme has been implemented in Australia, when widespread bush fires forced families from their homes near Sydney. It has also been used throughout the United States in communities struck by a variety of natural disasters, including fires, tornadoes and hurricanes. However, to date, the Silver Linings programme has not been run in the United Kingdom.

Following the terrorist attacks of 11 September 2001, a special edition of the programme, Silver Linings 2001, was created specifically to assist children and teenagers in responding to the crisis. Within months of the attack, the programme had been distributed to sites across America.

The current Silver Linings Crisis Response Programme, which incorporates elements from this rich and varied history, is available to schools, faith communities and social service organizations serving young people as well as to disaster relief organizations.

No matter what the precipitating event, Silver Linings helps children and teenagers:

- Look closely at the crisis or disaster that has occurred.
- Discuss their feelings with others who share the situation.
- Integrate into their personal lives the changes brought about by the event.

• Develop an atmosphere of hope and acceptance as they move towards rebuilding.

Youth Grief Support: RAINBOWS

RAINBOWS is an international non-profit organization dedicated solely to providing grief support services for children, teenagers and adults. We have five age-specific programmes that help participants cope with the emotional pain of loss, whether it's the result of death, divorce, separation, abandonment, chronic illness, imprisonment or some other loss. While RAINBOWS provides training, materials and ongoing support to community-based sites that implement our programmes, the sponsoring agencies provide the facilities and the volunteers. RAINBOWS is designed to be offered to youngsters at no charge. Sponsoring organizations pay a one-time, below-cost fee for training and startup materials.

I am often asked who sponsors RAINBOWS programmes. Here is a look at the kinds of sites where RAINBOWS is found.

Schools. Most RAINBOWS sites are school-based. Both state sector, independent primary and secondary schools offer RAINBOWS programmes. The programmes are adaptable for children with special educational needs and also for those with English as a second language.

Other agencies. The programme can also be offered in hospices, hospitals and through social services agencies, both statutory and voluntary such as YMCA, children's societies, On Track and Sure Start amongst others.

Get in touch with us at RAINBOWS to learn about our various programmes or for information on how you might start a group in your area

RAINBOWS INTERNATIONAL HEADQUARTERS
2100 Golf Road, #370
Rolling Meadows
IL 60008-4231
USA
Tel: +1 800 266 3206 or +1 847 952 1770
Fax: +1 847 952 1774
E-mail: info@rainbows.org
Web: www.rainbows.org

RAINBOWS UNITED KINGDOM
Rainbows Distribution Centre
Unit 7
High Town Enterprise Park
York Street
Luton LU2 0HA
UNITED KINGDOM
E-mail: rainbows.dc@virgin.net
Web: www.rainbowsgb.org

RAINBOWS IRELAND
Loreto Centre
Crumlin Road
Dublin 12
IRELAND
Tel: +353 1 4734175
Fax: +353 1 4734175
E-mail rainbows@eircom.net

RAINBOWS AUSTRALIA
c/o Mr Peter Rohr
Spectrum Publications
PO Box 75
Richmond
VIC 3121
AUSTRALIA
Tel: +61 (0)3 9429 1404 or +61 (0)3 9427 1190
Fax: +61 (0)3 9428 9407
E-mail: spectpub@ozemail.com.au

Epilogue

TODAY, MY FAMILY LOOKS ABSOLUTELY NOTHING LIKE the one in which I grew up and that I dreamed of having. I have been a spouse, an ex-spouse, and a remarried spouse. I have been a parent, a single parent, a co-parent and a step-parent. I am a grandmother of one whose mum and dad never married, another who came to us via a remarriage and a third who came two years after her mum and dad married. I love them all equally and completely.

Each of the six children I have parented are mine in my heart. I am devoted to them. My life was dedicated to raising them well and ensuring they know they are loved. The siblings and stepsiblings love each other and genuinely care about each other. Michael, Tom and Tim, my sons by birth, have grown into well-adjusted, successful young men. As adults, they are wonderful, generous human beings who are devoted to each other and to our family. Reared in a non-traditional family, they have each taken a different approach to creating their own new family units.

Michael is an educator and father of Tommy. Tom is a police officer, married, step-dad to Samantha and dad to Emma with another baby on the way. Both live close by, and I am fortunate to see them frequently. Tim is engaged and the Chief of Staff for a United States Senator.

Each of them has taken the greatest pain in his life — the long-ago divorce of his parents — and become wiser, stronger and gentler because of it.

Peter, David and Katie, my beloved stepchildren, have also become terrific young adults. Like my sons, they have all graduated from university, and all three are just starting out in their careers. They are beginning the process of moving out of the family home, an adjustment that can be particularly difficult for children of loss. It is another ending of family life as they knew it.

Often, over the many years we have been together, our family structure reminded me of a mobile — a dynamic structure that depends on balance to move smoothly. For a while, so many people were being introduced into the unit that our mobile hovered unsteadily. Now it moves gently, adjusting to the additions of new family members through love, marriage and children.

This network of solid relationships did not just develop because 'we were lucky', as many people have told us. We bonded as individuals and as a family because we worked at it every day. And we are still working at it each day. Family life continues to fluctuate because of engagements, weddings, babies and deaths. Life in a family means constant change. The goal is to have these changes be life-giving rather than life-threatening.

Our ex-partners helped to create this framework of love and support for the six children, too. Our former in-laws joined in as well. For some of my grandchildren, there are eight grandparents. Rather than a family tree, we have a family forest!

Collectively, we try to look through the lens of what is best for the children and grandchildren. Admittedly, sometimes the eyepiece gets clouded with hurt feelings or bad attitudes, but we just keep polishing the glass to keep it clear and focused on the children.

But our family is hardly alone in establishing loving, nurturing relationships in the midst of challenging family dynamics. Earlier, I introduced you to some of the remarkable families I've met through my work with RAINBOWS. Families like these are 'harbingers of hope' that continue to inspire me and my colleagues with their devotion to their children and the compassion they've shown during and beyond times of loss.

In much the same way, all of us need to be harbingers of hope to the young people in our midst — whether we are parents, grandparents, relatives, teachers, coaches, doctors and nurses, neighbours, family friends or caregivers. For the sake of our children and teenagers, we must assume the role of compassionate companions and reach out to grieving youngsters.

Children and teenagers have the capacity to feel deeply, love intensely, lose much, and accept help from others. Bereaved youngsters can grow into happy, healthy, responsible adults. But they need care, understanding, emotional support and love from caring adults around them to weather the storm of loss and move onto the path of success.

You can be the difference in healing their hurt and restoring their hope.

Recommended Reading

Abrams, Rebecca. *When Parents Die*. London: Routledge, 1999.

Benedek, Elissa P., and Catherine F. Brown. *How to Help Your Child Overcome Your Divorce*. New York: Newmarket Press, 1998.

Black, Dora. *Family Therapy and Life-Threatening Illness in Children or Parents*. London: Free Association Books, 1984.

Blau, Melinda. *Families Apart: Ten Keys to Successful Co-Parenting*. New York: G.P. Putman's Son's, 1994.

Brown, Erica. *Loss, Change and Grief*. London: David Fulton Publishers, 1999.

Brown, Erica. *Children with Post-traumatic Stress Disorder*. London: David Fulton Publishers, 2001.

Coloroso, Barbara. *Kids Are Worth It!* New York: Avon Books, 1994.

Doka, Kenneth J., ed. *Supporting Children Mourning, Mourning Children*. Hospice Foundation of America, 1995.

Elkind, David. *All Grown Up and No Place to Go*. Reading, Mass.: Addison-Wesley, 1998.

Emswiler, Mary Ann, and James Emswiler. *Guiding Your Child through Grief*. New York: Bantam Books, 2000.

Grollman, Earl. *Bereaved Children and Teens*. Boston: Beacon Press, 1995.

Hetherington, E. Mavis, and John Kelly. *For Better or for Worse*. New York: W.W. Norton and Company, 2002.

Hewlett, Sylvia Ann. *When the Bough Breaks*. New York: Basic Books, 1991.

Holyoke, Nancy. *Help! A Girl's Guide to Divorce and Stepfamilies*. Middleton, Wis.: Pleasant Company Publications, 1999.

Institute of Medicine: *Reducing Suicide, A National Imperative*. Washington, D.C.: The National Academics Press, 2002.

Irwin, Cait. *Conquering the Beast Within: How I Fought Depression and Won ... and How You Can, Too*. New York: Random House, 1999.

James, John W., and Russell Friedman. *When Children Grieve*. New York: Harper Collins Publishers, 2001.

Jewett, Claudia. *Helping Children Cope with Separation and Loss*. London: Free Association Books, 1984.

Lansky, Vicki. *Vicki Lansky's Divorce Book for Parents: Helping Your Children Cope with Divorce and Its Aftermath*. Minnetoka, Minn.: Bookpeddlars, 1996.

Levang, Elizabeth. *When Men Grieve*. Minneapolis: Fairview Press, 1998.

Neuman, M. Gary. *Helping Your Kids Cope with Divorce the Sandcastles Way*. New York: Random House, 1999.

Newman, Fran. *Children in Crisis*. Scholastic Canada, 1993.

Noel, Brook. *The Single Parent Resource*. Beverly Hills, Calif.: Champion Press, 1998.

Royko, David. *Voices of Children of Divorce*. New York: Golden Books, 1999.

Shaw, Eva. *What to Do When a Loved One Dies*. Irvine, Calif.: Dickens Press, 1994.

Staal, Stephanie. *The Love They Lost*. New York: Dell, 2000.

Wallerstein, Judith, Julia Lewis, and Sandra Blakeslee. *The Unexpected Legacy of Divorce*. New York: Hyperion, 2000.

Walsh, Froma. *Strengthening Family Resilience*. New York: The Guilford Press, 1998.

Wells, Rosemary. *Helping Children Cope with Grief*. London: Sheldon Press, 1998.

Wolfelt, Alan. *Helping Children Cope with Grief*. Muncie, Ind.: Accelerated Development, 1983.

Worden, J. William. *Children and Grief*. New York: Guilford Press, 1996.

Index

Underlined page references indicate sidebars. **Bold** references indicate illustrations.

Index

348

OTHER RODALE BOOKS
AVAILABLE FROM PAN MACMILLAN

1-4050-4182-X	The Doctors' Book of Home Remedies	*A Prevention Health Book*	£20.00
1-4050-2100-4	The Anorexia Diaries	*Tara Rio and Linda Rio*	£8.99
1-4050-0671-4	Laying Down the Law	*Dr Ruth Peters*	£8.99
1-4050-3337-1	The Acne Cure	*Dr Terry Dubrow and Brenda Adderly*	£10.99
1-4050-4103-X	The New Brain	*Dr Richard Restak*	£10.99
1-4050-3339-8	The Immune Advantage	*Ellen Mazo*	£14.99
1-4050-0675-7	The Secret Life of the Dyslexic Child	*Robert Frank with Kathryn Livingston*	£10.99
1-4050-3340-1	When Your Body Gets the Blues	*Marie-Annette Brown and Jo Robinson*	£10.99

All Pan Macmillan titles can be ordered from our website, *www.panmacmillan.com,* or from your local bookshop and are also available by post from:

Bookpost, PO Box 29, Douglas, Isle of Man IM99 1BQ
Credit cards accepted. For details:
Telephone: 01624 836000
Fax: 01624 670923
E-mail: bookshop@enterprise.net
www.bookpost.co.uk

Free postage and packing in the United Kingdom

Prices shown above were correct at time of going to press.
Pan Macmillan reserve the right to show new retail prices on covers which may differ from those previously advertised in the text or elsewhere.

For information about buying *Rodale* titles in **Australia**, contact Pan Macmillan Australia. Tel: 1300 135 113; fax: 1300 135 103; e-mail: *customer.service@macmillan.com.au*; or visit: *www.panmacmillan.com.au*

For information about buying *Rodale* titles in **New Zealand**, contact Macmillan Publishers New Zealand Limited. Tel: (09) 414 0356; fax: (09) 414 0352; e-mail: *lyn@macmillan.co.nz*; or visit: *www.macmillan.co.nz*